Date Due

IN ALL CONSCIENCE

In All Conscience

REFLECTIONS ON BOOKS AND CULTURE

HAROLD C. GARDINER, S.J.

HANOVER HOUSE

A DIVISION OF DOUBLEDAY & COMPANY, INC.

GARDEN CITY, NEW YORK

Imprimi potest: Thomas E. Henneberry, s.j.
Praepositus Provincialis
August 25, 1959
Nihil Obstat: James F. Rigney, s.t.d.
Censor Librorum
Imprimatur: ✠ Francis Cardinal Spellman
Archbishop of New York
August 22, 1959

41455

The nihil obstat and imprimatur are official declarations that a book or pamphlet is free of doctrinal or moral error. No implication is contained therein that those who have granted the nihil obstat and imprimatur agree with the contents, opinions or statements expressed.

CONTENTS

INTRODUCTION

It was Hilaire Belloc, I believe, who once remarked that after a long life in which he had read many, many books, he had come to the realization that he had, after all, read just one book. All the books he had read coalesced, so to speak, into one book—and its title was *On a Distant Country*. The distant country is the land, the realm of man's happiness, and every book worthy of the name of literature is questing for that land. What, ask the books, *is* the happiness that can fill man's heart and mind and soul? What is its name and its local habitation? What are the things, in human nature and the world, that can get in the way of that happiness? Can I find it through adventure or in human love? And if I find some happiness, will it be satisfying—will it be an ultimate happiness? Or can it at least point to a happiness beyond, and that in turn reveal another range of happiness—so that the infinite vistas open up and show the "distant country" toward which we are all inevitably wending our way?

This is the book that Hilaire Belloc realized he had been reading in all the disparate volumes; his ultimate realization, after all, was nothing new. Centuries ago, St. Augustine of Hippo had said the same thing, though, to be sure, he did not have books and literature specifically in mind. We seek this "distant country" of happiness because "Thou hast made us for Thyself, O God, and our hearts are restless until they rest in Thee."

This, I admit, is a rather solemn opening to a book that is hardly as pretentious as this beginning may lead the reader to suspect. The book is simply a collection of what used to be called in Victorian days "fugitive pieces." The selections (about one fourth of my total contributions to *America's* pages) have all appeared in the issues since 1940 of *America*, of which I have the honor and the pleasure of being literary editor. The pieces have, therefore, been written in large part to meet immediate needs: controversies of the moment, trends that may since have stopped trending, certain books, motion pictures, and the like which may seem very dead indeed by now. *America*, however, is very much alive: this is its fiftieth year of continuous publication. May my editor colleagues, past, present, and to come, find this collection not unworthy of *America*.

Yet I think there is a thread of unity running through all that follows. The basic unity, I like to feel, is that "distant country" motif. My criticism has always intended to be (however faithfully I may have lived up to the principle) a comment on how books and our culture generally mirror that basic craving for happiness, for fulfillment, that underlies and girds all our human hopes and fears, loves and aspirations. If books and other media of culture do not and cannot shed some light on that aspect of the "human condition," then they are hardly more than pastimes.

I probably have not read as widely and certainly not as wisely as Hilaire Belloc, but perhaps it may be of interest to note that in my position as literary editor I handle some 2,000 books a year— process for review, that is, not read all of that rather staggering number. I have never kept count of the number I read each year, but it is considerable. For my reader's peace of mind, however, let me state that any book discussed in these pages is one that I know thoroughly and judged with what critical acumen I could bring to the task.

From these collected pieces, then, I hope that some pattern will be discerned. The reviews and articles are a continuing comment on our American culture as it is mirrored in and influenced by literature and other communications media. Perhaps the picture that will take shape in a reader's mind is suggested by the title. The dictionary says of the phrase "in all conscience": 1. "in reason or fairness"; 2. "certainly." I use the phrase as the title in the first sense: I trust that my comment will be found to be fair and honest. Second, I intend an overtone as well. Conscience is our human faculty for judging the morality of an act. I trust that none of the following pieces will be found to be "moralizing" in tone; but I trust equally that a moral judgment will be in evidence whenever it was called for. I do not agree with that school of thought which holds that literature is susceptible to a partitioned evaluation: it can be artistic but immoral. I hold that the integral judgment is a composite judgment which includes both the artistic and the moral. This position will not be found fully explicated in these pages. I have written rather extensively on it, but the reader will have to turn to the pages of *Norms for the Novel* to follow the complete argument.

"In all conscience," then, I present these "fugitive" pieces. I can only hope that they will not prove to be fugitives from (literary) justice.

HAROLD C. GARDINER, S.J.

New York
Campion House
April 30, 1959

PART ONE

Books in our Culture

Chapter One

LOOKING A CULTURAL "GIFT HORSE" IN THE MOUTH

Hamlet once (and for all?) said that the player's vocation was to hold the mirror up to nature, to show the age its very form and feature. Had the melancholy Dane been proferring his sage advice today, he might well have directed it to writers, editors, and publishers, for certainly books are a most revealing mirror in our times in which to see our own countenances. Are we pleasant to behold? Are we amazed at the features that smile, grimace, or scowl back at the collective us?

To put it simply—to reflect on the reflection that fronts us in books as they show us to ourselves—a small introduction seems necessary. What is this American culture we speak of? Is there really any? What is distinctive about it? What is lamentable or laudable in the distinctiveness? This first section is somewhat in the nature of a running start; from its springboard we shall plunge splashingly in the following sections into the world of books and other media that shape our American culture.

So, holding our breath on the teeter-tottering edge of the diving board, here are some general reflections on the good and bad, the hopeful and the harrowing in the shimmering pool of American "company manners"—is our tie straight, is our face on attractively as it looks back at us from the mirror of mores?

THE "DANGERS" OF LITERATURE

Literature is not life. A book, no matter how great, is not the growth, the activities of body, mind, and soul, the hopes and fears and, above all, the love that make a human life. Literature is not religion. No book, not even the Bible, is the bond that ties us to God in the filial fear, devotion, and love that link creature to Creator. Literature is not morality. No words on a printed page constitute integrity, rectitude, honor, justice, or, above all again, the love on which all morality is based.

But literature is not a kind of death, either. It is not a means to deny or stunt growth; it is not a severance of the links that bind us to God. It is not a horribly fascinated introspection into dishonor, injustice, and the love of self that blot out the love of others and consequently the love of God.

Literature, in other words, is simply a means to an end, and any end must be clearly envisioned before means to attain it can be sensibly chosen. If I read a book, I ought to know why I am reading it. I may, indeed, read it for many subjective reasons: to pass the time, to ward off boredom, to satisfy curiosity, to gain knowledge, even, it may be, to indulge forbidden pleasures. But there is an objective reason, too, and that can be ascertained by asking the simple question: why is this book, in itself, worth reading?

Well, if literature is not life, religion, or morality, why is it worth reading? It is worth our attention and study precisely because it sheds light on life, religion, and morality. And how does it shed that light? By confirming or challenging the values we hold, values we have got, it is to be hoped, from sources other than literature itself—from the home, from education, from the Church.

It is exactly on this level that literature can fulfill its most vital role; it can be a means to deepen and enrich the values we already hold about life, religion, and morality. It can force us to ask ourselves why we hold, and how deeply we hold, what we have thought to be our most precious convictions. The reply we hear may, it is true, at times disquiet us. If our faith is not strong, infidelity in a book may sound alarmingly attractive. If our tolerance is but skin deep, dramatized intolerance in a book may woo us to agree that pigmentation makes the man. If our purity is not strong and virile, any depiction of impurity may amaze us by its solicitation.

But the mature reader of literature, and above all the teacher of literature, will know how to balance the lurking dangers and the obvious good. Any step in education involves the "calculated risk." If Johnny learns to spell, will he learn chiefly four-letter words? If Mary learns to read, will she read only *Black Beauty*? If Oscar learns anatomy in his premed courses, will he learn only curves and not cures?

It is this calculated risk to which Father Boyle addresses himself in his article this week. It is a risk which Catholic education in this country must confront boldly, humbly, and with many a prayer for guidance to the Holy Spirit. Catholic education, especially in its higher reaches, is not merely a protective coating applied to the moral and spiritual lives of students. It must prepare young men and women to meet the world and to transform that world into the spirit and image of Christ. And it is apposite to recall that when Christ was faced with the woman caught in the act of adultery, He did not flee the sight of her. Rather did He say to her, "Neither do I condemn thee."

We cannot refuse to condemn books that are glorifications of dirt, or books that treat dirt as casually as one might a smudge on a jaunty lapel. But we can say—and do—that books which truly, sincerely, even if startlingly, make us realize the stuff of which fallen human nature is made can be prudently taught in our colleges. If any serious reader of literature or any teacher has doubts on this score, let him read one of the books of Graham Greene that Father Boyle mentions in his article and then try to wade through such a book as John O'Hara's *From the Terrace*. Many a "dirty" book is great. No dirty book is.   (December 13, 1958)

This editorial was occasioned by an article, "Teaching 'Dirty' Books in College," by Reverend Robert Boyle, S.J., chairman of the English department at Regis College, Denver, which appeared in the December 13, 1958 issue of America. *My review of John O'Hara's* From the Terrace *will be found on page 141 of this collection. The challenges of literature and their impact on our culture, which will be the burden of discussion in the rest of this book, seem best introduced by this statement, which is an abbreviation of what I have written on extensively in* Norms for the Novel.

MASS CULTURE—GOOD OR BAD?

One of the most thoughtful scanners of contemporary United States culture is Gilbert Highet, Columbia University professor, humanist, author, critic, and radio commentator. His weekly broadcasts on current books are commonly judged to be among the most literate performances available to tuners-in. Over the air waves, Dr. Highet recently pondered the problem of our "mass culture," and his reflections could well be made the subject of a Lenten meditation. For during that season of reflection, one will—or can—grow, not only in God's grace but intellectually and culturally as well.

Dr. Highet is frankly appalled by some of the "benefits" that our practically universal education is said to have brought us. "It revolts me to know," he states, "that the only American author whose works have sold over ten million copies is Mickey Spillane." He goes on:

> You may say that Mr. Spillane is not a cause, but a symptom; yet I think I should disagree. Everyone who writes bears the responsibility for presenting a social picture and a set of moral beliefs to his readers; the simpler and stupider his readers are, the more receptive they will be, and the greater his responsibility; and very few modern authors can ever have offered a more debased and debasing picture of the world to their readers—or shall we say their victims?

To the charge that he may be unduly alarmist, since Spillane's books are taken seriously by only an "occasional moron," Dr. Highet responds:

> It seems to me that the kind of vulgarity which [Spillane's books] represent is spreading, by infection. In the twentieth century, because of the growth of mass communications and mass culture, people have become more easily impressible, more passively receptive. . . . Cultivated people have always been in a minority. But is this the first time in history when they have been made to feel ashamed of it? Can it be true that prosperity degrades us, that mass culture vulgarizes us, that freedom from want makes

us more like animals—like pigs in a filthy sty, with both feet in the full trough?

Strong words, to be sure, but a salutary reminder that one has constantly to fight against the drag of cultural mediocrity. It takes conscious effort to turn off the banal TV program and pick up the great book you have always promised yourself you would get around to reading. It takes an act of the will to pass by the cheap magazines and paper-covered books enticingly displayed on the newsstands.

But "mass culture" is not all bad. For side by side with Spillane's monstrosities in their racks at the corner drugstore there are reasonably priced good and great books, too. On the very next TV channel there is probably an excellent program to be seen by merely flicking the dial. But the deliberate choice has to be made. One's ideals must dictate the choice. (February 22, 1958)

"DAMNED" IS THE MISSING WORD

James Jones's novel is out, has been reviewed, and, sure enough, has created all the stir advance publicity assured us it would occasion. It is called *From Here to Eternity*, which is an echo of the famous Yale "Whiffenpoof Song," in turn a parody of Kipling's *Gentlemen-Rankers* from *Barrack-Room Ballads*.

Both songs, you will remember, say that the gentlemen in question, out on their spree, are damned from here to eternity. Their horrendous-sounding boast is a bit of rather adolescent bravado; Jones's title, if the "damned" be included as it should, is a shuddering prophecy. If his story is true, then its meaning and the reception thus far given to it by the reviewers ought to set us trembling for our American, and particularly for the U.S. military, soul.

The story, for all its Gargantuan 880 pages, is simply outlined. One young Robert E. Lee Prewitt, fugitive from poverty in the Harlan, Kentucky coal fields, joins the regular U. S. Army some years before Pearl Harbor. He finds he is a natural artist on the bugle, and he loves it with all his starved soul. Disgusted because he is passed over for a lesser artist, he transfers to another company, preceded by his other claim to fame, namely that he is a good welterweight boxer. Regimental championship bouts are coming up, and his new commanders and fellows think that he will be happy to bring glory to the company. But in an earlier fight Prewitt had blinded his opponent, and since he still remembered his drab, broken mother's plea that he never hurt another unless he had to, he refuses to box any more.

He is promptly labeled a Bolshevik and is accorded The Treatment, a fiendishly devised process of breaking his independent spirit. He goes berserk under it, attacks an officer, and is confined to The Stockade, the Army prison at Schofield Barracks, Honolulu, where all the action takes place. Witnessing there the brutally fatal beating administered to another prisoner, he resolves to kill the chief torturer when released. He does, and then goes "over the hill" to avoid capture and trial. He is still a deserter when the Japs strike Pearl Harbor. In an attempt to rejoin his outfit, he is killed by his own men. He ends ingloriously, but is, we are given to understand, a soldier to the last.

This bare outline gives no indication of the richness of the book. It is rich in two senses. It is literally packed with details of Army life—drill, tactics, weapons and their care, the bull sessions, bivouacs, canteens, and so on—caught with all the keen sensitivity of a born observer and recorder. It is also rich—nauseatingly so—with the filthiest language it has ever been my lot (or doom) to read. It is a solution supersaturated with sex. The talk of the soldiers (and of the officers) reeks with sex; there are detailed descriptions of brothels and the degraded commerce that goes on there; two sordid "love" stories are interwoven into the tenuous plot—the story of Prewitt and the outwardly lovely, inwardly noble-at-heart whore and that of Sergeant Warden and the wife of his commanding officer. Even the descriptions of nature are frequently couched in terms of sexual relationships. Another layer of this richness crops up in the sadistically brutal descriptions of the physical torture meted out to the prisoners in The Stockade.

Let me say unhesitatingly that I recognize, with many of the critics, that Mr. Jones can write—not flawlessly, but tempestuously, passionately, if almost maudlinly at times. I can even respect what is being called his "honesty." He has something to say and feels that he must say it. He has a love for the rough, brutalized companionship of the Army as he apparently knew it and a hatred for the "system" (as he also apparently knew it), and both clamor for voice. He has given them voice, all right—a raucous, obscene voice.

This may be the only voice Mr. Jones possesses or recognizes, and so, perhaps he himself is not too much to be censured.

But the reviewers and critics? That is another question. Early reviews at hand are practically unanimous in almost unqualified praise. In this, I am firmly convinced, reviewers have done a great disservice to the canons of their craft, to the young author, and to the cause of international stability in the face of the Communist threat. This is a large indictment. I hope what follows will substantiate it.

First, the artistic quality of the book. Is it quite as great as the critics say? Take the matter of the constantly recurring verbal obscenity. Lewis Gannett in the New York *Herald Tribune* says: "The four-letter words are used as casually as punctuation, so that they lose all sense of obscenity . . . you'll be shocked at first, and then, as happens to those who listen to Army talk, you'll get used to it." I had always thought that in good writing every word is to count, to carry its precise and enriching meaning. It is paucity of thought, imagination, and vocabulary that generally throws the uncultured into profane and obscene language; is that to be grounds for praise in an author?

Second, it is extremely doubtful that this is, as David Dempsey claims in the New York *Times Book Review*, a "deeply convincing" story of life in the peacetime Army. There is an ancient dictum (from Aristotle), which is still valid, to the effect that literary credibility rests more securely on an impossibility that is convincing than on a possibility that is unconvincing. It is theoretically possible that the peacetime Army was as Jones portrays it, but I, for one, am not at all convinced.

My intransigeance rises from the fact, not adverted to by the reviewers, that this sort of ultrarealism always yields diminishing returns. The first spate of foul language, the first lurid descriptions of the brothels do ring with a note of authenticity, but the very repetition of them, over and over again, becomes so flat and tedious that it all assumes an air of unreality. It is true in literature as in logic that he who proves too much proves nothing. It is also true that we begin to suspect the veracity of one who protests too much.

I don't believe that I am here violating the principle of not generalizing from particulars. Jones is not merely saying that some of his characters are lechers and drunkards. Every single one of them is, men and officers alike. He is unmistakably saying this is the Army.

And it is not a too-tender patriotism or puritanical squeamishness that makes me say this cannot be the Army. It is rather some fundamental knowledge of human nature and an elementary grasp of the theory of probabilities. Even in the peacetime Army there would have been some few decent men, motivated by more than the sub-human stubbornness that makes Jones's characters tick, and which is being called by the reviewers "manhood, dignity, and integrity."

All this injudicious and basically false praise heaped on the new author will inevitably settle him in the groove that can run nowhere else than downhill. Unless Jones shifts his viewpoint and begins to grasp what are literary probabilities, I have not the slightest hesitation in prophesying that he will end up in the dead end that has long since prisoned and frustrated James T. Farrell.

But there are still deeper criticisms to be bazookaed against this book and its praisers. Only one reviewer thus far has adverted to the fundamental philosophy of the story, and even he referred to it in praise rather than in condemnation. Says Gene Baro (New York Herald Tribune): "It [man's tragedy, I presume, for that is the only subject discernible] is man's need for individual dignity in an authoritarian world." "Authoritarian"—that is the tip-off. All Jones's characters are rebels against authority. That that authority was legitimate (though brutally exercised) makes no difference either to them or to the reviewers. The mere fact that authority is flouted somehow endows the mavericks with a great "dignity" and "nobility," and legitimate authority strangely becomes "authoritarianism." To put it briefly, the characters have absolutely no concept that obedience is a virtue, and the reviewers seem to share their blindness.

In this sense, to be sure, Jones's book is truly a mirroring of the times, for the concept of the duty of obedience to legitimate authority is certainly feeble in the American mind. We might, however, have expected the critics to distinguish between proper independence of the human spirit and an inarticulate, crazy hatred of superiors simply because they are superiors.

Whether Jones and his praisers realize it or not, to view authority as authoritarianism is to strip it of all moral force. It can then impose itself only by physical force—and we are plunk in the middle of Communist ideology. Not many modern U.S. novels get published in Russia—this one would keep them up happily at night in the Kremlin.

There are two other observations that impose themselves. They touch on the whole problem of the strength of the free world in the face of the slave threat. They may sound like exaggerations, and I hope they are, but they are at least results that might logically flow from this book.

We are expanding our armed forces. We are debating the age of inductees. Families all over the country are rightly concerned about the moral atmosphere that will surround the young men who will spend a year or more in uniform. If responsible mothers and fathers read this book (though likely most of them would not be caught dead with it), they will find themselves in a mood to move heaven and earth rather than have their sons plunged into such an Army. It will matter little to them that Jones is depicting the Regular Army. Is a peacetime Army, they will wonder, any different? If several million people read this book (and they will, many of them assisted by the Book-of-the-Month Club, which is distributing it as an alternate selection), the result could well be several million conscientious objectors.

Lastly, U.S. troops will be going abroad in larger numbers. If Europeans read *From Here to Eternity*, they would have legitimate grounds for doubting whether protection afforded by such U.S. officers and men would be one whit better than inundation by Soviet hordes. They would at least feel impelled to lock up their wives and daughters. This saga of foul-mouthedness, sex, brutality, contempt of authority, vapid and blasphemous "philosophizing" on marriage, love, and God adds another and powerful brush stroke to the picture some Europeans are all too fond of contemplating— the portrait of America as non-civilized.

One final remark. If West Point ever produced officers like the ones who wallow through these pages, it ought to be fumigated, blown into the Hudson, or—perhaps a worse fate—put through the wringer of a congressional investigation.   (March 10, 1951)

"THE BARBARIANS ARE WITHIN THE GATES"

The title above is the conclusion Ben Ray Redman reaches from a study of new trends in the American whodunit. The results of Mr. Redman's researches were published in the *Saturday Review of*

Literature under the title "Decline and Fall of the Whodunit." They deserve the serious consideration of all who are concerned with the culture of this country and especially with the role reading has to play in developing or polluting that culture. Almost simultaneously, a high-flown study of the whodunit, "Murder for the Millions," appeared in *Town & Country* from the pen of Charles J. Rolo. Its implications are not so serious, but serious enough to merit consideration.

Mr. Redman begins with a brief résumé of how the detective story started, how it attracted writers of real talent, and how, by a kind of common consent, those who were respectable came to observe certain rules. These rules were that violence and cruelty were not exploited for their own sake, that there had to be at "least as much detection as crime," that the solution should never be just blundered into, that romantic involvement of the detective was to be frowned on, and that the sleuth should do his work with his brains.

What has happened to these rules of the game? They have not only been junked; they have been replaced by their almost exact opposites. This process began, according to Mr. Redman, with Dashiell Hammett, was further developed by Raymond Chandler, and has been brought to a screaming climax by Mickey Spillane.

Spillane's private detective, Mike Hammer, is not a sleuth; he is a "killer with delusions of grandeur." In one book, Hammer revels in "the power of the gun and the obscene pleasure that was brutality and force, the spicy sweetness of murder sanctified by law." Not only is he a killer; he is driven by an insane blood lust; he is "driven by crazy, mad hatreds that tied my insides into knots." Hammer rejoices in subhuman brutality for its own sake, and one might pardonably wonder whether Spillane does, too. As we might well expect in a character such as Hammer, he frequently solves his crime by stupid stumbling onto clues.

That is bad enough, by all canons of detective writing, but there is worse, much worse in Spillane. According to Mr. Redman, Hammer "moves swiftly from bed to bed in a series of concupiscent episodes, on which his creator dwells with amorous emphasis. . . . In his own choice words, he is continually 'drooling' at the sight, or even the thought, of some choice fleshly morsel."

Mr. Redman's summing up of this school of whodunits will perhaps give a fuller idea of their characteristics than many quotations. He concludes:

> Detection, in the true sense of the word, has been bred almost out of existence; while crime, on the other hand, has become dominant. Stupidity and brutality have replaced intelligence. Salacity has replaced ingenuity. Probability is flouted, credibility scorned, absurdity honored. A routine narrative pattern has been developed in which sadism, exhibitionism, sexual intercourse, and murder recur at regular intervals, while homosexuality, flagellation, or some other attractive perversion occasionally adds zest to the whole.

Does Mr. Redman exaggerate? I checked by reading three of the Spillane best-selling pocketbooks, *The Long Wait*, *Vengeance Is Mine*, and *I, the Jury*. It is my considered judgment that Mr. Redman is all too right. The barbarians are indeed within the gates.

But who are the barbarians? They are more than merely Mickey Spillane and other writers of that stripe and their sadistic characters. The barbarians are, to a growing extent, readers of this stuff, and their number is staggering. Say the publishers of Spillane: "In three years over eleven million copies of his first five books have been published in 25¢ Signet editions."

This is a major social phenomenon. If this type of whodunit is as degenerate as Mr. Redman and I think it is, the barbarians within the gates are a veritable fifth column, effectively, if perhaps unwittingly, sapping the moral fiber of this country. This is certainly true if the youth of this nation are to any great extent among "the millions of loyal fans" Spillane has won.

But perhaps the millions of loyal fans read Spillane just for the excitement—of which there is a surfeit—and don't pay any attention to the cruelty, the brutality, the lust, and the perversion? Here we must turn for a moment to Charles Rolo, whose *Town & Country* article was alluded to above. He comes up with a rather exotic and silly explanation of the appeal of the whodunit. According to Rolo, "The detective story is modern man's Passion Play." The Hero has the call to set the world at rights (the world out of joint by the murder). He is the savior; the murderer is Everyman, the symbol of the guilt that is in all of us. The detective suffers, as a savior must, but he finally brings order into the world—truth has been made manifest and justice prevails. Moreover, the detective-savior is also a prophet, for he witnesses to a "system of belief, a secular credo, or a religious doctrine."

More than that, in the Rolo ratiocination: the reader also plays, vicariously, the role of savior; "he finds himself saving the world with a borrowed credo which is temporarily his . . . whatever system of belief the hero acts out will infuse something of itself into the reader."

It's a very neat psychological pattern. The only trouble with it is that Mr. Rolo is trying to apply it to two types of whodunits which are essentially different. The classic detectives, Holmes, Poirot, Peter Wimsey, are indeed interested in truth and justice, and they do set things to rights in their little worlds. The reader, if he likes to indulge in Mr. Rolo's fancy, may identify himself with the detective-savior.

But with the Hammers of the Spillanes, any thoughtful reader will feel that the world has been set all the more wrong because the murder is solved and the culprit brought to "justice" by means of brutality, lechery, insane blood lust. Hammer is actually a fouler creature than most of those from whom he is "saving" the world.

But Mr. Rolo does manage to say something that rings true, and it is the menace contained in that truth which points out how great is the threat of the barbarians within the gates. The system, the "credo" of the detective "will infuse something of itself into the reader," who borrows it temporarily.

But how do we know that the borrowing is temporary? How can Mr. Rolo or anybody else say that the spell of Hammer-Spillane lasts only so long as we are within the pages of the book? What if dozens, hundreds, of the "loyal fans," especially among the young and impressionable, "borrow" a creed of sadism and mayhem on a more permanent basis? Is it possible? Is it probable? Well, I for one would hate, before God and before decent public opinion in this country, to have the responsibility for saying it is not.

Apart from the strictly moral aspect of these books, what about cultural barbarism? If this type of book were not degenerate and foul, it would still be vulgar and crude. The irony of the situation is that Signet books ("Good reading for the millions") are published by the New American Library. This booming firm was written up at length in *Newsweek*. Though Spillane was alluded to in the write-up, it was nowhere stated that the NAL publishes him. The claim was made that NAL's experience (and that of other pocket-size book publishers) shows that the taste of the American reading public is rather high. That is true, and NAL and others do publish a great quantity of good books for the millions. But they are at the same time conscious, to quote *Newsweek*, that

> the staple product of the reprint publisher is not the book with the undressed girl on the cover and a sequence of murders and seductions inside, but the public thinks it is, and if the average man gets fed up with the sensational and erotic items, his distaste could easily spread to include them all.

The New American Library is apparently out to disabuse the average man of this impression. But it will certainly never disabuse him while it simultaneously pushes the sales of Spillane to greater and more astronomical heights. In fact, if the loyal fans of Mickey continue to spawn, the NAL will be publishing books, good books, for a reading public that has been so hopped up on brutality and lechery that it will find the sanity and serenity of good books as tasteless as pablum.

Then the barbarians will not only be within the gates. They will be ready to take over the city.   (June 28, 1952)

FAINTING WITH DAMN PRAISE

Granville Hicks planted a buzz bomb smack in the middle of the book-reviewing fraternity when he wrote in the *New Leader* his article "The New Yorker, Anthony West and the Sad State of Literary Journalism." The bomb has been ticking away ever since, but the full-fledged explosion, anticipated with horrid eagerness by many, has not yet come. True, there has been much sly button-holing among the literary brethren; much "say, have you read Hicks's blast yet?"—with a brave little hope peeping out and looking for a friendly pat on the head. Perhaps—oh, perhaps!—this time the smart-alecky *New Yorker* has really got its comeuppance.

But the *New Yorker* itself, and notably Anthony West, have preserved a dignified, discreet, or perhaps necessary, silence. There has been a small exchange of letters in the *Saturday Review*, but, by and large, Mr. Hicks's buzz bomb is still just ticking away. It will be a shame if a good, sizable explosion does not rip loose, for I believe that there is too much complacency among those whom Mr. Hicks calls the "literary journalists" to distinguish them from full-fledged critics. I believe that opinions on books do not arouse the healthy discussion that ought to make the pages of book-review media more vital and challenging than they are. I believe that there is entirely too much "yea, man" attitude among reviewers. And I am ready to suggest, for the sake of the argument and because I feel that there is more than a suspicion of truth in the charge, that the ungoverned enthusiasm and high-voltage language of the blurb writers influence, perhaps all unperceived, the judgments of the literary journalists.

In other words, I agree with Mr. Hicks that there is at least the beginning of a "sad state" among the reviewers, and if this addition to the controversy will nudge Mr. Hicks's buzz bomb into an early explosion, I will not, as prefaces so often say, have written in vain.

But my charge is different from Mr. Hicks's. He thinks, if I may streamline his argument a bit, that the *New Yorker* and especially Mr. West are too strict in judgment—snobbishly and unfairly strict. My indictment is that all too many reviewers are too ready to award greatness and immortality. One often has the impression that a first healthy reaction to the book under review has been polished and pruned (for, after all, it is to appear in print and may perchance win for itself an accolade of greatness) to such an extent that the reviewer does not say what he really would say in a less formal and full-dress moment.

However that may be, it is instructive and suggestive to compare reviews of the same books in the American journals and in, say, the London *Times Literary Supplement*. As a fairly steady phenomenon, the English review will be much more temperate and cautious. It will be much charier in seeing greatness; the fifth or sixth book of a prominent author will not automatically become "the apex" of his writing career. The English literary journalist, one feels, approaches his task with a healthy and constructive skepticism, whereas his American counterpart is apt to be widely eyed naïve—or more malleable to the jargon of the sales department of the publishing house.

The only way to give evidence to support this impression is to quote. I have before me a sizable stack of reviews from the American and English papers. I can't use all the material but these samples may serve to establish my point..

Recently, the National Book Awards went to John O'Hara's *Ten North Frederick* for the best fiction and to Herbert Kubly's *Stranger in Italy* for the top non-fiction. The books had been winnowed out for the vote of the jury by a poll among all the leading reviewers, publishers, book sellers, etc., in the country. Obviously the winning volumes had come in for some high praise from the literary journalists.

But what do the *Literary Supplement* reviews say? Admitting quite graciously Mr. O'Hara's skill "as a reporter" and "his considerable art in the selection and ordering of detail," the review concludes:

> By the end of the book, it might be said unkindly, we know all about Joe Chapin [the story's protagonist], but we still do not know Mr. O'Hara's reason for writing a book about him. Such a criticism would be unfair, for to Mr. O'Hara people are interesting only as part of the social pattern.

Kindly or not, the criticism raises a question the American adjudicators obviously did not suspect—was the award made for fiction or was it made for a sociological study?

Even more pertinent to my theme are respective reviews of *Stranger in Italy*. Again, since the book got the National Book Awards laurel, I shall not quote specific American evaluations. But here is a final paragraph of the *Literary Supplement* judgment:

> An insufficient knowledge of Italy, her history, and institutions would not necessarily be fatal to a collection of character sketches and travel notes, but they are fatal to Mr. Kubly's grandiose plan of explaining Italy and America to each other. Sentimentality, a superficial approach to the gravest of problems, and a belief that anyone who speaks to an American must infallibly be telling the truth have combined to make a muddled book which . . . presents almost as misleading an impression of Italy as any of the Hollywood films the author castigates.

Earlier, as an example of how Mr. Kubly "gives the impression of loving the Italians without understanding their background, their values, or their religion," the reviewer had pointed out:

Italy is defined, without qualification, as "Latin, pagan, Catholic, and poor," and, when the Romans cheer the Holy Father, Mr. Kubly comments: "To the people the man was divine; their emotions could be aroused by none less than a god."

Would the cool—to say the least—reception of our two "best" books of the year perhaps suggest that the American critics were a little too generous in their praise?

But let us press on. Irwin Shaw's *Lucy Crown* has been greeted by American reviewers like this: "The best of Shaw's novels" (New York *Herald Tribune*); "sharply drawn, highly charged, continuously absorbing" (New York *Times Book Review*); "a remarkably apt comment on modern, high-style marriage" (*Saturday Review*); "compelling and personal" (*Newsweek*); "a first-rate novel of real depth and power" (New York *World-Telegram*).

The *Literary Supplement* devotes exactly twenty-two lines to *Lucy Crown* and concludes:

> Mr. Shaw treats his subject with desperate seriousness, but unhappily one is never convinced that his characters would behave as he makes them do in their moments of crisis. From a writer so talented, *Lucy Crown* must be called a disappointment.

Or let's take A. J. Cronin's recent A *Thing of Beauty*. The New York *Times Book Review* calls it "one of the most moving novels of the year"; the *Chicago Tribune* avers that it "keeps the reader's eyes glued to the page"; the New York *Herald Tribune Book Review* puts it "in the company of *Lust for Life*" (a trick of casual "see how much I know" reference that Mr. Hicks finds especially annoying and irrelevant as practiced by Mr. West). But the *Literary Supplement* will have none of this fanfare. It allots twenty chilly lines to *Crusader's Tomb* (the English title), ending with the estimate that this is a "well-padded tale."

This sturdy refusal to be overenthusiastic about books hot off the press is not a new thing in English reviewing circles. Several years ago, for instance, when the American critics were knocking themselves out to find in *From Here to Eternity* some literary veneer that might camouflage the dirt (the editorial board of the Book-of-the-Month Club beat the drum for the book's "genuine literary importance"), the London *Times*, the *Daily Express*, *John O'London's Weekly* all concurred with the *Standard's* opinion: "It is a mistake for the novelist to have his ear so close to the ground that he can only hear noises in the sewer."

Again, after the American reviewing fraternity had generally praised Remarque's *Spark of Life*, the *Literary Supplement* lamented that "this hashed-up story of an imaginary concentration camp continues Mr. Remarque's decline as a novelist."

My reader, by this time perhaps not so gentle, may be with difficulty suppressing the suspicion that I am an Anglophile and that all I have proved so far is that English reviewers would rather abolish overnight the partition of Ireland than give a laudatory review to an American book, particularly an American novel. Not so, reader. English reviewers, by and large, don't seem to suffer from Yankeephobia. Witness, for example, the fine praise accorded to Sloan Wilson's *The Man in the Gray Flannel Suit* ("fresh, authentic talent"; "an important, absorbing book that deals in ideas and conflicts with an extraordinary deceptive readability").

Such examples could be multiplied, and further, the nice balance of judgment that will not fly immediately to hucksters' phrases is manifest in the English critics' approach to both their own literature and to that of non-English-speaking lands as well. Here, for instance, are some phrases from a review of *Un Certain Sourire*. After conceding the undoubted and rather extraordinary talent of Françoise Sagan (*Bonjour Tristesse*), the review goes on to pose the question whether this is legitimate novel writing or "exhibitionism on paper—and at times a rather dreary and repugnant exhibition. Time alone will tell whether Mlle. Sagan is enjoying a *succès de scandale* or a success really worthy of her exceptional gifts." The book will be published in the United States this month under the title *A Certain Smile*. I shall be greatly surprised if even one American reviewer will be able to temper his justified praise with any suggestion that perhaps what Mlle. Sagan says so well is really not worth saying.

One of the bones Mr. Hicks has to pick with the *New Yorker's* literary journalism are the reviews that appear in the "Briefly Noted" section. Among other complaints, Mr. Hicks thinks that the anonymity of these reviews "seems to encourage bad taste, and the brief reviewer, trying hard to be smart, succeeds merely in being vulgar." Could be, as they say. But, on the other hand, the reviews in the *Literary Supplement* are all anonymous and, whatever else we may think of them, they are not in bad taste. Could it be that if more American reviews were not signed, the critic would be a little more fearless in saying what he really thinks? Could it be that no reviewer was ready, by signing his name to a statement that Mr. O'Hara had not written a good novel, to lay himself open to the possible scorn of his fellow critics?

The *New Yorker* and Mr. West are a fair target for the charge of snootily singing *extra chorum*. But a great many other reviewers often sing too obediently with the chorus. My contention is that there is too much of follow-the-leader in American literary journalism, and that the leader too often speaks with the accents of Madison Avenue.   (August 18, 1956)

GET-RICH-QUICK LURE OF
"CONDENSED BOOKS"

Older readers—into whose ranks we are rapidly being winnowed by remorseless time—may remember a redoubtable character whose escapades used to grace the pages of an older *Saturday Evening Post,* if our reading memory does not play us false. He was Get-Rich-Quick Wallingford, who came up every week or so with some scheme, plausible and even seductive on the surface but hare-brained beneath, for becoming a millionaire practically overnight and most painlessly. Mr. Wallingford has long succumbed to oblivion, perhaps because the attractions of becoming a mere millionaire do not loom so large in these days of high taxes. He still lingers in the older reader's mind and affections, however, as a type of American who wanted, and wants, big results fast—with a minimum of effort.

There is nothing wrong, of course, with a man making a million dollars fast, providing neither the sum nor the speed entails immoral means or ends. And if American technical methods can assure the erecting of a skyscraper over a weekend, well and good, provided it is a well and safely built building. But when we get into the realms of the mind and the spirit, into the fields of culture in general, problems arise. Is it possible to get culturally rich quick? Can one become really well educated in a hurry? Can wine truly be mellowed by electronic bombardments?

It has long been a suspicion in some quarters that one of the characteristic features of American civilization has been exactly this passion to get culturally rich quick. Much of this passion, of course, is most admirable. We, as a culture, had a late start and, in our determination to catch up, often felt that we could prove our cultural equality merely by attracting, mainly *because* we could afford to buy them, works of art, great artists and musicians. In the days when we were not producing many evidences of deep culture, we thought commendably that at least we could give culture a haven and a hearing.

But other aspects of this zeal for a cultural speed-up raise some questions. One of the reasons for the success of the *Reader's Digest*, for example, would seem to be the impression many people have that if they read only the fascinating articles over a relatively small period of time, they will have the equivalent of a university education. Readers would hear, in a year or so, of all the latest developments in science, philosophy, religion, the arts, public affairs, sports, amusements, crime, and what not. The magazine, of course, never promised all this, but how many a reader has unconsciously, wistfully been all along anticipating just about that?

The newest promise that culture—or one aspect of it—can be got quick-like seems to be the proliferation of the "condensed-book" clubs. It is a phenomenon about a year and a half old; it seems to be with us to stay; it perhaps deserves at this time some thought and criticism. What does the phenomenon promise; what can it deliver?

Here is, to begin with, a rundown on some of the major "condensed-book" clubs. The giant among them is the Reader's Digest Condensed Book Club. It began in 1950 with a "modest" 200,000 members; by the middle of 1954, it had burgeoned to 1,600,000 members. For the price of two dollars these members get every three months four books condensed into one volume (the four complete books would have cost $14.45). This condensed-book club extended its operations to England in the summer of 1954; one English reaction will be commented on later.

Doubleday's Best-in-Books offers to its 200,000 members (as of August 1954) up to eight books, shortened into one volume, six times a year at $1.49. A subsidiary of the Book-of-the-Month Club, Books Abridged, charges $1.95 a month for four condensed books. Other competitors in the field include Condensed Religious Books, which culls Protestant thought, and a Condensed Classics Club, whose abridgements, it is announced, will be "educator approved."

There are very probably other "condensed-book" clubs which have not yet come within purview—how could there not be, when the pioneers have met with such staggering success? But this brief survey will at least show that an estimate would not be far wrong which concluded that today there are millions of Americans who, if they read anything save the daily paper and a popular magazine, must spend their book-reading time keeping up with the 600-odd pages into whose compass four to eight books have been condensed.

Is any judgment of this trend proper to make at this time? We have one reaction, one judgment, which I would like to pass on to those who are concerned with the proper place of the book in American cultural life. It appeared in the London *Times Literary Supplement* for July 30, 1954, and viewed somewhat askance the news that the Reader's Digest Condensed Book Club would soon invade the British Isles. An editorial in the eminent journal noted somewhat ungraciously that the process of condensing books was possible because

> . . . skilled condensers, trained in a technique analogous to those used by the Oriental growers of miniature trees and the head-shrinkers of the Amazon, will employ their art in compressing five full works into the compass of one ordinary book. So, there is no reason to doubt, the number of books "read" will be much increased, and for author and publisher of the original there will flow, so to speak, a second pressing of the grape.

After going on to admit that some kinds of books are admirably suited to condensation for some kinds of readers—books that merely give information, for example: "matters of fact (a field in which shortest written is usually best read)"—the editorial poses the larger question of "why we read and write books at all?" If we read for pleasure and delight and some need of wisdom (which is far wider and deeper than mere instruction), then who is to condense into us these fruits of reading? Most experienced readers, indeed, develop "some powers of condensation and need no separate condenser," and, moreover, the whole scheme raises the problem "whether a skilled condenser, faced with half a million words on which to apply his art, must, to play fair, read every one of them."

How, for instance, would even a most professional "shrinker of heads" go about condensing Waugh's *Officers and Gentlemen?* This is my query, not that of the *Literary Supplement.* If a novel is a good novel, does its excellence rest only in a plot? If so, it could probably be condensed into a sentence, just as *Macbeth* could be so shrunken. But if atmosphere, more or less leisurely character development, philosophical and descriptive asides, the beauty of language, and keenness of observation mean anything today, as they have meant much down through the history of literature—then how can all this be simmered, boiled, stewed, or reduced by any other process to bare bones? Admitted that many a modern novel would be improved by being reduced by a third, to maintain, as the condensed-book pushers seem to do, that any book can be improved or at least essentially transmitted is like claiming that the shrunken head still keeps the faculties of sight, taste, and smell.

Those who literally do not have time to read and who still would like to be able to "keep up with the books" may find some value in condensed books, but certainly no one who has ever truly enjoyed the pleasures of reading will consider that he is getting more in the boiled-down books than the leftovers of what might well have been a sumptuous literary banquet.

In the face of this trend, which seems the latest spasm in the endemic American get-rich-quick fever, I would like to underline the suggestions Frank Sheed makes at the conclusion of his admirable little pamphlet, *Reading for Catholic Parents.* He advises:

1. A real book cannot be read at the same speed as a pass-time book, any more than a steak can be eaten at the same speed as ice cream . . . Take a book as slowly as you need to understand it.

2. It helps tremendously to have someone else reading the same book, so that you can discuss it together . . . You are not bound to agree with everything the author says. Listen to what he says, but use your own mind. It is not essential that you think what he thinks. But it is essential that you should know what you think.

3. Read with a pencil. Mark in the margin passages that seem to you to say something that you had not realized before, or to express some already known truth particularly winningly.

4. When reading, you will every so often come across a phrase

which sheds a great shaft of light upon your own experience.
. . . You never know when the truth will strike home. When that
happens, stop reading, shut the book, put it away. Let the phrase
sink into you. Many a book is of less value than one of its phrases.

Obviously, one who makes his reading a steady diet of condensed
books will never read in that way. Indeed, the phrase that may have
shed a "shaft of light" will probably have been already carefully
condensed out of existence, and the passages that might have been
thoughtfully pencil-marked already blue-penciled into oblivion.

The parting counsel—which may have been gathered by now—
is this. Be chary about plunging into a constant reading of condensed books alone. They may serve a purpose, but it is not the
purpose that good books have served down through the ages. They
can supply mere information, but the cultural riches they seem to
promise are, generally speaking, riches that are panned, even in
this age of speed reading, ounce by ounce, and not gathered from
bulging bonanzas that yield huge nuggets at every stroke of the
pick. Wisdom, which books, after all, are supposed to make grow
in us, is a slow growth. I am sure that even Mr. Wallingford, who
never actually got rich quick, would agree.   (August 13, 1955)

CLICHÉS ARE DANGEROUS

To our prejudiced eye, one of the most sparkling articles to appear
in *America's* pages in recent years was Thurston N. Davis's
"Scrabble on Madison Avenue" (January 15, 1955). It's always
politic, of course, to speak well of the work of one's editor-in-chief,
but, quite apart from that, we honestly feel that Father Davis did
a great service by calling attention to the "slow corruption of language" injected into our linguistic blood stream by admen who
place no limit on "this meretricious use of sounds and syllables to
titillate a jaded public."

This Madison Avenue scrabble is perhaps mere smart-aleck sales-
manship. But there is a serious side to this playfulness with language. The simple fact is that

words are meant to have meaning. They are conventional symbols for the spiritual realities we call ideas. Until the recent past,

a kind of abiding respect for language kept us from permitting its disintegration through arbitrary combinations of its mangled elements. . . . There was a time, before we got to exploiting language as a set of purely evocative symbols, when we would not have dared to bastardize a glorious name like Marathon into a monsterlike "phonathon." Now anything goes.

Whether or not the advertisers' attitude of "anything goes" points to a softened moral fiber, there is a field in which a lazy or dishonest misuse of words does pose a threat to standards of moral judgment on the part of students (especially in the secular colleges and universities) and of the ordinary reader. I refer to the jargon, the clichés, the short cuts to thoughtful criticism which seem to me more and more employed by literary critics and book reviewers. Three words in particular have been consistently debased, and their debasement suggests that a sort of moral relativism is the only standard a reader need bring to the perceptive reading of literature. Those words are symbolism, mysticism, and compassion.

A most slipshod and misleading use of the word symbol, or symbolism, has cropped up in the vocabulary of hitherto careful critics in connection with the sensational novel *Lolita*. This book, "proudly" published by G. P. Putnam's Sons (a feat that wins an accolade from a critic for its "courage"), is, without the slightest doubt in my mind, the most obscene lucubration to disgrace U.S. publishing in many a decade. The theme itself is distasteful enough: it concerns the perversions of a middle-aged European émigré who has an ineluctable fondness for what he calls "nymphets"—teen-age girls. The story deals in detail with his motel-to-motel dalliance with twelve-year-old Lolita, who, to be frank about it, is a spoiled, even vicious, sexually precocious brat. The details are, as one critic opines, quite "delicately" treated; that is to say, there are none of the "obscene" four-letter words. It is all very sophisticated, dripping with phony "culture," written in an arch style that pleads for "understanding." But it is weary, cynical, degenerate, and, precisely because of its veneer of blasé charm, emits more noisomely than a cruder tale would the nauseating odor of festering lilies. Incidentally, it proves admirably the wise dictum that "only the truly vulgar don't see that pornography is utterly boring."

The book has had a strange history. After four U.S. publishers had refused to touch it, author Vladimir Nabokov sent it to France, where it was issued in English by the Olympia Press, only to run into a ban by the French Government. Then the U. S. Customs authorities declared that the book did not come under restrictions against the importation of "obscene" material, and some copies found their way into the hands of those who apparently lie in wait for this type of under-the-counter stuff. G. P. Putnam's Sons now has the dubious distinction of raising the book to over-the-counter stature. It will have quite a monetary stature, too; watch the sales figures after publication on August 18.

It ought to be adverted to, I suppose, that the story is told in the first person by the pervert, who has already spent several spells in asylums and who writes his tale while waiting the verdict for having murdered the "monster" who wins Lolita away from him. This heart-wringing circumstance, some of the critics have been telling us, adds to the "immensely funny" story a dimension of "tragedy." Elizabeth Janeway (New York *Times Book Review*), in particular, sees the narrator as "the hero with a tragic flaw." We might as well refer to a putrescent corpse as a "noble human body with a flaw."

This is all cause enough for headshaking, but now I come to a more serious matter, namely, the evasions, subterfuges, and plain double talk to which a good number of critics have resorted to whitewash this decadent book. A dozen or more such statements can be unearthed in the little brochure with which the publishers are "proudly" announcing its appearance.

The most amazing debasement of critical vocabulary, however, appears in the statement of Professor Harry Levin of Harvard: "[It is] not primarily sexual at all. [It is] a symbol of the aging European intellectual coming to America, falling in love with it but finding it, sadly, a little immature. . . ." One can wonder, incidentally, whether Professor Levin read Mr. Nabokov's own epilogue, in which the author states that ". . . everybody should know that I detest symbols and allegories . . ." (p. 316); but let that go.

The main point is that symbolism is an ancient and respected technique. A symbol, say the dictionaries, stands for something else; it is a sign that suggests more than it actually denotes. A flag is actually a piece of cloth, but it stands for love of country, national heroes, even respect for God. But the prime fact about a flag is that it *is* a piece of cloth; it *is not* love of country. Symbols, in other words, have a twofold significance; they mean what they actually are and they connote something they actually are not. When Gerard Manley Hopkins described the windhover in his famous poem, he was first meditating on the actual flight of an actual bird; he saw beyond that, in the grace and mastery of the flight, a suggestion, a connotation, a symbolism of the majesty of Christ.

But a newer interpretation of symbolism, of which Professor Levin's is, if I am not mistaken, an extreme example, seems to be that anything can be said if only something else is intended. The imagery of *Lolita* is not "meant" to be sexual; therefore the obvious sexual implications can be, must be, overlooked because there is a "deeper" meaning. This is a strange application to literary criticism of the end justifying the means.

But let me go on to another catchword that you will find in just about every other review of a book that deals with the more sordid aspects of life. Sure enough, this overworked word crops up in one estimate of our *Lolita*. Said that critic: "By high art [this novel] transmutes persons, motives, and actions which in ordinary life are considered indecent into objects of delight, compassion, and contemplation. . . ." There, the word is out—it is "compassion."

Madame de Staël once wrote that *tout comprendre rend très indulgent* (to know all makes one tolerant). This may be true and even desirable in life, but it is no way for a man to write a "compassionate" book. It may be quite clear to me why the "hero" in a novel runs off with his neighbor's wife, or takes up dope pushing, or does any number of reprehensible things; but this is not enough to make me "tolerant" of these sadder aspects of human nature. Understanding, in other words, is not enough of itself to engender compassion.

Compassion connotes, in addition, a desire to help, and in order to help, I must have some idea of what to do; I must pass some at least inchoative judgment. Edmund Fuller has an admirable and incisive treatment of this "new compassion in the American novel" in Chapter 3 of his recent *Man in Modern Fiction*. He states, in part:

Now we see increasingly a technique of simple identification with the degraded [the "lovable bum" of Steinbeck and others, says Mr. Fuller, "began to slip away, and in his place emerged

the genial rapist, the jolly slasher, the fun-loving dope pusher"]
which is miscalled compassion. . . .

What is compassion, anyhow? It means the sharing of a sorrow,
a pity, and a sympathy, a desire to help. . . . It applies to a
man's moral as well as material or physical breakdown. In the
moral realm it recognizes the sharing of all human guilt, the
potentiality of evil in the most blameless, the element which
the Christian calls original sin and the analyst calls the id.

A distinct set of values is necessary to establish compassion.
. . . Compassion is not a suspension of judgment; it is a judgment tempered and chastened according to the facts under some
definable theory of the human condition . . . Mercy follows a
judgment; it does not precede it.

Mr. Fuller's analysis is a trenchant dissection of the moral relativism—there's no real good or evil, or if there is, who's to say just
where?—that vitiates much of U.S. fiction writing. Let the reader,
both of the novels and of the critics, beware.

As a last bit of evidence for the prosecution, I would like to
adduce the misuse of the word "mysticism." This is indeed a large
and involved field and I don't have either space or equipment to
discuss that intuitive grasp of God which is real mysticism. But I do
know this: mysticism is not the word to describe the spiritual processes of such characters as those who held the stage in Maugham's
The Razor's Edge. They were religiously at sea, they were searching
for a meaning to life, and something between Confucianism to Zen,
with a few excursions into Trappist monasteries thrown in, was the
watery reach of their spiritual wanderings. Such characters, dubbed
"mystics" by mystified critics, remind one of Daniel Boone. When
asked, so the tale goes, whether he had ever been lost in all his
wanderings in the wilderness, he replied after considerable thought:
"Well, no; but I can remember being considerably confused for
three days."

Frankly, I know of very few novels that contain the character of
a real mystic. Some of the French masterpieces come perhaps close
—Bernanos's *Joy* and *The Diary of a Country Priest*, Bloy's *The
Woman Who Was Poor*—but real mysticism is a subject not easily
treated in a novel.

These are the three words a serious reader ought to beware of.
Symbols mean first of all what they directly say; the plus value

presupposes the actual denotation; otherwise we are in the no man's land of "the meaning of meaning." Compassion is not maudlin, anything-goes-if-understood sentimentality. Mysticism means a foretaste of the Beatific Vision; it is not a miasma of neon ads proclaiming an earthly paradise, seen through the mellow mists of religious indifferentism. Watch the critics' fuzzy words and you may read better than Johnny.

(August 30, 1958)

SOME WRITERS REVERENCE LOVE

It's a perennial temptation for a literary critic to think of himself as a sort of one-man Trendex. Set before him two novels, say, that deal with a similar theme or manifest a like slant on this or that, and immediately he heralds the beginnings of a "trend." The same critic, being naturally well versed in the sayings of the ancients, would be the first to admit that two swallows do not make a spring, but he will insist that a few trickles do make a trend.

This is very understandable, really. The man who tries to keep abreast of the output of books—and this is especially true in the field of fiction—begins to wonder if he is reading in all directions at once. He longs to find a center, a vantage point from which he can bring the disparate books under some common viewpoint. Styles obviously differ, story lines are poles apart, locales can be palaces or slums—and yet, feels the critic, yielding to the common human urge to synthesize, all these books must have something in common.

He knows, of course, that any novel worth its salt will inevitably be talking about perennial human condition, as we somewhat loftily say today, or about the basic conflict between good and evil, right and wrong, sin and virtue. This, however, is a bit too general for our Trendex-minded critic, and so he is on the rather nervous lookout for some concrete social situation or viewpoint, and if he finds it in two or three almost simultaneously produced novels— bingo!—he is the literary Sherlock Holmes of the moment.

As a matter of fact, two Holmeses are right now donning their deer-stalker caps and arming themselves with magnifying glass and fingerprint kit to examine the corpus of American fiction. Robert Elliot Fitch has entitled his study of the state of U.S. novels *The*

Decline and Fall of Sex. Dr. Fitch (he is a Congregational minister) has given critics of the U.S. cultural scene much to think about. His style is witty, but his conclusions are lugubrious. In brief, he charges that sex, as portrayed by American novelists, has degenerated to the point that it is now considered merely a plaything. Gone is any sense that sex can be glorious or tragic, a source of realized and generously embraced duty, a nurse of nobility and a pedagogue of virtue.

Dr. Fitch makes out a good case but, try as I may, I cannot quite see that there is the "trend" he claims to discover. For one thing, many of his examples are taken from the long-since fizzled-out sensationalism of Elinor Glyn and Anita Loos (remember *Three Weeks* and *Gentlemen Prefer Blondes?*—I doubt you do). When it comes to naming contemporary U.S. authors, critic Fitch is hard put to come up with more than three or four names.

Robert Raynolds is similarly equipped with gumshoes, but his magnifying glass is even less high-powered than Dr. Fitch's. Mr. Raynolds has written, among other works, the distinguished novel *The Sinner of St. Ambrose.* It appears that Mr. Raynolds is now waging singlehanded a crusade to alert the reading public to his forthcoming novel *Far Flight of Love,* which, he says, has "been ennobled by eleven years of defeat at the hands of publishers." House after house has turned his novel down because, he claims, it is too clean and idealistic a love story. So he has turned to a "vanity publishing" house (a term he indignantly repudiates) and meanwhile is writing to reviewers, critics, and journals to enlist support.

From what I know of Mr. Raynolds's work, I expect that his book will be a noble statement of the nobility of marriage. But in striving to assure us that it is, Mr. Raynolds comes up with the detection of a "trend" I doubt exists—at most it's a tiny trend, not a towering one. In general terms, Mr. Raynolds's charge is that

> many of the novels [which publishers claim] to be importantly
> concerned with love, and back with liberal advertising, show that
> [the publishers] are willing to traduce the name of love to catch
> a market in the salacious.

This is a sweeping and serious charge. To document it, Mr. Raynolds adduces only four novels, of which a bare two are by American novelists, *Hecate County* by Edmund Wilson, and *Pey-*

ton Place, which is without doubt as rotten as anything in Denmark.

I am by no means blaming the resentment of Dr. Fitch and Mr. Raynolds at the annual appearance of a number of salacious books that do actually defile any Christian concept of sex and marriage; it is indeed the unpleasant duty of our review columns to lash such offerings with whips and scorpions. But there is not a *flood* of such books. It is lamentable that a reputable publishing house will let one *Peyton Place* or one *Deer Park* soil its lists, but I don't believe we should cry "wolf" too readily, because when the really malodorous book comes along, the wolf—in more senses than one—is ready and able to gobble up a reading public weary of warnings. Or if we must follow out the figure, the reading public is ready to gobble up the wolf.

To counterbalance the trend discerned by Dr. Fitch and Mr. Raynolds, I have Sherlocked a bit, too, and can come up with a "trend" that gives as persuasively, I hope, a cheerier picture. If there are a number (not great) of books that "traduce the name of love" in recent U.S. literary history, there have also been a greater number of books that proclaim the nobility of sex and love.

It is by no means true that among the American fiction-writing fraternity only Catholic novelists still regard sex and love and the family as noble and sacred—Mr. Raynolds himself is proof to the contrary. But my trend does center on Catholic authors, and I think that it is a most significant sign that these authors consistently refute the opposite "trend" toward the debasement of love.

We may mention first the body of Richard Sullivan's fiction, with especial emphasis on *The World of Idella May*. It features a marriage that would have been a farce, that would have been portrayed by another author not deeply convinced of the union's sacramental character, as naturally leading to many an extramarital foray. All of Mr. Sullivan's novels are steeped in this realization, and his basic attitude is admirably expressed in his recent review of *The World of Suzie Wong*, by Richard Mason, which is being hailed as "a memorable and original love story." Mr. Sullivan's estimate (New York *Times Book Review*) is:

Love and art are very high matters. They demand appropriate treatment. Some altitude, some elevation, is required when love and art are looked at, for they cannot be seen from a level of shock and sentimentality. As a rendering of the artist and of artistic endeavor, *The World of Suzie Wong* is regrettably absurd. As a rendering of love, which subsumes art, it is merely topical, superficial, and thin.

Paul Horgan is another Catholic novelist who constantly gazes at love from "some elevation," as will certainly strike the reader of *Give Me Possession*. In that book the elevation is perhaps all the more convincing because a realization of the responsibilities of love comes slowly to the almost pagan young "golden" Americans in the book. Another veteran Catholic practitioner in fiction, Margaret Culkin Banning, treats uncompromisingly and explicitly the problem of love (this time as a barrier to conversion to the faith) in *The Convert*, a story that is surprisingly gripping despite its overt didacticism.

Nor do we have to bolster our trend by looking to the established Catholic authors. A young writer whose two novels have received high praise shows forth the same realization that sex and love are not mere toys but carry consequences of supreme importance for time and eternity. He is Charles Bracelen Flood, and his *Love Is a Bridge* and *A Distant Drum* evidence a talent and—perhaps more important—a point of view that surely, as far as we can judge now, will lend no countenance to a debasement of human love.

Finally, as evidence of my trend hunting, let me alert you to a book that will be coming along in December, *Even As You Love*, by Elizabeth Barton de Trevino. Rarely have I read a statement (dramatic, not dogmatic) on marriage that is more moving and almost sublime.

I believe that here is one great challenge to the Catholic author. In an age when love, sex, and marriage have, to some extent at least, lost their meaning and their direction, the Christian and Catholic ideals must be restated time and again in the context of today's world. This challenge is being superbly met in the more scholarly fields, through the sociological work of such authors as Reverend John L. Thomas, S.J., Reverend Lucius Cervantes, S.J., A. H. Clemens, Clement S. Mihanovich, and others. It is being met in such concrete activities as the Cana and Christian Family movements. And I believe it is being met with growing frequency in the work of creative Catholic writers.

It was recently announced in the press that a French sociologist, Dr. Arnold Léger, was coming to the United States to find out how sex obsessed we Americans are. It is commonly charged in Europe, and especially in the Iron Curtain countries, he stated, that we are so ridden by a sex mania that we betray that "we are too adolescent to be trusted as a nation." One of his observations bears on my "trend." He remarked:

To us, one of the most puzzling things about American life is the attention [those] just reaching adult status give to sex. . . . In Europe, young men and women of university age don't have much to do with one another. That is the time for absorbing ideas and knowledge, and sex waits until later. The European idea really is that sex is meant for mature persons. In America it apparently becomes less important in maturity.

I don't know whether the good professor has yet landed on our shores, but I hope part of his study will lead him to some of our American Catholic writers. He will find that, whatever be their stature in the pantheon of the immortals, they are at least mature in their dealing with sex, love, and marriage. If I'm right, that's a healthy trend, friend, in American letters.   (August 31, 1957)

MODERN AUTHORS CAN BE GENTLEMEN

Style is to writing what graciousness is to deportment. One can, after all, get along in life with few major altercations, and even with a tolerable amount of pleasant and amicable relationships, without shedding around oneself that rare and winy bouquet of manners that we call graciousness, consideration of others. And one may write, too, in phrases that are intelligible, even forceful and emotion charged, without writing a single sentence that has about it that lovely and inevitable felicity that we call style.

As graciousness in deportment is not a superfluity, a sort of vestigial organ, but rather the fine fructification and flower of politeness, so this mysterious thing called style is not something that overlards the expression. It is the fine glow on the countenance of words, suffusing them in the same way that a fine soul lights up a beautiful face and quickens it to lovelier life.

Not only is style comparable to graciousness, but it depends to some extent, I think, on that quality, if not in the individual author's life, then at least in the social atmosphere of the age. Now, jeremiad groanings are distasteful to all of us, but is it not true that graciousness is little thought of in these our days, save as a quaint and stuffy relic of a somewhat saccharine past? How often do you hear a man praised nowadays as being a "gentleman?" That rather carries to our cynical ears the implication of "stuffed shirt"; instead, we lavish our meed of praise in terms like "a great guy," or admit that "he's tops." And as for referring to a feminine friend as a "gentlewoman" . . . !

Modern life has indubitably gained much in transition, but it has lost much, too—and a great and greatly to be lamented part of that much is graciousness.

As we regret this, so I think that we have also, and as a consequence, to wring our hands over the decline of style in very much modern writing. This observation has been made before, of course. It was made, for example, at a meeting of the English Association held in London last July. The president, Viscount Samuel, lamented the parlous state of modern poetry, attributing its anemia to one factor, indifference to literary style, which has led the poets "into a habit of intellectual contortion" and "contracted the appeal of poetry from the mind and heart to the languid interest of a sophisticated clique."

Recently, there appeared a most instructive criticism of Hemingway on this score of style. Marcus Goodrich, the author of *Delilah*, experimented for months in translating Conrad into the Hemingway rhythm and vocabulary, and came to the conclusion:

When writers limit themselves to the vocabulary of sixth graders, they abandon one of the greatest instruments of their profession. You can't write treatises for tough sophomores and hope to have your work endure. The sophomores will learn how to read, and despise you.

Here is an example of what he means. The original from which Hemingway took his title *For Whom the Bell Tolls* runs, in the stately sermon by John Donne:

No man is an Iland, intire of itself; every man is a peece of the Continent, a part of the maine: if a clod be washed away by the Sea, Europe is the lesse, as well as if a promontorie were, as well as if a Manor of thy friends or of thine were; any man's death

diminishes me, because I am involved in Mankinde; therefore
never send to know for whom the bell tolls; it tolls for thee.

Translated into Hemingway's manner, it might go thus, says Mr.
Goodrich:

Listen, what is important to you is important to me. We're all
mixed up together and if you die, that's a bad break for me. Same
if I die. You die a little when I die; I die a little when you die.
So don't send around to the church to find out who's dead. Part
of you is dead.

This simplification of expression, this avoiding all complexities
of language and hewing it down to the bare bones of thought, is
concomitant with and affected by the simplification of social intercourse, which is bringing about the decline in graciousness. For
graciousness does imply complexity: it entails allowances and compromises to be made; it demands consideration for others. It means
charity, and that queen of virtues, though simple in essence, is
infinitely detailed and complex in application.

But as social intercourse reduces more and more into a simple
man-to-man and man-to-woman brusk straightforwardness, and
loses more and more a gentleman-to-gentleman and gentleman-to-
lady relationship, the language that expresses that civilization is going to degenerate, too.

This is more or less the point made in a penetrating study of
Hemingway which appeared in the defunct *American Review*
(Summer issue, 1934). Wyndham Lewis, the author, concluded
that Hemingway "is inclined to gravitate stylistically toward the national underdog dialect. . . . Take up any book of his," he continues, and

you will find stuff that is, considered in isolation, valueless as
writing. It is not written: it is lifted out of nature and very art-
fully and adroitly tumbled out upon the page: it is the *brut*
material of everyday proletarian speech and feeling. The *matière*
is cheap and coarse: but not because it is proletarian speech
merely, but because it is *the prose of reality*—the prose of the
street-car or of the provincial newspaper or of the five-and-ten-cent
store.

It is not writing. . . . The cumulative effect is impressive, as the events themselves would be. . . . But if you say anyone could write it, you are mistaken.

Hemingway and his school, then, do have a style that is unique. That must be admitted, but the admission that this style is vastly popular today is at once a confession, for, as Mr. Lewis concludes: "If we take this to be the typical art of a civilization, then we are by the same token saying something very definite about that civilization."

Urbanity, then, would seem to be flickering out in much modern writing precisely because it is a vanishing quality in much modern life, and as it shows its decline in life by ever increasing social simplifications, by the constantly shrugging off of many of the complex social niceties of a generation ago, so it betrays its degeneration in writing by excessive simplifications in expression.

Hemingway can write, for example, a passage like this, in his *The Snows of Kilimanjaro:*

> No, that's not snow. It's too cloudy for snow. And the Secretary repeating to the other girls, No, you see. It's not snow, and them all saying, It's not snow we were mistaken. But it was snow all right and he sent them out into it.

This is simple and direct and so performs one of the great duties of style, to express thought clearly. But page after page of it inevitably leads one to echo Mr. Goodrich's bewilderment:

> Why, when the subtle language of civilization is at our hand, should we limit ourselves, particularly when writing a complex psychological novel, to the language of some not too bright primitives who never heard of the subtleties we are talking about?

This connection, tenuous but, I think, very real between graciousness of life and excellence in style can be further illuminated if we remark that most of the recent novels really distinguished for their style did not deal with the contemporary American scene; they treated other cultures than our own (Nina Federova's *The Family,* Kate O'Brien's *Land of Spices*), or our culture of other generations (Willa Cather's *Sapphira and the Slave Girl*). And it may be pertinent to add that many of the best contemporary stylists are women, whom we expect to mirror forth longest and most clearly true graciousness in life.

Is the conclusion, then, to be that no one can write a contemporary American novel in a style that is subtle and gracious and urbane? Well, if graciousness of life were absolutely extinct among us, it would be. But fortunately there are still thousands of Americans for whom these values have a meaning; those for whom their meaning is deepest and finest are our American Catholics. Because you see, our faith is instinct with graciousness because it is born of and lives in the grace of God—His graciousness toward us.

From that great initial grace spring our obligations of graciousness toward one another, so that strong and virile faith inevitably means that one is thoughtful and considerate of others, is kindly urbane and gracious—in a word, is charitable. It is from such a group of Americans, I am convinced, that we can hope for the renascence of a more civilized style. Hope? No, we can actually see it budding; some of the finest poetry of today is coming from our cloisters; one of the most distinguished magazines of verse is *Spirit*, the organ of the Catholic Poetry Society.

How lamentable, then, are the attempts of Catholic writers to imitate the adolescent simplicity of a Hemingway. His style springs from a culture that just is not ours. When we think that we are writing a Catholic novel, simply because we teach Catholic dogma in tough language (a recent example of this is *We Who Died Last Night*, by Quentin Morrow Philip), we reveal that we have been betrayed by a superficially "realistic" attitude into throwing overboard the deepest realism of all, the realism of Christian civilization, which demands a certain amount of subtlety and complexity, in language as well as in life, to be gracious.

Do you recall Belloc's lovely poem, *Courtesy?* It says much better all that I have been trying to say:

Of courtesy, it is much less
Than courage of heart or holiness,
Yet in my walks it seems to me
That the Grace of God is in courtesy.
On monks I did in Storrington fall,
They took me straight into their hall;
I saw three pictures on a wall,
And courtesy was in them all.
   The first, Annunciation;
The second, the Visitation;

The third, the Consolation
Of God that was Our Lady's Son.
    The first was of Saint Gabriel;
On wings a-flame from Heaven he fell;
And as he bent upon one knee
He shone with heavenly courtesy.
    Our Lady out of Nazareth rode——
It was her month of heavy load;
Yet was her face both great and kind,
For courtesy was in her mind.
    The third it was our little Lord,
Whom all the Kings in arms adored;
He was so small you could not see
His large intent of courtesy.
    Our Lord, that was Our Lady's Son,
Go bless you, people, one by one;
My rhyme is written, my work is done.

When courtesy (graciousness) becomes again popular in life, we
will in all likelihood have popular writers who will address us in the
language, not of ill-mannered adolescents, but of gentlemen speaking to gentlemen.   (February 7, 1942)

FICTION AND THE LIBERAL ARTS

Athene was the Greek goddess of both learning and war. Why
there is no male equivalent in all the Pantheon is indeed a
point of embarrassment for us members of that sex, and the chagrin
is all the more felt today, for Athene can be the patron of the
Waves' and Wacs' training colleges, but the men's colleges must go
patronless (unless we chose patrons that are popish, not pagan).

It is a shame, for war has taken over education. That is just the
fact, and one which we welcome, if it will help us out of chaos
quicker. What will happen to education after the war is something
to cause no small concern. President Conant of Harvard has expressed the conviction that "the study of the liberal arts will not
only survive this war, but prosper in the days of peace." Other
educators have doubts: technical education may have become so
taken for granted, so necessary in the increasingly industrialized

world of the future, that an education which is not practical, in that sense, will be thought no education at all.

How fervently we should hope that Conant's prophecy is correct may, perhaps, be brought home with some newness by a few remarks on the phalanx of our modern novelists.

Now the past of American literature is what it is, and no amount of criticism, of pointing out its deficiencies (an easy matter when one is not engaged in creative work oneself) will change what has been written. The whole stream of realistic, naturalistic fiction that has characterized American literature for the past two decades and more is a phenomenon that cannot be dismissed, as we are too often inclined to do, simply by saying that the authors are nasty and wicked men. Hemingway, Farrell, Faulkner, Caldwell, O'Hara, for all that they write too many passages that are simple dirt, do manifest on page after page a sort of tortuous and tortured interest in ideals. Farrell, in particular, racks his own soul in a straining self-exorcism; it is as though he is trying to get rid of the evil by talking it out.

This capital point was made in masterly fashion by Alfred Kazin in his monumental study of modern American prose, *On Native Grounds*. Summing up the general characteristics of that literature, he says:

> Nowhere has there been so tumultuous a subterranean life of the spirit, so much inchoate religion, with so self-assured a refusal on the part of so many sensitive writers to admit the reality of a spiritual life. Nowhere has there appeared so appalling a fear of "emotionalism" and mysticism among the hard-boiled, and nowhere have there been so many substitutes for them.

Further on he remarks: "There is sickness in contemporary literature, a very great sickness; but it is hardly self-willed, and it is bound up with the situation of contemporary humanity."

The moral and artistic integrity of authors is, of course, their own personal responsibility, and any deviation from it is inevitably, to some degree at least, self-willed. But it is quite true, on the other hand, that much modern fiction is simply conditioned by the whole social environment that surrounds the author.

Here it is that the matter of education plays a vitally formative role. It is not, perhaps, the primary role; religion, home influences, social milieus—all play their part, too, but I think one great reason for the spiritual rootlessness of much modern fiction can be found in the fact that the author's education and development have been a clean break from the traditional education that has shaped Western culture for centuries—the tradition of the liberal arts.

This break is not a thing that can be traced just by consulting a Who's Who to find the educational background of the individual authors, though it is interesting to note that Hemingway, the most influential in this group, had only a public high-school education, and our public schools have certainly broken fairly thoroughly from the classical tradition. Rather is it to be discovered in the whole range of style and content. The lack of fullness in the use of our English tongue is a break from the tradition of the liberal arts to produce a *perfecta eloquentia*. The sweep and resources of the language lie barren under the pen of a Farrell, for example; when that point was made in an earlier article, "Modern Authors Can Be Gentlemen" (see p. 44), Willa Cather wrote to me in agreement:

> It is rather alarming to see the magnificent reach of the language silent except for one octave, on which little boys seem to be pounding the same keys over and over with one finger.

Deeper than this lies the break with the culture of the liberal arts in the matter of personal responsibility. As President Conant well puts it:

> The ideal educational process should include at each level of maturity some continuing contact with those problems of human nature and human destiny which man has assembled under the headings of literature, history, and philosophy. The student . . . should be concerned, in part at least, with the words "right" and "wrong" in both the ethical and mathematical sense.

This is a concept that the modern novelists we are discussing have relegated to the scrap heap, and it is not the scrap heap to which we ought to contribute to win the war. They all suffer from the blight that Kazin singles out as a characteristic of the "documentary" writers, that of "not knowing, of society's not knowing, but only guessing and suspecting and trying to ignore what goes on irreconcilably, subversively, beneath the vast smug surface," both of society and of their own souls.

The values of a humane and liberal education would have saved them from the narrowness of their vision. They might still not have had the sweep and grandeur of vision that the Faith can give to artistry, as it did in *Kristin Lavransdatter*, but the humanist—"I am a man, nothing human is beyond my interest"—might have humanized a Hemingway and the others who "lost, and forever writing the history of their loss . . . became specialists in anguish."

This flabbiness in personal responsibility is seen clearest in Hemingway, who was penetratingly docketed long ago by Wyndham Lewis as "the man that things are done to." Society, the times, force of circumstances, the stress of the moment—all impel the Hemingway hero, so that we long for a dash even of the Henley braggadocio, "I am the captain of my soul." In Dos Passos, too, to quote Kazin again, though he is "interested in the larger concerns of humanity" and identifies himself with society as Hemingway (writing his "epics of self-consciousness") could not, the heroes are still pawns; society shapes and distorts them; they groan and writhe; they do not determine and act.

Now, as we admitted above, there is little to be gained by flogging the past. That school of novelists carried the day, and their sun is not yet set. What of the future? How best can we encourage and train writers who will have some roots in the past? How avoid that craze for "liberation" which became the all in all for the American writers who emerged in the twenties?

The result of this craze to break away from the past is summed up by Kazin: "Nowhere . . . has there been so obvious a subjection to the latest dictum, the contemporary rage, such as has pulled American literary thought from pole to pole for fifty years." The latest social problem, the latest war, the newest trumpetings of "science"—these have all been seized upon, but poorly related to the problem of man and his complete humanity.

Two books recently published provide the best key to the solution. In them we can follow the majestic sweep of humane and Christian tradition for a thousand years and more. Had a Faulkner and a Caldwell been trained in this tradition, how different would be their approach to the problem of human lives and human destiny! Were all intelligent Catholic readers familiar with it, how judicious and sound, and not merely contemptuous, would be their criticism of the rebellious moderns. The two books are *The World's Great Catholic Literature*, compiled by George N. Shuster, and *Poetry and Life*, a new anthology of English Catholic poetry. The

41455

first aims to "illustrate the impact of Catholic thought and feeling upon world literature since the days of the Apostles"; the second "to see what man's life has looked like to the Catholic poets." In this connection, Frank J. Sheed, the compiler, remarks: "It is marvelous to see how little difference a thousand years makes in that. Early or late, these poets are all fellow Catholics, fellow to one another, fellow to us." Surely, here is a tradition that no modern author can afford to ignore.

This tradition will, of course, be ignored by our future Hemingways and Farrells. But if, at least, they can be brought back to the tradition of the liberal arts, there will be hope that the coming postwar period will not stand aghast at a wave of cynical disillusionment, such as engulfed American literature after World War I.

Here, then, is another reason for working and planning for the fulfillment of Conant's hope, the return and reflowering of the liberal arts. If they do not return strong and fructifying, it is to be feared that all our writers of the future will be but poor imitations of spiritually immature realists.

Quite apart, moreover, from a matter of mere literary desirability, American literature must grow in appreciation of the whole man, in its ability to "see life steadily and see it whole," if it is to escape intellectual totalitarianism. As President Conant remarks:

> A student reared on deficient spiritual and intellectual diet is an easy prey for proponents of the totalitarianism view. If his skills only are developed and his mind filled only with technical information, he will know nothing of man's emotional history or his practical experience as a gregarious animal. Not realizing the profound truth of Pascal's saying that human nature is both the glory and scandal of the universe, he will tend to the extremes of blind utopianism or bitter cynicism. His development as a free man is crippled.

Crippled. That is exactly what so much modern American writing has been. It has been strong and stark and honest; it has been bitter and bawdy; it has been agonizing for spiritual truth and contemptuous of moral values. Through all its defects and merits runs the crippling paralysis of a truncated view of human nature, the lack of realizing that "literature lives by something more than literature."

The liberal arts alone cannot play Sister Kenny to this paralysis; for its true glory literature must be stirred by One who stirred the pool of Bethsaida. Until such time, the leaven of the liberal arts can develop nature—that grace may find a fertile ground.

(March 6, 1943)

THE HOLLOW MEN GIVE WAY TO HEROES?

Fiction—at least of the home-grown variety—has admittedly been pretty peaked for the past year or more. Back at the turn of the year, Harvey Breit's "In and Out of Books" column in the New York *Times* was quoting editors-in-chief of major publishing houses as lamenting the "continual shortage of first-rate fiction" and charging that "during the fall of 1953, impressive fiction disappeared from sight to the point where second-rate books were topping the best-seller lists."

The flush of health has not notably mantled the novel's wan countenance since those wry observations were made. Some novels, to be sure, have not succumbed to the anemia that is afflicting other members of the family. Harriette Arnow's *The Dollmaker*, for example, is a healthy specimen, and so are Igor Gouzenko's *The Fall of a Titan* and Pamela Frankau's *A Wreath for the Enemy*, but their very health is a rebuke to such pallid brothers and cousins as John Steinbeck's *Sweet Thursday*, Erich Remarque's *A Time to Love and a Time to Die*, Frances Parkinson Keyes's slick *The Royal Box*, and Daphne du Maurier's slicker *Mary Anne*.

Some months ago, in the June issue of the London *New Statesman and Nation*, England's veteran and doughty practitioner of the novelist's craft, J. B. Priestley, became for the while a practitioner of the craft of the literary medico when he tried to diagnose the illness afflicting the modern novel. He finds that "most younger novelists" suffer from

> two major weaknesses. . . . I am never quite convinced that what they tell me is happening really is happening. It is rather like being in a dream and reminding oneself that it is a dream. . . . My second objection is that as a rule their central characters are too deliberately unheroic and often seem such bumbling nitwits that it is hard to sympathize with them in their misfortunes.

The vague first impression that Mr. Priestley is largely right in his criticism grows into almost a conviction when one casts back in his mind and tries to recall a notable character in recent fiction who has been conceived and portrayed in anything like heroic stature. Sinclair Lewis's Babbitt and T. S. Eliot's "hollow men" have cast long shadows, indeed, and it would seem that all too many fictional characters still lurk under the gloomy penumbra.

Saul Bellows's *The Adventures of Augie March,* for instance, won the National Book Award blue ribbon as the best novel of the past year, but Augie, its hero, is most emphatically "deliberately unheroic," if not with equal deliberation a downright heel. It is practically impossible, I believe, to find in the whole gamut of American fiction for the past two years a character who approaches within a light-year the heroic stature of Robert Aske in H. F. M. Prescott's *The Man on a Donkey.*

This observation is not by any stretch of the imagination meant to be a plea for novels peopled only with Galahads and other knights (even in shining business suits) who are *sans peur et sans reproche.* But it is to pose the question whether the modern novelist, in his search for characters who will embody some of the social, political, and cultural tensions and struggles in which a world striving toward a democracy is engaged, has not got so fascinated with the "common man" as to become blind to the minuscule heroism of which even the common man is at times capable. *Is the Common Man Too Common?* (as the title of a recent book puts it) in the conception of today's novelist—so common as to be cheap and mean?

This myopia in the novelists' view of human nature has not afflicted the historical novel to such an extent. Characters in such works as Dorothy Roberts's *The Enchanted Cup* and *My Brother, Launcelot,* and Alfred Duggan's novels (*Lady for Ransom, The Conscience of the King,* etc.) are still nobly conceived and drawn with the mark of heroism upon them. But it would seem that that mark, easily captured in a portrayal of the more aristocratic past, escapes the authors who try to interpret in their characters our egalitarian present.

But there are signs, I believe, that a change of weather is making up on the horizon. It is rather noteworthy that in non-fiction for the past year or so the trend has been to books whose main characteristic has been their portrayal of heroism—either the more glamorous heroism of high adventure or the more modest-violet type of perseverance and devotion to duty under adverse circumstances.

Whether it is a spirit of asceticism or of escapism or just plain human cussedness that inspires men to climb mountains and go down to the perilous seas in ships, their exploits do carry with them the flavor of heroism—and this type of book has been prevalent and popular while the novel has been playing down the heroic element. We have had almost incredible feats of endurance described in such mountaineering books as *The Conquest of Everest*, by Sir John Hunt, and *Anapurna*, by Maurice Herzog. Similar courage bulks large in *Of Whales and Men*, by R. B. Robertson; in *Yankee Whalers in the South Seas*, by A. B. C. Whipple; in *Savage Papua*, by André Dupeyrat (an epic of the higher heroism of Catholic missionaries); in *Journey to the Far Amazon*, by Alain Gheerbrant. There is even the foolhardy bravery (if that be heroism) of the charge of the Light Brigade in *The Reason Why*, by Cecil Woodham-Smith.

It is fairly easy to understand how this more spectacular heroism appeals to most of us whose lives are considerably more humdrum. A more significant sign, perhaps, that readers are getting bored with the too common man and look for some heroism even in more ordinary lives is the popularity of books that tell of the courage of people like your next-door neighbors in overcoming terrific physical and moral handicaps.

One of the finest of these was Marie Killilea's *Karen* of several years back, in which the young wife and mother movingly recounts the efforts to give the little daughter, suffering from cerebral palsy, a normal and happy life. Since then there have been a dozen or more books on similar themes. Several now on the best-seller lists include *I'll Cry Tomorrow*, Lillian Roth's account of conquering alcoholism; *Reach for the Sky*, Paul Brickhill's life of Douglas Bader, the famous legless ace of Britain's RAF; *The Cliff's Edge*, by Marie Hackett, the story of family devotion and solidarity under the strain of the father's mental illness.

It's not to be thought that just because these books deal with heroism of a kind they are therefore great literature—though the point could be made that all great literature has dealt with heroism. The point here, however, is that the appearance of this kind of book here and now seems to give ground for hope that a gradual shift in reading interest is taking place. The reader is seeking—and finding in non-fiction—books that are more affirmative, more positive, in which somebody has the courage of his convictions, a will and a heart to try something loyal or daring or challenging, books in which drifting with the tide is not the main character's chief form of exercise.

Will our present-day novelists catch up with the trend? After all, perhaps they are not too much to be blamed for having set their sights so unheroically low. The novelist, we are told with much truth, does not shape his age; he reflects it and—depending on his greatness—illuminates it. If an age has made its heroes out of the stuff of cynicism, disillusion, and debunkery, if the smart guy who knows all the short cuts to getting ahead without prior scruple or subsequent qualm—or the ruthless tycoon, the demagogue, or the self-serving do-gooder—are an age's tacitly accepted and sneakingly imitated paragons, then the novelist will cut his characters to their pattern.

But perhaps the interest our times are now showing in reading about the heroic in human nature may be a timid little swallow which, if it does not make the spring, at least chirps that a spring may be coming. Could it be that such things as the recent outlawing of racial segregation—welcomed by the majority of Americans, if blatantly opposed by some "leaders"—have shown readers that heroism (the quiet heroism of little, if not common, people) finally pays off?

This is not to say that there is no drift in today's American world toward secularism, toward floating in the standard-of-living stream. It is not to say that there is no need to throw up moral levees to dam the tide of immorality that threatens the home, the family, the children, the free world. These threats are real and imminent, but we would not give the picture in proper perspective unless we also represented the myriads of Americans who thirst to hear accounts of courage, bravery, heroism. The novelists have not, by and large, given us such accounts; perhaps they will soon if they gauge better what readers want.

The heroic nurse of Dien Bien Phu, who was cheered by thousands of U.S. citizens, is perhaps the exact symbol of what novelists have been missing and what the reading public wants. She simply did her duty, she protested—but the duty was heroic. Will

American novelists catch up with the fact that the "common man" can be and is often not a heel, but a humble hero?

(September 11, 1954)

THE SUPREME ROLE OF LITERATURE

To whet your appetite for a very nourishing and succulent literary dish, only to tell you that it is still, so to speak, in the kitchen and will not be served up for some months, is, I confess, a somewhat churlish trick. But having caught the aromas streaming out from its preparation, I hope the hint of a coming treat may not keep you in too cruel a state of anticipation.

The week this issue of *America* reaches you, the Institute for Religious and Social Studies will be meeting at Columbia University. One of the papers read there will be Howard Mumford Jones's "Literature As an Aid to Intercultural Understanding"; later on, this paper and others will be published in book form.

But the remarks made by Dr. Jones are so sane and stimulating and will, or ought to, cause teachers of literature to engage in so salutary an examination of conscience that I would like to provide a preview of his thesis and then go on to some thoughts suggested by it. The preview, I hope, will give a glimpse of Dr. Jones's well-knit and realistic thought; the suggestions, I am convinced, will at least open up for discussion the question of what is the real role of literature, and particularly what is the role of Catholic letters as an apostolate.

Dr. Jones starts by remarking that the whole "genteel tradition affirms, the teaching profession assumes, and the publishing business promises, that literature is a guide to intercultural understanding." The unwary reader, then, is impelled to say: "Why, of course, it is quite obvious that the more I know about the Russians, the French, the Chinese; the more I know about how they live and their ways of thought, the more I will understand them. It is through literature, among other channels, that I will learn these things; therefore, literature is a bridge to this intercultural understanding."

But Dr. Jones will go neither so fast nor so simply. First of all, he cautions that it must be remembered that literature is but part of any national or racial culture, and that while literature may be building this bridge of understanding, other elements (economic, political) may be working just as fast to tear it down. Further, he goes on to show, with frequent concrete examples, that literature has often proved a source of misunderstanding and concludes this section of his analysis by remarking that

> . . . if literature is a real guide to intercultural understanding, the greatest literary monument of the Western world is awkward evidence. That monument is, of course, the Bible. But if any work of literature has done more to divide mankind than the Bible, I do not know what it is; and if as a record of the culture of the Jewish people, the Bible be put in evidence as an instrument of intercultural understanding, one can only marvel at anti-Semitism. In sum, the more one studies the problem, the more baffling it becomes.

The bafflement grows when one recalls that literatures, being couched in national tongues and enshrining national achievements and spirit, have done no Lilliputian job when it comes to the matter of fostering excessive nationalism.

The author then goes on to break the problem into two aspects, for the sake of clarity. He conceives that literature as a means to intercultural understanding can be studied in what he calls its horizontal movements, by which he means an "exchange of comprehensions among races or nations"; and in its vertical workings, which operate toward an "exchange of comprehensions within a given race or nation."

To consider the second aspect first, Dr. Jones admits, for example, that the upper classes nowadays know a great deal more about the lower than they did two centuries ago, and that the great tide of humanitarian, social-minded literature has been largely responsible for this happy state.

One particular example that springs obviously to mind is the wide contemporary knowledge that literature gives of conditions among our Negro population. But the bridge of cultural understanding ought to be for two-way traffic, the author reminds us, and he wonders if literature has fostered understanding of the upper classes by the lower to any comparable degree. In this sphere of literature's vertical operations, then, we cannot claim too much.

What of the horizontal movements? Has literature ever stimulated an exchange of understanding among races and nations? Here Dr. Jones admits that the eighteenth-century Western world

> . . . nourished a truly cosmopolitan culture operative among a literate minority in some nations . . . who were products of the same literary and philosophical system. . . . But what quality of intercultural understanding this fact exhibits is not clear. These persons and others like them were, to the extent that they participated in this cosmopolitanism, products of a single culture and not of the several national cultures to which they geographically were born.

Finally Dr. Jones remarks rather wryly that the real culture of any nation trickles across a bridge built, not of literature, in the sense of works of art, but of the subliterary popular magazines.

The whole of the thesis is clearly, cogently stated. It is not elaborated for the sake of debunking, but simply as a caution against the making of airy and exaggerated claims for the social function of literature. It is, at the same time, as I have suggested, a challenge to teachers and writers to clarify their own thoughts about the function of literature in its social consequences. Catholic professors of literature, in particular, will welcome Dr. Jones's examination and would be well advised to discuss it.

I say Catholic teachers especially, because it strikes me that several of Dr. Jones's arguments throw some light on the function of Catholic letters. First of all, an examination of Catholic letters under the aspect of their horizontal movement will reveal that the reasons adduced by Dr. Jones for the success of an exchange of comprehensions among races and nations in the eighteenth century are the same reasons that make Catholic literature today a broad, frequently used bridge. If, as he remarked, Horace Walpole, Frederick the Great, Catherine the Great, Benjamin Franklin, and Voltaire could participate in a common understanding through literature because they were products of the same literary and philosophical system, Catholic literary men today can share an intercultural understanding for the same reason—they, too, are products of a common literary and philosophical system.

To go a step further, not only do a Waugh, a Mauriac, a Greene, a Merton, a Hopkins overleap national boundaries and share an understanding based on the same principles, but today, far more widely than in the age of Ben Franklin, a great mass of Catholic readers participate in that understanding. I think it is undeniable that there is a vast field of mutual understanding which is being increasingly cultivated among the Catholics of all nations through literature. Fifty years ago or less, it would have been a rare American of Irish descent who could have stomached the very British atmosphere of *Brideshead Revisited*; the French approach in fiction to the psychology of sanctity won few American enthusiasts a decade ago; the probings of the French mind seemed too morbidly introspective to a bluffer, more external American approach. Now Bernanos, Claudel, Bloy, Péguy are current coin of the American Catholic intellectual realm.

This—and much more along the same line—is all possible for the precise reason that these authors and the growing body of their readers are all products of the same literary and philosophical system. On the ultimate values which these authors pose and try to resolve in their works, Catholics are all in agreement; the language of sin and temptation, of grace and hope, of human struggle and divine compassion is a veritable *lingua franca* of the Catholic literary world. And on the purely literary side there is a common body of principle, a common approach to criticism which, perhaps all unconsciously, is held by Catholic authors and readers.

Keeping Dr. Jones's caution against exaggeration in mind, it is at the same time possible to point out that literature, in its Catholic manifestation, is actually continuing and broadening the work of intercultural understanding.

But it is doing still more than that. My argument thus far has been based rather openly, though not exclusively, on a matter of quantity. There is also the quality of intercultural understanding to be reckoned with. Dr. Jones gives occasion for this consideration when he concedes that "a given literature will yield to the sympathetic reader glimpses into persons and customs other than his own—that gives insight into an alien way of life." But that is not precisely to state the function of literature as a bridge to understanding; it is not by revealing the alienness of another way of life that literature will bridge the gap—it is by revealing the similarities, the common interests, the common destinies, the kinship.

And this is the exact point where Catholic literature enters into its true function and glory, namely, its intrinsic purpose of being a channel for the deepening of charity, charity as a theological virtue with immediate regard to God, yes, but perhaps more pertinently charity as the overflow of love of God into love of His creatures for His sake. It is not enough for Catholic literature merely to widen an "understanding" between and among peoples and nations; if, with the "understanding" there do not grow sympathy, consideration, respect, reverence, love, any literature will have failed, and a Catholic-inspired literature will then have failed most ingloriously.

But it has not thus failed. I feel that any sympathetic reader today (and, as the more quantitative argument above indicated, there are thousands and thousands of them) will put down a *Brideshead Revisited*, a *The World, the Flesh and Father Smith*, a *Star of Satan*, a *The Labyrinthine Ways* with a deepened realization of the frail majesty, the eternal grandeur and infinite lovableness of human souls because God loves them—and that is a deepening of the bases for and motives of charity, of love.

In these two aspects, then, of Catholic literature, we are close to the heart of the purposes and goals of the apostolate of the pen; we are also closest to any actual realization of making literature an instrument in the work of cultural understanding. If Catholic literature can first swell the numbers in every land and country who will read from a common literary and philosophical approach, it will continue and widen the work of understanding that Dr. Jones praises in the eighteenth century; if, while increasing the numbers of those who can so understand, it further makes understanding burgeon into love, it will build the only bridge that can be built across the gulf of human mistrusts and hates—the bridge of Christianity, wherein "there is neither Jew nor Greek: there is neither bond nor free: there is neither male nor female. For [we] are all one in Christ Jesus."   (September 14, 1946)

This essay is one of some eight (the others are not included in this volume) all centering around the artistic and moral aspects of the novel, which, after their initial appearance in America, *were first gathered into a booklet,* Tenets for Readers and Reviewers, *published by The America Press in 1942 and since reissued in many editions. This booklet was expanded and revised and published under the title* Norms for the Novel (The America Press, 1953). *A further revision of this book, under the same title, will be published by Hanover House in 1960.*

Chapter Two

CHRISTIAN THOUGHT AND THE PAST

Historical novels are a type of literature that depends largely for its validity on a proper assessment of the past—an assessment first of the actual historical facts, and an assessment, second and more important, of what we may call the psychology of the past: how did the people think and feel? what were their responses to the temporal and spiritual values of their day? It would be invalid and uncraftsmanlike for an historical novelist—if not so obviously for the technical historian—to try to recapture the spirit of the Middle Ages, for example, by writing about them in terms of how we now feel about them, rather than in terms of how the people of that time thought about themselves, their problems, and their values.

Yet this literary rewriting of history from the wrong end is a common shortcoming of some otherwise excellent novelists. This springs very frequently from the fact that the teachings and the practices of the Christian past are but vaguely understood or appreciated by many who essay a literary re-creation of the past.

The following essays and reviews are a sampling of how I have been impelled to point out this viewing from the wrong end of the historical telescope. The most revealing view from the right end in recent years was the magnificent achievement of H. F. M. Prescott in her The Man on a Donkey (see p. 106), to which wonderful historical novel I strongly and hopefully refer my readers. One who savors this book will be truly "happy though medieval"— happy with the joy a great book gives, and medieval, almost literally plunged into the very life stream of those turbulent days.

Such is the magic of great historical fiction; in its way it makes us citizens of the ages, rapt out of the narrow circle of our small days.

ON VIEWING HISTORY BACKWARDS

I have a minor bone to pick with some fellow Catholic reviewers. The bone may, indeed, be minor, but I feel that the principle on which I will pick it is an important one and of particular relevance here and now.

The bone emerges from other reviews of a book titled *The Daughter of Jairus*, by Paul Fox, and from correspondence received on the occasion of my review of it. The story concerns, as the title indicates, the little girl Our Lord raised from the dead, and the impression He made on her as she meets Him later on in life as her path, Judas's, and His strangely and fatefully cross. This is a very brief indication of what the book is about, but it is enough for my purpose here, for the bone to be picked lies precisely in that "impression" made by Our Lord, as Mr. Fox portrays it.

The Catholic reviewers with whom I disagree on principle have condemned the book, more or less, because it gives no indication, they say, that Jairus's daughter ever saw anything more in Christ than a marvelously interesting man, a fascinating "personality," as we would say in today's sense. This, the charge goes on, amounts to a "whittling away" of belief in the divinity of Christ, is, in fact, a surreptitious denial of it.

This charge, I hold, amounts to a demand that the author ought to have written history backwards. That is no way to write history honestly; Catholic critics are—or ought to be—the first to repudiate that sort of approach to the past. They do repudiate it when it crops up in fields of writing other than that which deals with Our Lord.

The question of the precise time at which Our Lord revealed His divinity to His contemporaries—both His followers and His antagonists—is one for Scriptural exegesis. For our purpose, it is necessary to remember only these truths: that Our Lord certainly revealed His divinity during His public life; that He did so rather gradually, in order not to excite death-dealing opposition before His time had come; and that some few of His followers believed Him to be in very truth the Son of God, while most of the people who knew Him did not. I am not referring to His post-Resurrection life, but to that stage in His public ministry when He raised the daughter of Jairus to life. She was, after all, a young girl. Is it conceivable that the little daughter of Jairus might have met Christ many a time and still not have seen Him to be what we know He in truth was? Again, obviously yes. Well, then, was the author under any obligation to hint that although little Naomi did not realize who Christ really was, he, the author, does? This might be debatable, but it does not seem to me that we can require an author to inject his own religious beliefs into a story which he chose to tell simply in terms of the reactions of those pictured as meeting Christ.

But is not such a story evidence that the author himself does not believe in the divinity of Christ? I cannot see how, and, really, from a literary point of view, it does not matter. What would matter is if that disbelief (if it exists) were projected into the story. It would matter tremendously if there were some denial on the part of the author of that divinity. A character could, of course, be portrayed as denying it. The Pharisees, remember, did.

No, I cannot see how the attitudes toward Christ portrayed in this book had to be other than they are, unless we are ready to demand that Mr. Fox should have written history backwards.

It is this principle which is at stake, and Catholic critics ought to be as ready to uphold it when it bears on the story of things most sacred to us as when it is pertinent in books that touch us less intimately.

That principle was invoked by many Catholic reviewers, if I remember rightly—and properly invoked—as criticism of the late Lloyd Douglas's *The Robe* and *The Big Fisherman*. Not only was there a psychological backward writing of history in these books—the mentality of the twentieth century was siphoned into the brains of the first-century characters—but the jargon of nineteenth-century non-Catholic Biblical "scholarship" (the "higher criticism") was put into the mouths of those, for example, who tried to explain away Our Lord's miracles.

This not-too-neat trick of writing of yesterday in today's terms, and so of distorting our view of the past, is a favorite of Communists and fellow travelers. Howard Fast, our Communist novelist, has indulged in it in such a book as *The American*. There he puts straight Communist phraseology into the mouths of turn-of-the-century American radicals, making it appear that they, who were actually fighting for their personal liberty, were doing so precisely because they were Communists—several decades at least before they could have been. If you want a classic example of how the writing of history backwards can be used to undermine our American heritage, I believe the U. S. Supreme Court's interpretation of the First Amendment affords it. As I understand the legal issues involved, the learned justices set out in the Everson case (1947) to define for the first time exactly what is meant by the phrase, "an establishment of religion." Instead of resorting to the origins of the First Amendment in 1789–91, they latched onto a phrase in a letter Thomas Jefferson wrote in 1802, in which Jefferson said the First Amendment set up "a wall of separation" between Church and State. They then proceeded to define not what "an establishment of religion" originally meant but what "separation of Church and State" means today to those who insist that it must be absolute. Even Jefferson's restricted meaning got lost in the shuffle.

No, it won't wash. There is the principle that history has to be written as it happened. It cannot honestly be written as we would now like it to have happened. And if that is a principle, then it has to be held, no matter what the species of writing to which it applies. In all reverence, it applies to writing about Our Lord. He must be portrayed as men then saw Him, not as we now see Him and wish that all men did.

I believe that it's Chesterton who once lampooned in his hearty fashion the naïveté (or dishonesty) of those who see history from the wrong end of the glass. He pictures a group of men of, say, the thirteenth century, gathered to plan some revolt or reform. In their midst rises one who harangues them, and he begins his rallying speech with: "We men of the Middle Ages must stick together. . . ."!

(March 24, 1951)

RATIONALISTIC THEOLOGY IN MODERN FICTION

Theology, the schoolmen tell us, is the queen of the sciences, and though I do not know that they said it in so neat a phrase, they did imply that she is the mother of the arts. Even the modern art of fiction with its too frequent estrangement, both in time and spirit, from the roots and truths of Christianity has not been able to shake off entirely this maternal relationship. Often, indeed, modern fiction that has reached close to the pinnacle of greatness has achieved that height precisely because the natural gifts of the author have been transported above themselves and immeasurably heightened by the theology implicit in his theme. Even more than from its characterization and superb storytelling, Werfel's *The Song of Bernadette* draws its greatness from the theology of grace; more than from its atmosphere and tension, Greene's *The Labyrinthine Ways* takes its profundity from the theology of vocation.

But too frequently this mother of the arts undergoes a sea change and wanders through the art of fiction not in maternal and queenly dominance but in the tatters and squalor of a "greasy Joan" who "doth keel the pot." Even so, modern fiction often bears a sort of perverted testimony to the fact that it has not been able to shake off her presence; even in her degradation and shame, she is still wedded to the arts.

It is particularly in modern novels that deal with Christ that we see this strange tenacity of theology; it is in them that we have the spectacle of theology no longer the mother and mistress, but the slave. It is from this point of view that I would like to discuss some of these recent works.

The Robe by Lloyd Douglas, as you know, is setting records as a best seller; Catholics by the thousands have read it, and perhaps been helped and edified by it, but I will herewith be bold and challenging enough to say that their edification was and is in inverse ratio to their knowledge of Christ. For one who has studied or even read attentively the Gospels, the book cannot possibly, I feel, appear other than a caricature of Christ. Theology enters the book, for any attempt to delineate Him, to unfold His character must touch upon the mystery of His Personality, and that is a matter for the queen of the sciences; but it is a theology that has become humbled and distorted in *The Robe* and similar books.

That this is the character of the book need not cause much amazement; that this character has not been recognized for what it is by Catholics should cause a little heart searching.

First of all, though it be regretted, the distortion of theology in *The Robe* and kindred books need cause no wonder. Several years ago, the eminent apologist and Christologist, Father Hilarin Felder, in his book, *Jesus of Nazareth*, summed up the results of the rationalistic criticism of the Gospels by saying: "Since each individual critic rejects whatever does not suit him in the Gospels and substitutes his own ideas, Jesus is made a constantly changing representative, a kaleidoscopic image, of modern religious individualism." Quoting a German critic, he continues:

> Modern Protestant theology has become entirely involved in one thought—to project its religious ideals upon Jesus. . . . Each one transports his more or less finished picture of the ideal religion and the ideal founder, and endeavors to interpret this out of the Gospels.

So little does theology live in a vacuum, so readily does theology, even bad theology, run quicksilverlike to fill the emptiness and cravings of daily life, that this rationalistic theology of Protestantism has found its way quickly into literature, and particularly into fiction. In our days, all the novels about Christ that I know are perfect literary fruits of the tree of the so-called higher criticism, and of them perhaps *The Robe* is the classic example.

For what has Mr. Douglas done to Christ in that book? He has spun his ideas of Christ out of his own mind, or perhaps out of a one-sided reading of the Gospels. He has formed the idea that Christ was essentially a social reformer, whose blueprint, be it remarked, was extremely vague and shadowy in His own mind— at least, if that mind was understood by the Apostles. Peter, the "Big Fisherman," and all his companions knew only that they were to gather some sort of communities about them, and that their great care was to be the succoring of the poor and interminable talk about peace, for all the world like a group of modern pacifists. This is not to present Christ as He historically was; this is to construct an imaginary Christ first and then to turn to the Gospels to cull passages and incidents that apparently put flesh and blood upon that phantasm.

Precisely the same literary rationalism vitiates the attempt of the Congregationalist minister, J. R. Perkins, to deal with Christ in his *The Emperor's Physician*. Here Christ is the Great Healer, and though the author does refer to the cures as miracles, Christ remains on his pages still a mere man, working, it is true, with divinely given powers, but not speaking out with that majestic sense of His own, proper, absolute divine power which flashes forth in the Gospel pages, as when He replies with the serene certainty of omnipotence, "I will. Be thou clean," to the leper's, "Lord, if thou wilt, thou canst make me clean."

Again, Sholem Asch's *The Nazarene* presents Christ under the exclusive aspect of being the greatest of the rabbis. This distortion runs through his later *The Apostle* as well, though it is not so dominant for the simple reason that Christ is not an actual character in the book. If it be interjected here that Asch cannot well be tarred with the brush of liberal Protestantism, since he is a Jew, the answer is that *The Apostle* is unmistakable evidence that, Protestant or not, Asch has been infected with the rationalism of the "higher criticism." His insistence, in this second novel, on the dichotomy of the early Church into Petrine and Pauline factions stems directly from the German critical rationalism of the nineteenth century.

One further example is at hand. It is a book that will not attract much attention, for it is quite second-rate, but it is another clear instance of liberal theology influencing the arts. In Dorothy Clarke Wilson's *The Brother* (yes, again the weary, hoary myth of Our Lady's children—this time seven!) Christ is simply a Jew of his day, motivated by "the Dream" to establish the "God-fearing community." This is to be done by what we would call these days an underground movement. And so Christ emerges from these mediocre pages as simply a temporal liberator.

Two other books soon to be published will deal with Christ. They are *The Impostor* and *The Way*, and I think it is safe to predict that they will be the same story over again—the characterization of Christ not according to the objective facts as history gives them, but according to the rationalistic preconception that it is simply impossible and absurd to think that God ever did or could become Man.

Of the Christ of fiction, then, no less than of the Christ of modern liberal theology and precisely because of that theology, it can be said, again in Felder's words:

> Thus Jesus appears to one as a poet, to another as a mystic enthusiast, to the third as a valiant fighter for the freedom and dignity of man, to the fourth as an organizer of a new church and church morals, to the fifth as a rationalistic enlightener,

etc., etc., but to none as the historical facts actually reveal Him— *Deum verum de Deo vero*.

That the corruptions of theology have so worked their way into literature (and, of course, they have done so even more flagrantly in the field of morals) need not, as I said, cause surprise; indeed, the fact that even a truncated "theology" is thus operative is, in one sense, a consoling testimony to the essential need of men and art for some sort of theology. But the amazing thing is that Catholic readers do not seem to recognize the errors in this fictionalizing of Christ with the same quick and sure instincts with which they spot immorality. Frequently enough it is only dogmatic errors which verge onto morals that draw their fire—as when the perpetual virginity of Our Lady is called into question. Yet I think that it is even more dangerous to form one's faith on the Christ of *The Robe* than to mold one's morals after *Studs Lonigan*. Because, if my whole mental grasp and appreciation of Christ is true and full and complete, then I have the means at hand to shape my morals after the only pattern given to men and that is Christ; whereas, if my realization of what and Who He is is awry, then my morals rest essentially on a foundation of sand.

But is it not tolerable and even good to have these partial portraits of Christ? After all, He *was* a great healer; He *was* a social reformer, in the sense that His Gospel contains the seed and spirit for the remaking of society into a Christian community. What harm to be told in story form that which, being more or less vivid and gripping, may make me realize more intimately one particular phase of His character?

No harm, certainly, if only the author himself realizes and brings the reader to realize that there are other elements in the explanation of Christ; if, in treating Him as the healer or what you will, there is the unmistakable thread running through the book that, healer or reformer or whatever else Christ was, He was first and foremost and essentially God Himself. And it is precisely because the lacunae in the picture of Christ drawn for us by these modern novels do not spring from the mere limitations of the novelist's craft, but from the corruptions of a rationalistic theology, that their inadequacies become not a negative but rather a positive denial.

There is a further question which we may attempt later. It is: can the character of Christ legitimately and successfully be made central in a work of fiction? Do the exigencies and limitations of the novelist's craft lend themselves to that portrayal? I think the answer is no, for the simple reason that the author, even a superbly

Catholic one, would be under an insuperable embarrassment of riches.

However that may be, the non-Catholic author who writes novels about Christ without betraying how the poison of modern Protestant theology has seeped down into literature is the rarest of *rarae aves.*   (September 2, 1944)

TWO NOVELS THAT DISTORT THE PAST

Two novels whose publication will open wide the sluice gates of criticism, debate, condemnation, and acclaim are Thomas Mann's *The Holy Sinner* and Sholem Asch's *Moses.* Though I have no idea what the verdict of the jury will be, I believe that each novel merits examination on a ground that will very likely be largely ignored. That ground is each author's sense of history. It is my conviction that both Mr. Mann and Mr. Asch are deficient in such a sense.

It may sound ungracious to subject Mr. Mann to a little preliminary investigation before discussing his book, particularly as I have written elsewhere that a reviewer's job is to review the book under discussion and not the man. However, I believe that *The Holy Sinner* makes imperative some prior remarks on Mr. Mann's sense of historical fact and the psychology of an era.

Mann has demonstrated his deficiencies in this regard many times in the past by his gullibility, to say the least, in the face of Communist propaganda. In a visit to the eastern zone of Germany in 1949, to give one instance, Mann was so little attuned to historical reality that he could repeat with relish the affirmations made to him that "popular democracy" was well received among the mass of Germans under Russian domination. He believed that "the Government provides well for the intellectual life of the workers," that that intellectual life was "a challenge of a Europe that could not be bought, that would no longer be the kept woman of the man with the money bags." In the face of what was actually happening in Germany in those days, this naïveté of Mann was sufficient to engender the suspicion that perhaps he did not realize what history—even current history—has to say.

This suspicion is confirmed, I believe, in this novel. There need be no particular alarm—though I think needless tocsins will be set asounding—over Mann's choice of subject matter. The story of an incestuous union between brother and sister whose offspring, later named Gregorius, in turn marries his own mother and begets further offspring, only to end up as penitent, Pope, and saint, is, strange as it may seem, a legend long enshrined in the literature of Catholic ages.

This legend is a Christian variation of the Oedipus motif which seems to have a fascination (and indeed quite an innocent fascination for the ages before Freud) for every age of storyteller. Mann is careful to indicate in a postscript that his embroidery of the tale is based on a verse epic, *Gregorius auf dem Steine*, by the Middle High German poet Hartmann von Aue (c. 1165–1210). Hartmann in turn had taken this legend of chivalry from old French versions. A Middle English version was included in a volume called *Legendae Catholicae: A Lytle Boke of Seyntlie Gestes*, edited and published in 1840 in Edinburgh by W. B. Trunbull, Esquire and Advocate. This volume, incidentally, and as though to indicate what many a modern critic will fail to realize—namely, that the story was not considered at all shocking—was dedicated by the editor to the memory of Peter Ribadeneira of the Society of Jesus.

Indeed, this particular Gregorius theme is but one of the changes the medieval mind used to love to ring on the larger wheel-of-fortune motif: a man is today pinnacled on the highest peak of human good fortune; he is rich, handsome, powerful, princely. Tomorrow the wheel swings round and he is plunged into poverty, lowliness, and disgrace. The Gregorius legend is simply a somewhat sensational treatment of this theme.

Nor need the fact that Mann's variation contains many an inaccuracy in both dogmatic and moral theology cause a flurry in the dovecotes of heresy watchers. The original tales in German, French, and English are likewise rather cavalier in matters of orthodoxy. One most glaring example is that in all versions of the tale the innocent fruit of the incestuous union considers himself, and is considered, as sharing the guilt. There are other deficiencies as well which need not be pointed out, as the perceptive reader will certainly spot them for himself.

These preliminary remarks are intended to clear away what I believe are non-essentials in a criticism of *The Holy Sinner*. The essential criticism is that Mann has entirely shifted the tone of the medieval legend. This is partly achieved by the style. Mann is hardly noted for a lightsome touch, and so his humor tends to be rather sardonic and cynical. This in turn is further accentuated by a burlesque medieval phraseology which is indeed a scintillating tour de force but which makes even more obvious the tongue in cheek. Again, the device of having the story told by a medieval monk who professes a distaste for and ignorance of the horrible things he must treat, and yet seems to enjoy himself no end in the treatment, further deepens the impression of a leer.

All these elements seem to me to weaken, if they do not totally vitiate, Mann's profession through the mouth of the narrator that he is telling a tale "at once frightful and highly edifying."

For this is precisely where Mann's historical sense fails. These medieval tales were designed explicitly for edification. They were cautionary tales—illuminated, it is true, by all the hues of medieval romance—but yet obviously didactic in tone. This startling contrast with Mann's sly technique may be seen nowhere better than in the relationship between Gregorius and his mother at the time of their marriage. Mann's treatment gives ground for the suspicion that they knew one another as mother and son and yet, with this guilty knowledge, effected the union. That this is not my own impression only is shown by Henry Seidel Canby's review in a Book-of-the-Month Club newsletter in which he says: "Both confess in their hearts that they had known who the other was at the time of the incestuous marriage." The medieval tale is explicit, however, in saying, according to the English version: "Bot nothing sche him knewe / So long he hadde ben hir fro." (But she knew him not at all, so long had he been away.)

All this may seem like a captious hullabaloo over fine points and I will admit that my criticism turns on a matter of emphasis or accent. A writer is free to take a medieval tale and vest it in current psychology, sociology, or what not. But if in so doing he destroys the genius of the tale; if his modernization contradicts its spirit and purpose, then he is really no longer merely adapting but rather prostituting. I believe that Mann's lack of feeling for the simplicity with which the Middle Ages read the Gregorius legend is evidence of a lack of historical sense.

Mr. Asch's reading of history in *Moses* is more seriously at fault because it involves not merely a matter of false accent but rather of false essentials. This springs from a bias not too uncommon among historical novelists, namely, the habit of reading history in reverse. Concepts, attitudes, and ideologies which are current and endemic today are projected into the thinking of the past. Asch is a "modern" Jew and not orthodox in the full sense of that term as applied to Judaism. Hence he is impelled to read into historic, primitive Judaism what the "modern" Jew now thinks of Judaism. Moses is, indeed, a most austerely sincere testimony to the existence of God and to God's supreme place in Jewish life. The idea of God's providence, of His overriding concern for all the details of Jewish national and religious life, is superbly set forth. But when Asch comes to portray Moses's grasp of God's intentions with regard to the priesthood and to sacrifice, it is the modern Jew speaking through the lips of Moses and not Moses speaking from God's direction and command. We are told, for example (p. 217):

> The bringing of sacrifice was the only form of Divine service which the world at that time knew. The lips of man were locked and a heart overflowing with love and awe of God, finding no utterance in prayer, found it in sacrifice; but in his heart Moses believed that the desire of God was not for sacrifices but for good deeds and a life of justice.

This idea runs through the book. We are told, to give other instances, that the Tabernacle was only a concession to the weakness of the people, not yet ready for "pure union with God, through the will alone"; that the later prophets protested against sacrifice; that later generations replaced sacrifice by prayer.

As regards the priesthood, Moses thinks as Asch would have him think, not as the historical accounts in Scripture portray his thought. So, it is said:

> It had never occurred to Moses that the priesthood would constitute a caste . . . with a great and costly sanctuary and a golden altar on which there would always be smoking the sacrifices of sheep and oxen.

The Jewish priesthood, as Asch describes it in origin and function, is simply a social development which kept pace with the desires and needs of the Israelites. Whereas the historical accounts, as contained in the Old Testament books of Exodus, Leviticus, and Numbers, clearly portray, for one who is not reading today's rationalistic viewpoints into a past age, that the Jewish priesthood was consecrated first and foremost at God's command and that the sacrifices of the Old Law were likewise not simply Moses's yielding to social pressure but a ritual instituted at God's express order.

That Asch believes most sincerely that the Jewish people still are the channel for redemption to the world need cause no particular critical dissent, though it is an historical anachronism. In his present state of conviction we could not well expect Asch to admit that redemption is now no longer through the Jews but through one who, Jewish in His humanity, is the Son of God. A Christian reader will here find a note of unintended poignancy running through Asch's superb but tragically inadequate testimony to God's dealings with His children.

Mann will probably be accused of irreverence, Asch of an anti-Christian bias. Whatever justification there may be for these indictments, the fundamental failure of both authors is a lack of complete grasp of the inner spirit of the times and movements of which they write.   (September 29, 1951)

A BOOK, SOME THOUGHTS ON THE MIDDLE AGES

Zoë Oldenbourg, author of *The World Is Not Enough*, an historical novel of the Middle Ages, followed up that widely acclaimed work with a sequel, *The Cornerstone*, which is certain to rouse equally enthusiastic critical "bravos," and which will, moreover, attract a much wider reading audience, for it is the January selection of the Book-of-the-Month Club.

This is all to the good, for *The Cornerstone* is a magnificent book, if somewhat tedious in long, detailed passages. Its magnificence springs from the patent authenticity with which the author, long an historical student of the Middle Ages, brings to teeming, throbbing life both the misery and the glory of those colorful times.

Pennants stream in the wind before the galleries filled with the magnificently gowned court ladies; the jousters charge to the shock on their caparisoned horses; waves of chant rise in the dim aisles of the great cathedrals aglow with their stained-glass windows. But poor wretches in their hovels quail before the threats of brutal lords who wring from them all but the crusts and gruel that will barely keep them alive during the wolf-winter, and some venal priests and bishops do not raise their voices in protest. The whole panorama spread before the reader is stunning, and in more senses than one —it is both exhilarating and shocking.

The tedious portions of the book, it seems to me, are those that deal with the tradition of courtly love, that strange institution by which a man could be well and truly married and faithful in all things, yet give the innermost devotion of his heart to another lady and prove it outwardly through incredible tasks performed at her command. This is indeed a fascinating subject for study, as C. S. Lewis has shown in his *Allegory of Love*, but the long descriptions in *The Cornerstone* tend to be repetitious and clog the otherwise superb pace. In these passages, I feel, the antiquarian lore intrudes.

The story deals with a single French family of knights in the thirteenth century and is about equally divided in following the fates of three of them: Ansiau, the grandfather; Herbert le Gros, the son; Haguenier, the grandson. The old man, nearly blind and feeling that his days draw to their close, leaves home to make a pilgrimage on foot to the Holy Land, where he had fought in the Crusades. Haguenier does his stint of crusading, too, but it is in France against the fanatic devotees of the Catharist heresy. His story and that of his father, Herbert, however, center mainly around the home estates and deal with family intrigues, deaths and marryings, the protection of the lands, dealings with the peasants.

The magnificence of the book comes through predominantly in the character of Ansiau, who, blind, wandering with some equally wretched companions, is captured by the Moors, endures a long martyrdom, and dies in a desperate attempt to escape. Through it all he comes ever closer to God and to Our Lord, who, as the title of the book seems to suggest, was the cornerstone not only of the old man's life but of the whole fabric of the civilization we know as Christendom. There are truly superb passages in the old man's interior monologue that clamor for quotation, but I would call especial attention to the section in which Ansiau, dying alone in the desert and driven by a passionate desire to receive the Blessed Eucharist, to experience in his agony the physical presence of Christ, hits on the idea, which he prays may not be sacrilegious, of "consecrating" a blade of grass, all he can find to consume, to represent the Host.

"O my God, You are here, it is You who will do what must be done. For You are also a priest, the only true priest. Here is this grass, grown where You, perhaps, once walked, for You lived in these parts. Now I make the sign of the Cross upon this thing You created. . . .

"By the power I possess in virtue of baptism, I consecrate this grass which I hold in my hands that it may be the image and likeness of Your body. The words of power I do not say, I have not the right, but You will say them for me.

"A man dying alone has no choice. You will not let me die of hunger.

"And my hunger for Your body is as great as my thirst, God. I have no power, but bless, I pray You, this thing of Your Creation, that I may receive it as Your image."

Slowly, he broke the blade of grass in two and raised it to his bruised and swollen lips.

It is the portrayal of such faith that gives the book its greatness, as it was indeed the existence of such faith that is a key to the understanding of the Middle Ages. And yet, it is to be feared that many a critic will not grasp the book in its true inwardness but consider it only as another, if superior, cloak-and-dagger tale, precisely because the faith of the Middle Ages will not be understood. Even so perceptive a commentator as Gilbert Highet, writing in the Book-of-the-Month Club *News* for December 1954, summarizes by saying:

Gracious and brutal, devoutly pious and shockingly profane, self-seeking and self-forgetful, grossly materialistic and airily fanciful and remotely mystical, often cruel and often tenderly charitable, the soul of the Middle Ages is a mystery to us today . . . we can scarcely begin to comprehend people so unlike ourselves. . . .

The first remark suggested by such a commentary is that the Middle Ages were ridden by no more mutually contradictory qualities than our own age is, in so far as it can be viewed as a whole. If the Middle Ages were "gracious and brutal," is not the twentieth century refined and humanitarian—and cursed with concentration camps and slave-labor battalions? If the Middle Ages were "self-seeking and self-forgetful," is not our age remarkable for its organized and international charity and indictable for widespread economic oppression? And so on; the war within the human heart has not changed since the thirteenth century, and in every age and clime the terrible contradictions can be found.

But Mr. Highet's thought may well lead the incautious reader of the book to another and more incorrect conclusion. The history that a vast number of Americans have been taught equates in their minds the Middle Ages with the "Dark Ages." The Middle Ages are therefore seen under a pejorative light, and to insist that they are so vastly different from our own times in their inner qualities is practically the same as to say that their difference means that they were worse, physically, intellectually, and morally.

Such thinking about the Middle Ages has not by any means become as scarce as the dodo. It is still commonplace in various popularizations and is certainly stock in the intellectual trade of the famous man in the street. In an article, for example, in the December 11, 1954 *Saturday Review*, Warren Weaver writes on "Peace of Mind" and makes some devastating and, I feel, much needed criticisms of the best-selling *The Power of Positive Thinking*, by Norman Vincent Peale. The peace of mind, says Mr. Weaver, that Dr. Peale and other authors like him advocate is really a sort of stagnation, craving a "world at complete rest." And then, in come the poor Middle Ages; Mr. Weaver quotes approvingly from *The Common Sense of Science*, by Bronowski:

> Medieval philosophical and religious thought considered that the then unfortunately disorderly world [is ours not disorderly?] seeks its order in the great ideal hierarchy of how it ought to be. And it ought to be a still perfection.

Undoubtedly the Middle Ages did conceive of society as ideally ranged into a hierarchy, but to call it a "still perfection" is indeed wide of the mark. The concept was rather one of a hierarchy composed of graduated and balancing tensions.

Again, Mr. Weaver calls on Albert Schweitzer to testify that the Middle Ages were dominated by the principle of non-activity, which in turn flowed from "a negation of the world" that contrasts sadly with the modern attitude, which is one "of passionate affirmation . . . interesting oneself in the things in this world and in the life we lead in it."

If one would like to judge the exactitude of this remark and of the general thinking about the Middle Ages that underlies it, one has but to browse through such a book as *Literature and Pulpit in Medieval England,* by G. R. Owst. In the chapters on "The Preaching of Satire and Complaint" and "A Literary Echo of the Social Gospel" are hundreds of practical, concrete examples of how the Church of medieval England (and the same was true on the continent) was indeed "passionately interested" in the world and in the lives men were called on to live in it.

> Here, then [says Dr. Owst], the message of the English pulpit, stored in a thousand manuscripts, bursts in upon us with an invigorating freshness. It reveals a Church striving by word of mouth . . . to curb wild passions and vicious habits, to educate the masses in a higher way of life, to reunite a discordant society in brotherly love and common service, to establish, according to its lights, a City of God upon earth, in every home and community, warning, pleading, arguing, now with a show of learning, now with quaint symbolism, now with threats, now with pathos, now with humor, a very human as well as a very formidable Church.

No, there is no call to be smug when we look back on the Middle Ages. We might rather cast the retrospective glance with humility, for there was one thing in which the Middle Ages were different and better. If they were "devoutly pious and shockingly profane," they at least knew the difference between right and wrong. They would have found simply unintelligible the statement of Arnold Toynbee in *This I Believe:*

> I believe we have no certain knowledge of what is right and wrong; and, even if we had, I believe we should find it just as hard as ever to do something that we knew for certain to be right in the teeth of our personal interests and inclinations.

The pages of *The Cornerstone* reveal vividly how the saints and the sinners, the superstitious, the rich and the poor, priests and laity, knew the right, however they freely shaped their lives.

One final thought. I'm wondering how many Catholic college graduates know enough about the real character of the Middle Ages really to appreciate the achievement in *The Cornerstone.*

(January 15, 1955)

TODAY'S WRITER AND THE MIDDLE AGES

Van Wyck Brooks, the distinguished American literary historian (*Makers and Finders, The Ordeal of Mark Twain,* etc.), has just written a book which assesses the problems, the successes, and failures of the creative writer in the United States. It is called *The Writer in America,* and I recommend it to the attention of all who would hear an eloquent plea (if at times a rather shrill and repetitious one) for the rebirth of a spirit of nobility, particularly in American fiction.

Mr. Brooks is tired of the younger American novelists who, living off a "dreary legacy" left them by such oldsters as Dos Passos, Hemingway, Faulkner, et al., have become "unable to see active goodness in developed human beings, or, rather, scarcely able to see developed types at all, or anything but 'irresponsible criminals.'" He is weary of the influence of those authors who, like F. Scott Fitzgerald, never advanced beyond adolescence. He is filled with ennui of writers whose "cult of youth . . . has filled them with a fear of growing old that almost precludes at the outset any regard for the uses of growing old."

He longs for the return of the spirit which, he says, was the informing genius of whatever great American literature we have had, just as it has always been, in the long run, the informing genius of any great literature in the world. That is a spirit of affirmation, of assertion of the eternal human values, of pride in the dignity of man. "To rehumanize literature," he states,

> the first step is to think better of man, to celebrate the grandeur of humanity and rejoice in its nature, to repudiate the meanness of the minds that love to dwell on the "stale thoughts" which are all one with the "stale food moldering in the larder." We should elevate and honor men, proud of the great things they have done since their anthropoid forbears climbed down from the jungle trees; since, discarding their tails and fur and walking forth as human, they looked before and after, knowing good from evil.

Not a few defendants are haled into Mr. Brooks's literary dock and charged with having been responsible for this contemporary assault on humanity and this debauching of the literature that is supposed to picture humanity. One of the worst offenders, the indictment runs, is the school of "new" critics. By concentrating their attention exclusively on the "form," the "word," they have ingrained the impression in all too many minds that what literature says is of no account. By insisting on the heresy "spread abroad by Valéry, who said that 'the matter is of small importance,' that 'nothing is of any importance but method and form,' these critics have disregarded the vital fact in writing that the subject is a 'challenge' which evokes the writer's 'response.'" Brooks charges, too, the contemporary creative American artist with preserving and stubbornly fostering a love for the "closed society," by which he means the modern state with its claims to absolute sovereignty—and this at a time when the cultural trend in all other fields is moving toward the internationalism of an "open" society.

But basic to all these charges, it seems to me, are Mr. Brooks's accusations that the writer in America is false to the ideals of literature because he has sought security by fleeing back to the spirit of the Middle Ages and reviving that period's belief in and concern with "original sin." This fundamental regression, as Mr. Brooks sees it, is what has brought in its train all the other ills which have dehumanized literature.

No one will cavil at Mr. Brooks's plea that literature be "rehumanized," though I do believe that he makes out too black a case against such a novelist as Faulkner, to take but one instance. But I believe even more strongly that Mr. Brooks is quite off the beam in this fundamental matter of the spirit of the Middle Ages. He is vulnerable on other points as well—for example, in the unabashed and earthbound humanitarianism which leads him to quote with no reservations Swinburne's "glory to man in the highest, for man is the master of things," and to add:

When Swinburne wrote [this] he stood at the culminating point of a long evolution that began with the Renaissance four centuries before; and for many minds fifty years of human failure and human thought has served to reverse the whole of this evolution. They see man not as the master of things but as the victim of original sin, just as man saw himself in the Middle Ages.

Mr. Brooks will little note nor long remember what I might

have to say about the spirit of the Middle Ages, which I submit he grossly misunderstands. Happily, however, a novelist whom I'm sure he must acknowledge to be great, though perhaps he may not admire her (there is no mention of her in his volume's rather extensive index of names), has recently had a critical study devoted to her by one who is himself a professor of the history of philosophy at Oslo. Sigrid Undset is the novelist; she was, in addition, an admitted authority on the Middle Ages, particularly in her native Norway. Her greatest novels dealt precisely with that period of Norwegian history. The study is *Sigrid Undset: a Study in Christian Realism*, by A. H. Winsnes. Perhaps Mr. Brooks may give them a hearing.

What do Sigrid Undset and her biographer, interpreting her, have to say about the spirit of the Middle Ages? Were those centuries a glum and gloomy time in which man's brooding on original sin so drove him to such "other-worldliness" that he despaired of this world? Did the doctrine of original sin tell medieval man that "men are more radically evil than potentially good" (Mr. Brooks's interpretation—and one for which I believe he would search in vain in any Catholic source)? Were the Middle Ages, with their climate of "authority, hierarchy, and order" *ipso facto* wedded to the "closed society" and disdainful, if not ignorant, of the "open society?"

Mr. Winsnes's book gives rich refutation to all these assumptions and statements of Mr. Brooks. I can only urge the reader who would like to have more solid reasons for embracing Mr. Brooks's noble crusade than he himself adduces to read the whole Winsnes book for this purpose—as well as, of course, for the fine appreciation of Sigrid Undset that it is.

Here are some of the main points on which Undset-Winsnes are corrective of Brooks. It was precisely the

religious idea which, at the beginning of the medieval period, had been formulated in terms of historical philosophy by the genius of Augustine that, through the expansion of the Church, had created on a wholly spiritual basis a European universalism. The truth glimmered in men's minds [that is, in the minds of the later historians] that it was in the Middle Ages that the real European community was born.

These same historians began to realize that "the Middle Ages are not simply the dark ages or *medium aevum*, which, for the humanists of the Renaissance and later for the rationalists, cast, as it were, a shadow between them and the glories of classical antiquity or the sun of the 'enlightenment.'" It would seem dubious that Mr. Brooks has ever heard of this more recent trend in historical studies.

Sigrid Undset and her appraiser would, again, have looked askance at Mr. Brooks's charge that the Middle Ages, because of their insistence on man's sinfulness, were bogged down in despair, a lack of nerve, a lack of inventive to strive. They say, rather: "Not the Viking forays, but the creative and constructive will towards peace and order, the desire for the beautiful and the spiritual elevation of existence—aspirations liberated by Christianity—came into the foreground as marking the greatest effort of the Norwegian medieval period."

Again, Mr. Winsnes remarks:

Nowhere is Sigrid Undset's realism more merciless and searching than in her account of the last years of Kristin's [*Kristin Lavransdatter's*] life. There is grandeur in this truthfulness which will not suffer any embellishment. She sees through the frailty of human nature, the wickedness of man and his divided will, the source of his disease. But this realism is not pessimistic in effect—it does not leave a character bound and helpless. It knows that escape can be made, that freedom does exist, that it is always possible to break through and win the strength which gives that freedom.

Even more telling are Mr. Winsnes's remarks on *The Master of Hestviken:*

What in particular makes this book unique in our Norwegian literature is its description of contrition as a rejuvenating power in the human mind [and certainly contrition presupposes a sense of sin]. . . . Sigrid Undset is not the first Norwegian author in whose writing contrition, in the Christian sense, plays such an essential part. It is a leading motive in Henrik Wergeland and Henrik Ibsen . . . but neither of these authors has seen so deeply into the nature of remorse as Sigrid Undset . . . nor have they shown us how conscience, with all its imperfections, demonstrates the existence of an invisible order with which man is connected. Contrition is presented to us as the fountainhead of health—those stirrings of the conscience which are characterized by the desire to re-establish inner harmony by rehearsing before God all that is past.

From this brief sampling of how the spirit of the Middle Ages gave strength and glory to Sigrid Undset's medieval novels it might appear that Mr. Brooks could well revise his estimate of what "the return to the Middle Ages" has done to our younger writers. It may well be, of course, that if indeed those younger writers thought at all about the Middle Ages they did so in the inexact and misleading terms that color Mr. Brooks's estimate of the period. The point is, however, that the Middle Ages ought not to be thought of in that way. If younger writers would return to the true spirit of the Middle Ages, they would find them far from being a debilitating influence. They might even see what Sigrid Undset saw:

Her inspiration is not simply Norway's past, but the history of Europe and Christendom. None of her contemporaries has heard the voices of the past as she has done; neither has any of them seen further into the future and been more aware of the darkness which lies before them and *of the way through to the light beyond* [emphasis added].

It is lamentable that Mr. Brooks, in pleading for a return to the accents of nobility in literature, has written off the spirit of an age when man's aspirations (if not his achievements) were perhaps noblest.

(May 2, 1953)

HOW TO BE HAPPY THOUGH MEDIEVAL

Suppose you found yourself one day just standing in the middle of a long road, knowing neither where you had come from nor where you were. It would be rather difficult to know where you were going, would it not? And yet, the makers and planners of the bright future that is, they say, to emerge out of the present world chaos and confusion are not infrequently in a similar plight. Finding the world as it is in 1942, with but a sketchy idea of how it got there, of how its present condition emerged, it becomes an impossible task for them to map intelligently the direction it is to take.

And, of course, one of the best ways of knowing the past is to know its literature. Ignorance of this gives rise at times to fantastic conceptions of the culture of the past; with that comes a distortion of history and the consequent emasculation of plans for the future which pretend to rest on an historical basis.

A beautiful example of this (beautiful in the sense in which a pathologist speaks of a beautiful specimen of cancer) was provided in a past issue of the *Saturday Review*. The feature article for that week was "The Idea of Happiness," by Raoul de Roussy de Sales, and is part of a chapter of his new book, *The Making of Tomorrow*. Just what he is to make of tomorrow I do not yet know, but if that making is not a more sensible job than his reconstruction of the past, his planning will spawn a monster.

His thesis in the article is that it was only in the eighteenth century, when the "concept of progress, such as we understand it today, became sufficiently clear to influence the course of history," that "men deliberately turned toward the future and expressed the faith that the condition of mankind could be improved by human means."

To establish this presumed fact, the author tells us what he thinks the Middle Ages had to say about this business of improving man's earthly condition. His account will leave his readers with the definite and distorted impression, if they take his word for it (and they will, for, you see, he has written a book), that all the world in the Middle Ages was a sorry, lachrymose lot of "what's-the-use"-ers.

This defeatist attitude was due to the fact that our strange western European forefathers were of the species "Theological Man." For them "the pursuit of happiness on this earth was neither conscious nor encouraged." This was because "men placed their hopes in a life hereafter." Hence, they were incapable of conceiving any happiness as possible here in this vale of tears. After all, "the dogma of Original Sin permeated all thinking. Man was born wicked and his only hope was for a better life after death." He did not expect "that life on this earth could be anything but miserable. To live was admittedly a punishment." They were a generation of men "to whom the notion that humanity as a whole could become happier on this earth through its own efforts was still foreign."

Now it really does not seem unreasonably captious to ask that if anyone writes about the Middle Ages he be equipped with a fairly wide and deep knowledge of the period. Certainly we would expect this if an author were expatiating on the strategy of tiddlywinks or the raising of rabbits. But apparently history is of less importance. If only the author, for example, had some familiarity with such a work as Langland's *The Vision of Piers Plowman.* No one can discourse authoritatively on the history of ideas and culture in the Middle Ages without knowing this poem. Because it is more than a poem—it is the "quintessence of medieval preaching"; it is in "perfect accord with the most commonplace orthodox preaching of the times, indeed, a perfect echo in every respect of the Church's message to the world."

Here, then, was no voice crying in the wilderness; Langland's message was no preachment of a ragged-haired rebel listened to by the "Theological Man" in bewildered and scandalized awe at its daring heresy. It was the same message he heard week after week from the pulpits.

And what is this preaching's message? By no means exclusively the hopeless groaning that "man's only hope was for a better life after death." Medieval "other worldliness" is in the poem, of course; its eye and heart are fixed on the fair shore of Heaven—but the great and clamorous-tongued message of the poem is a social message, an impassioned plea for the righting of the temporal wrongs of the realm. These wrongs, injustice, oppression of the poor, discord, and many another, can be righted if each of the three orders of society performs its proper functions well.

These three orders, in the medieval concept, were priesthood, knighthood, and laborers. Each, in its own divinely constituted sphere, had its definite duties, and in their zealous performance society was to find its harmony and well-being, was to give forth, as a thirteenth-century preacher put it, the sweet melody of a well-strung harp. Each order, and each man in it, "by doing his work faithfully, was serving a supreme common good"—and that common good was, yes, happiness hereafter, but also, very *much* also, the temporal welfare, the temporal progress, the temporal happiness of the community and of the men who were its members.

The medieval idea of the three orders of society may strike us nowadays as quaint, but the ideal there enshrined has never been even approximated in the political and social theories of a world since devoted to unadulterated progress. The medieval vision of the Christian commonwealth was "that of a battleline *'constipata et compensata,*' in which no gap appears, but all stand shoulder to shoulder in a common love to God and to their fellows."

And this concept was not exclusively wrapped up in dreams of celestial happiness—it envisioned happiness here, and not mere individual felicity only but a corporate happiness, depending upon and attainable through the ordered, rational, corporate efforts of a society that had a duty to strive constantly to ameliorate its condition.

It is the conclusion of two French scholars, Guérard and Delisle, from their study of the medieval sermons of their native land, that the voice of these preachers "was a continual appeal to the emancipation of the people," and this interest of the Church in the temporal welfare of the little folk has not by any means been confined to recent times and the social encyclicals of the recent Popes. Why would the preachers of those far ages bother to preach improved human conditions if "to live was admittedly a punishment?" We cannot forget that not only long-suffering but joy, too, was, even for the medieval Church, one of the fruits of the Holy Ghost.

Space limitations prevent lengthy quotations from *Piers Plowman* or from the medieval preachers, but to prospective writers about the Middle Ages and to readers who have believed, or who have, perhaps, by this time been brought to believe that a knowledge of the past is a help to understanding the present, I recommend the reading of such a book as *Literature and Pulpit in Medieval England,* by G. R. Owst, particularly the chapter, "A Literary Echo of the Social Gospel."

So much, though rather sketchily, about the incontestable fact that even a superficial knowledge of the literature of the Middle Ages will give the quietus to the impression that the people of the age were fervent Manichees to whom life was but a punishment, a miserable affair to be dragged out in whinings and blubberings until death brought release into the only life that could possibly be at all happy, life in Heaven.

A further sane guide to the social and cultural ideas of the Middle Ages can be obtained by a study of medieval art. Here again, the same truth, though in more indirect fashion, is brought home. Glance through, for example, Émile Mâle's classic three volumes on religious art in the Middle Ages, and you will find that the idea of earthly happiness was not a stranger to men's thoughts. If Heaven were the only happiness to the medieval mind, certainly in missals and "books of hours" of the time, books devoted to heavenly things, we should expect to find illustrations of heavenly happiness only.

But what do we see? Strange, whimsical, humorous marginal drawings and illuminations depicting the hurly-burly and fun and joy of the times—scenes from animal life, scenes of village feasts, caricatures, and even lampooning, all on the sacred pages. Speaking of these so human and appealing side lights on the habits of the times, Mâle concludes: "Joy shines through everywhere—Christianity of the Middle Ages took human nature to itself in all its entirety . . . profound faith gave to those ages gaiety and the serenity of infancy." And he reminds us that Dante, who certainly knew the times, has a special circle in Hell for those who "wept, when they could have been joyous."

The admission, if it is that, must be made, of course, that from the fifteenth century on, Christian art takes on more and more a somber and tragic note. The suffering Christ begins to dominate the scene and representations of death, sometimes in very lurid form, appear, and so on. But to take these new directions in art as being representative of the whole Middle Ages is singularly to misread the record of the past.

Up to this period, the fifteenth century (and the reasons for its rise cannot be gone into here), "all the luminous sides of Christianity" had been reflected in art—rarely was there a representation of pain and death; Christ upon His Cross was almost exclusively Christ triumphant; all art portrayed a Christianity which could be summed up "in a single secret word—love."

These remarks may open up some vistas on the Middle Ages for our readers and, we hope, even for authors like the one with whose summary of the period we can by no means agree. That much defamed era in history has been so indefatigably misinterpreted by non-Catholic historians that it comes as no shock (though it is a shame) to read facile and false summations like those which have led to the writing of this article.

It is doubly a shame that those distortions should come from one who claims kinship with a saintly and noble soul, whose life span bridges over from the late Middle Ages into the so-called modern times. Saint Francis de Sales (1567–1622), an ancestor of M. Raoul de Roussy de Sales, would have understood the Ages of Faith much better. (March 28, 1942)

Chapter Three

WHY I LIKED SOME

There is no good reason in the world why anyone in the world should be interested in why I liked some books. Liking is a purely personal matter and one might and really ought to be as disinterested in whether I like green socks as in the mere fact that I liked some novels.

The operative word in the title above, accordingly, is not the "like" but the "why." Are there objective grounds on which fiction may be judged? What precisely in the book provides the basis on which the reader or the critic may reasonably say he likes it? Is it the style or what is said—or a combination of the two? Can a book be rationally liked for one aspect of the whole complex that goes into the making of a piece of literature and yet disliked because of some other less well-handled aspect? How does one strike a balance?

The selections that follow by no means cover all the good, fine, and even great books I have read in the past two decades. The reader will probably raise an eyebrow at the omission of many near classics—the coverage of the French novelists which I have tried to achieve in the pages of America, for instance, is not represented here. But I can do no more than refer the reader who would like to discover why I have liked more books than appear here to the weekly columns of America.

A few of the books discussed below are not by any means of towering stature, but they have at least been catalytic agents—they have provoked much discussion and controversy, and they are included for that reason. Incidentally, it may be of interest to point out that the most violent winds of dissent have swirled around the

criticism I accorded to The Scarlet Lily, A Tree Grows in Brooklyn,
The Keys of the Kingdom, The End of the Affair, *and* The Nun's
Story. *My head survived—bloody (very slightly) but unbowed
(very stubbornly)—because I feel that in each case I could and did
point out the objective "why" that justified the "I like."*

"NIGH DRAWS THE CHASE"

The Loi don *Tablet* for July 9, 1945, headed its review of Evelyn
Waugh's book, *Brideshead Revisited,* "A Great Catholic Novel."
With that high estimate I am inclined to agree; it is undoubtedly
a remarkable achievement; whether you will think it great will depend mainly on whether you think Waugh's meticulous, aristocratic
style, his sardonic objectivity are happily wedded to a theme that
is sober and ascetic. There is no question that the style, in itself,
is admirable; there is no doubt that the book's theme is profound
and moving; but some, I fear, will find the book irritating, particularly if they read it with memories of Waugh's earlier work
lurking in the crannies of their heads to whisper that, after all,
Waugh is a satirist and writes tongue in cheek.

But in this book he has undoubtedly added a cubit to his stature.
This is more than satire; it is very much more. The satire is there,
but it plays around the edges of his central theme. That theme is
touched with reverence, though the reverence is not a solemnly
impressive one. Indeed, a sincere artist, as Waugh undoubtedly is,
could not touch the theme save with reverence, for it is of all themes
perhaps the world's most poignant. Our Lord Himself quite astonishingly painted its beauty and heartbreak when, after His loveliest
parables on the Good Shepherd and the Prodigal Son, He told us
of the joy there is in Heaven over a sinner's doing penance.

That is the core of the tale that Waugh puts in the mouth of
Charles Ryder, a British Army officer billeted by a quirk of chance
on the estate of the Marchmains, Brideshead. The sight of the
gracious old manor and of the lovely vistaed lawns sets his memory
in train and the story unfolds of his first meeting with the family,
the tumultuous quarrels and loves, the sins and repentances.
Charles had met Sebastian, the younger son, at Oxford. Spoiled,
engagingly innocent under his sophistication, the young son is stub-

bornly mistrustful of his mother's devout Catholicism. It is the
kind of devotion that all unconsciously dominates, or tries to, the
lives of those around her. Under it, her husband had left her to
live in Byronic fashion in Naples with a mistress. It causes a wall
of aloofness between mother and Julia, the older daughter. But
actually what all were trying to escape was not the mother's all-
pervading devotion but the clear demands of holiness that God
was making on them.

Charles is introduced into this strangely divided household.
Bridey, the eldest son is there, stodgy, logical, kind but unimagina-
tive; Cordelia, the younger sister, naïve, wise, and wholesome in
the simplicity of her faith. Sebastian finally wanders off to strange
places and ends up as a lay helper in a foreign monastery, still a
mild dipsomaniac but committed now to the shifting battle to
achieve his sanctity. Years pass. Charles, now a famous painter,
marries. On the boat to England from South America he meets
Julia, long since married to a Canadian politician residing in England. There is a liaison between Charles and Julia; on returning to
England they plan mutual divorces and marriage. Lady Marchmain
has died; the renegade lord comes home to die; Julia breaks off
with Charles irrevocably.

I regret exceedingly that bare skeleton of an outline. It gives no
hint of the richness of this book. I know, for example, of no death-
bed scene in recent literature to compare with the deeply moving
scene of the haughty, stubborn, long-calloused-in-sin Lord Marchmain as he lifts his dying hand to the chrism of the Last Sacrament
on his brow. He had refused to see a priest—what will that lifted
hand do? Wipe the Unction away in final repudiation or complete
the sign of his salvation? There is the agony of Julia when, through
Bridey's clumsy but grace-fraught remark, she is appalled at her
realization of the horrific truth of what it means to be living in sin.

There are, throughout, these intensely dramatic and dogma-
laden depths. There are passages that light up the meaning of
obedience, of suffering, of sin. And yet, Waugh is still Waugh; the
social satire, of the silly, golden boys of post-World War I Oxford;
of the utter blank of the secularist mind in matters of religion; of
modern ostentation—all these are marvelously detailed, caustic,
devastating, but never narrow-minded.

Yes, adultery, intellectual pride, debauchery feature in the book.
One or two of the characters are touched by darker vices, but they

are the ones in whose souls there is no struggle; they have settled comfortably into their degeneracy. The others have fallen and, as Julia says, "probably I shall be bad again, punished again. But the worse I am, the more I need God. . . . It may be a private bargain between me and God, that if I give up this one thing I want so much, He won't quite despair of me in the end."

So the tumultuous memories of Charles Ryder come to an end, to be replaced by the reality he won through those struggles and sins of the years gone by; the reality is that, as he stepped once again into the manor chapel, he found there

> a small red flame—a beaten-copper lamp of deplorable design, relit before the beaten-copper doors of a tabernacle. . . . It could not have been lit but for the builders and the tragedians, and there I found it this morning, burning anew among the old stones.

This is a profoundly Catholic work. It will reward thoughtful reading. Perhaps a hint may help you to be aware of the set of its current from the very first chapter. It is this: turn to the title of Book II and then look back to the bottom of page 220. This will give you a hint as to the structure of the book; with this in mind, it will be indeed only the very insensitive reader who will fail to catch the inexorable development and explication of the splendid tragicomedy. Here is the key to the book that so many critics have missed.

(January 12, 1946)

WAUGH'S AWRY CRITICS

Something has happened to the Book-of-the-Month Club. Twice within three months it has chosen for its accolade (and for its almost a million members) two books distinctly Catholic in theme and atmosphere. It is doubtless true that Catholic books have been chosen in the past by this most Gargantuan of all our book clubs, but unless I am yielding to a too ready optimism, I seem to detect nowadays among the Summi Pontifices of the club more of a readiness to recognize books on their own merits, whether written by Catholics and on Catholic themes or not.

How to account for this more discriminating, more catholic attitude I do not quite know. It may be that the recent replacements on the editorial board have brought about a wider sympathy. I have long thought that Christopher Morley's urbanity and wide knowledge of literature was one of the finest assets the club possessed; perhaps that, together with John Marquand's rather Brahmin tolerance, has been enough to tip the scales against what I feel might have been the club's choices had Clifton Fadiman and Sinclair Lewis had a free hand.

Whatever be the soundness of this diagnosis of the strategy of the club's guiding geniuses, their last three selections have been excellent and even startling to a Catholic critic (and I say "three" here, for I had forgotten in my first paragraph above that Robert Gibbings's *Lovely Is the Lee* is markedly Catholic, too).

But let us not leap to the conclusion that these books have been selected because they are Catholic. It is rather despite the fact, and because they have been witty, humane, pungent, tolerant—whatever epithet you will—and not because they had something fresh and compelling to say that was essentially bound up with some profound Catholic dogma. So while we laud the choices that have recently been made, the grounds on which they have been made give but added proof of the fact that has been pointed out in these columns from time to time—namely, that when any book, and particularly a novel, touches on anything like spiritual depth and significance, the non-Catholic critic and the Catholic critic cannot evaluate it in the same terms simply because their standards of judgment differ.

This fact was treated at some length several years ago when I gathered together some of the non-Catholic critical appraisals of Werfel's *The Song of Bernadette* and discovered that many of the eminent critics had, I felt sure, utterly missed the point of that masterpiece. It was impossible, it seemed to me, to judge the book properly without a knowledge of the doctrine of the distribution of grace; this the reviewers, generally, lacked; though they spoke about a Bernadette who was simple, strong, winning, and all the rest, they could not know the real Bernadette of life nor the remarkably alive Bernadette of the novel.

Now the opening of 1946 brings us another book which has, thus far, fallen upon the same unhappy fate. As I write, it has not been reviewed by all the leading critics whose statements I would have to examine before I could reach a complete induction; but I venture the guess that most of the subsequent criticisms will labor from the blind spots I shall point out in the reviews that have up to now appeared.

The book is Evelyn Waugh's *Brideshead Revisited*. How I value it will be found in this week's leading review; here I am concerned only with how others have misvalued it, but to lay the groundwork I shall have to reveal the review sufficiently to say that to my mind the essential theme of the book is that contained in the bold imagery of the "Hound of Heaven"—God's relentless love that pursues the sinner and will not be shaken off.

What have the critics to date made out of this tremendous concept? One of the most sensitive of our authorities these days, Christopher Morley, is summarized in the Book-of-the-Month Club *News* as dubbing the book "the story of a noble old Catholic family that fell from grace." Nor is the summation unfair to Mr. Morley; in all his extended review there is not a single suggestion that there is any deeper theme to the book than that of the decline of gracious English manor houses and the coming of a cruder, more mechanized, more efficient way of life. In fact, Mr. Morley states quite openly that there is no serious theme unless one reads such into the book: "If you need to put social and serious feeling into it [the plot and manner] you've got to put it there mostly for yourself."

Mr. Morley has been, it would appear, so fascinated by the style, by the exquisiteness of the minutiae, by the at times sardonic tone and satiric overtones that he has missed any deep meaning. A fall from grace is indeed there, but that is but the point of departure; it is the tortuous climb *out of* the morass that is the story.

Two other critics, both writing briefly in the same *News*, see that there is a deeper meaning, but they are puzzled with it. Glenway Wescott sees that the book is serious in its dealings with "at least the longing for religion," but he finds the religious theme so objectively presented that "neo-pagan readers may think that the point is anti-Catholic, and Protestant readers may be deeply puzzled." Whichever of these two Mr. Wescott may himself be, he has not, as far as I can see, caught the meaning of the structure of the book, which moves inevitably toward the splendid climax.

Louis Kronenberger, on the other hand, seeing the religious aspect of the book, thinks that it "has the feel of propaganda, damages the tone . . . and rather deadens the impact." But that is rather like saying that the soul damages the body and deadens its impact, for the theme of God's pursuit is the soul of the book.

Writing the leading review in the New York *Times Book Review*, John K. Hutchens surveys Waugh's progress rather than this specific book. However, in his approach to *Brideshead Revisited*, he acknowledges to some extent the seriousness of the theme, but he straitens it unduly to make it state "that faith is a saving answer to anyone who has it or has had it." This, he contends as against Mr. Kronenberger, can "scarcely be called propaganda," but neither, on the other hand, can it truly be called the kernel of the book's seriousness. The significance of this Waugh work cannot be found in any such terms that can be construed as a statement of mere humanitarianism. Faith? Yes, but faith in what, in whom, how got, whence given, how bludgeoned into stubborn souls? Waugh's novel grapples with those questions: it does not glibly and unconvincingly lisp that "faith is a saving answer."

The anonymous reviewer in *Newsweek* has a hard time making up his mind. He claims that "in essence *Brideshead Revisited* is just another story of an old English family of wealth, culture, and social standing which has fallen victim to the evils of the times" (and "evils of the times" is certainly a surprising way to describe the gravely deliberate wrongdoing by which the several members of the family bring the greatest evils on themselves). He can say in the next breath, however, that "the major theme" of the novel is "faith in the ancient verities and in the reclamation of the beautiful and the damned." This reviewer, for all his inconsistencies, hits nearest to the truth, for he realizes that this last novel of Waugh's is not a study in decadence; the decadence that there is in it is but a foil to the imperativeness, the terrible insistence of God's grace. But neither does "reclamation" strike the key to the book's theme; that word smacks of social-service agencies, of juvenile-delinquency commissions and boards of do-gooders. Waugh's story does not deal with man's or society's efforts at correcting wrongs; it deals with how God at times steps in and, by bringing one's dearest, wrongheaded hopes and ambitions crashing down, overwhelms evil by the fierceness of His love.

After all, however, the *Newsweek* critic would think all this striving to grasp the real point of the book rather a fatuous labor, for he ends the review with the rather startling statement that "the reader should probably not look for too much in *Brideshead Re-*

WHY I LIKED SOME 95

visited, but be content with a story beautifully told by one of the most exhilarating stylists in our times." Again, the same reviewer echoes the fear, as others quoted above stated it, that "one is, in some mysterious way, being introduced to the subtleties of the faith." These critics fear so readily and unfoundedly that any book that touches on points of Catholic dogma must be a sectarian tract! And the fear that dogma is sectarian makes them miss the artistic sinews and bone structure, and rhapsodize only on the graceful and seductive external planes and curves.

Perhaps it is not fair to take Miss Patterson's chatty column, "Turns with a Bookworm," too seriously, but if her remarks in the New York *Herald Tribune Books* do reflect a serious judgment, that judgment is singularly shallow. Miss Patterson fears that "blue-moulders of literary opinion are going to go solemn again over a rather light-weight satirist . . . whereas we simply read the novel and amused ourselves analyzing the ingredients." Very good, but would you be led to suspect from this cavalier attitude that one of the ingredients was precisely God's refusal to let the sinner go?

Lewis Gannett, also in the New York *Herald Tribune*, comes along to swell the number of those who have not caught the central core of the book. "If it is anything," he writes, "it is a threnody upon adolescence, a nostalgic lament for the epicine intoxications of gilded Oxford youth in the early 1920s." Confusing, as the others have, the surface with the substance, he finds that this latest Waugh book is "his most fundamentally decadent." But certainly the whole architecture builds up to a thunderous affirmation; true, there are vertiginous falls from grace in the book, but the only persevering moral decadence in the story (as contrasted with the social decadence in gracious living) is in the characters who seem to be blinded to the truth; the weak souls have the essential goodness and the essential strength to tear down at last the barriers they had thrown up against the stern demands they knew all along God was making on them. Of this there is not a hint in Mr. Gannett's evaluation.

The New York *Times'* Orville Prescott comes closer to a proper estimate when he admits that "if the point of view of *Brideshead Revisited* is a fastidious detachment, analyzing and re-creating the past, its theme is religious." He sees how important the faith is to the Marchmains, "how it arched across the universe of their thought and action." But he falters when he goes on to say that it seems

Waugh "has painted a picture of Catholicism in decay." It is not Catholicism that has decayed; it is the social stratum and the discipline and fervor of some Catholics, and it is precisely the might, and not the decay, of the faith that makes its stern and insistent demands heard and obeyed at last after years of self-indulgence, self-delusion, and evasion. That I take to be a theme of regeneration, not of corruption.

These, then, are the critical judgments I have been able to gather as we go to press. I do not deny that many of the critics quoted above have written cleverly, discerningly, about many of Waugh's gifts. There is almost universal agreement that he is a masterly craftsman; the flash and bite of his satire, the richness of his allusions, his mastery of detail have all been appreciated. But I have not yet read a criticism in the secular press which has glimpsed what the book is really about. A few critics have managed to say the theme is religious, but in what specific way it is religious—that will still remain a mystery to those who take their opinion on the book from critics who, in these matters where ultimate spiritual values are under treatment, simply do not speak our language, the language of the faith.

As a footnote, may I say that two last-minute reviews, Harry Hansen's in the New York *World-Telegram* and William McFee's in the same city's *Sun* still leave me unconvinced that critics have thus far understood the book.   (January 12, 1946)

MR. GREENE DOES IT AGAIN

If for no other reason, Graham Greene will have a permanent niche in the history of English literature—and particularly of Catholic literature—because he manages to write provocative and controversial novels. But the controversy that swirled around *The Labyrinthine Ways* (*The Power and the Glory*) and *The Heart of the Matter* will sound like a muted murmur compared with the storms that will thunder around *The End of the Affair*. I feel that the book demands rather extended treatment, both for its intrinsic importance and to forestall criticism that gets off on the wrong foot.

Perhaps the best way to start is to quote from a very perceptive article on Greene (by Edward Sackville-West in the *Month*, Lon-

don, September, 1951). It is called "The Electric Hare—Some
Aspects of Graham Greene" and is largely a review of Greene's
volume of essays, *The Lost Childhood*. Says Mr. West: "Every
page of this book is saturated in the belief that original sin is the
most important fact about human beings." Now the point is, for
a judgment of Greene, not precisely whether this is theologically
true or not—for certainly the fact of sanctifying grace is equally
important—but whether this is actually Greene's view. I believe it
is, and I believe that it explains the eschatological tone of all his
work. He is not interested, so to say, in the mere problem of good
and evil, of sin and virtue, as worked out in this situation by these
characters. His attention is constantly turned to the ultimate end
of this situation, of these actions—he writes always in terms of
heaven and hell.

This is what makes his books, to many tastes, so grim and dour.
But that they are Catholic, in the sense that they have as a theme
some of the great truths of Christian revelation, I believe cannot
be doubted. Whether or not those truths are couched in terms that
find acceptance on grounds of propriety and so on is another
matter.

That will be the crucial point of criticism of *The End of the
Affair*. What Greene is saying in this story is as eternally true as
much of what St. Augustine said in his *Confessions*, for the burden
of the tale is that God is often the unthought of but ever present finality of all loves. Even illegitimate love is a blind, fumbling,
misdirected search for God. How Greene says this will very probably—and with a lot of justification—be disliked.

The story of the book is simple. The title tells it, really. An
adultery that has been carried on for years comes to an end because, in the London blitz, the woman, thinking her lover has been
killed in an air raid, promises God—in whom she really does not
believe—that she will end the affair if he is given life. He lives and
she—living up to her nebulous idea of obligation—finds herself
drawn to the Church and to holiness (it turns out that she had
been baptized as a young child). After her early death a number
of apparently miraculous cures seem to be due to her intercession.
The man in the affair (who is the narrator of the story) had been
even more a disbeliever than the woman, but when his tale ends,
he has come to the point where he can at least think that he hates
God, Who has stepped in to end the affair. Hatred, Greene seems

to be saying, argues belief—an echo of the Biblical "neither hot nor cold."

So much for the plot. However, I must admit that much of Greene's language is a stumbling block even to those who may be called mature readers. It must be remembered in all fairness that the story is told by a long-term lecher. His phrases—objectively blasphemous at times—are his own and fit his character, but they are such that the book is by no means to be commended to the attention of all. It is a shame and could have been avoided by a different narrative device.

Evelyn Waugh, reviewing the book in the same issue of the London *Month*, says: "*The End of the Affair* is addressed to the Gentiles. It shows them the Church as something in their midst, mysterious and triumphant and working for their good." That, I feel, is true, but the book will also be read by Catholics, who are not accustomed to having the Church referred to in terms that spring from a philanderer's mind. That is the ultimate novelistic problem of this controversial book—how can profound spiritual truth (which Greene touches) be told in terms of stark realism? I wish I knew the answer. Until it is a little clearer than at present, I would say that *The End of the Affair* is definitely for the perusal of those professionally interested in the study of the novel.

(October 27, 1951)

SECOND THOUGHTS ON GREENE'S LATEST

The time for temporizing is over, it seems. The original notice given to *The End of the Affair* was rather in the form of an interim report and was not decisive enough to satisfy either myself or the many who have written in to ask "what gave?" Further, it is worthwhile expending some second thoughts on this book, I believe, because Graham Greene is an extraordinary phenomenon in the world of letters. In modern times there has never been an author so uncompromisingly Catholic in his statements who is at the same time admittedly—by Catholic and non-Catholic critics alike—one of the greatest living novelists.

His work is, then, something of a touchstone for criticism. If Catholic critics, above all, get him wrong, if they demand from him what they cannot justly seek, if they miss what he is valiantly saying, they will be both unfair to Greene and false to themselves.

What, accordingly, will second thoughts reveal? Perhaps I can best start by adverting to some critical opinions that seem to me to stress the wrong emphasis in their judgment of *The End of the Affair*. Riley Hughes, for instance, writing in *Best Sellers*, thinks that the images of evil are so vivid and tangible (as it were), while the images of good are so "unclothed in the novelist's skill," that "sense wins out over spirit." I believe that I delivered much the same verdict when I wrote that the profound spiritual truths of the book were couched in "terms of stark realism." I would like to withdraw my own verdict while commenting on Mr. Hughes's.

The images of evil *are* more vivid than the images of good— but how can that be otherwise, particularly when the evil wears the trappings of sensuality? It is the drear heritage of our fallen nature that things of sense are more immediately alluring than things of the spirit. Human love is, in a sense, easier to grasp and understand and enjoy than the love of God. And so, it is to make a psychologically unfair and impossible demand of Greene to ask him to make the woman's struggles toward belief in God and love of Him as charged with the immediacy and urgency of actual experience as were her passionate meetings with her lover.

But that is not the whole gist of the matter. Actually, one of the triumphs of the book, as I see it, lies precisely in the growth depicted in Sarah. It is an interesting and key fact that once the reader turns, with the narrator, to the pages of the diary in which Sarah recounts her agony to be true to her promise to end the affair, the sensuousness of the language progressively gives way to a reflected and filtered treatment of passion that removes even the slightest suspicion of undue preoccupation with sense at the expense of spirit. As Sarah's realization of real love and purity grows, Greene's style mirrors the purity of her new-found world.

But in so doing, Greene achieves the further remarkable feat of keeping the character true to herself. She does not become, at one leap, a tinsel saint, basking securely in the love of God. She is still the passionate woman; she still feels the imperious call of the flesh. And here I cannot refrain from remarking (perhaps annoyingly, for the comparison is somewhat overworked) how inevitably Greene recalls St. Augustine to mind.

One of the marvels of that great saint's *Confessions* lies precisely here—the humble frankness with which he depicts himself after his conversion as still the same passionate man. But he is now the passionate man who can ask:

> But what is it that I love when I love You? Not the beauty of any bodily thing, nor the order of the seasons, nor the brightness of light that rejoices the eye, nor the sweet melodies of all songs, nor the sweet fragrance of flowers and ointments and spices: not manna nor honey, nor the limbs that carnal love embraces. Yet in a sense I do love light and melody and fragrance and food and embrace when I love my God—the light and the voice and the fragrance and the food and the embrace in the soul, when that light shines upon my soul which no place can contain, that voice sounds which no time can take from me, I breathe that fragrance which no wind scatters, I eat that food which is not lessened by eating, and I lie in that embrace which satiety never comes to sunder. This is what I love, when I love my God.

If this is not the exact tone that runs through the diary of Sarah, and if it is not a testimony not that "sense wins out over spirit" but that sense, still being sense, can reflect the beauty of spirit, then I have misread both Augustine and Greene.

This leads immediately, I think, into another criticism leveled at Greene which I conceive to be unfounded. Martin Turnell, the English Catholic critic, writing in the *Commonweal* on "The Religious Novel," calls both Mauriac and Greene to task. "It is impossible," he states, "not to be struck by the vast place occupied by hate and the tiny place reserved for charity in the work of contemporary Catholic novelists. . . . That is the crucial point. They seek not the good points, the redeeming features of their neighbors, but something that will give the right to hate."

However this castigation may apply to Mauriac, I believe that it is utterly false of Greene. The judgment, it would appear, springs from a confusion between characters who hate and the author who hates. It is true that Greene does portray (though much less frequently than Mauriac) characters ridden by some type of hatred, whether for themselves and their environment (like the priest in *The Power and the Glory* or Scobie in *The Heart of the Matter*) or for someone else (like Bendrix in the present novel). But that is not to say that the author himself is exercising "the right to hate."

In fact, it is pretty hard to discover that Greene hates anything in his novels. For one thing, the very objectivity of his portrayal of sin has struck many a Catholic critic (unreasonably, I think) as being a sort of tacit condonation. And, so far from hating the characters he creates, Greene's most moving characteristic is a deep compassion and understanding. The best one-sentence summary of Greene I know of is given by one of his own characters. When Bendrix, in *The End of the Affair*, hating (he thinks) Sarah's memory and desiring to hurt her through her husband Henry, blurts out the whole sordid story to Henry before Father Crompton, Henry, embarrassed for his guest, says to the priest, "I'm sorry, Father." "You don't need to be," said the priest. "I know when a man's in pain."

Graham Greene knows when a man's in pain. The pain most of his characters are in is the pain of loss or of lack. The significant forward step in *The End of the Affair* is that one character, at least, stands at last horrified at the edge of the chasm and through God's grace goes about filling it with God's grace. "I might have taken a lifetime spending a little love at a time, doling it out here and there, on this man and that," says Sarah. "But even the first time . . . we spent all we had. You were there, teaching us to squander . . . so that one day we might have nothing left except this love of You."

Surprisingly enough, it was the slick and sophisticated *New Yorker* (in a review by Anthony West) that caught most clearly this positive facet of Greene's novel. "The negative aspects of belief," says Mr. West, "have gone into the discard." Unfortunately, in trying to show how different from Greene's earlier novels *The End of the Affair* is, the critic builds up a largely fictitious case against *Brighton Rock*, *The Power and the Glory*, and *The Heart of the Matter*. In all three, we are told, the pivotal point is that the protagonist is undone

by contact with female flesh . . . It is this fear of life and creativity taking the form of fear of woman, so often found in religious writing, that makes religion repulsive to so many people . . . Until now Greene has allowed one to see behind his work only a faith that is an instrument of torture calculated to make any relationship between men and women, and life in the flesh, intolerable.

That is very neat—the only trouble is that it is not true. Mr.

West's whole argument fails for the simple reason that Scobie in *The Heart of the Matter* and the priest in *The Power and the Glory* are well on the way to being undone long before they reach the "pivotal" point of "contact with female flesh." Further, the torture suffered by both characters was not caused by the faith, but by an unlived faith. It was exactly when the priest finally began to live his faith that he was restored to the possibility of finding life tolerable; it was exactly because Scobie failed to live his faith that human fellowship became so intolerable that suicide seemed the only out.

Mr. West is right, I think, about his estimate of *The End of the Affair*, but he is right, unfortunately, for the wrong reasons.

I hope I'm right—and for the right reasons—when, to end, I revise my earlier verdict on the book. It is powerful writing and most rewarding reading and certainly fare for the mature reader—and not only for those professionally interested, as I had overcautiously cautioned. The language is explicit enough to cause some uneasiness in only two or three sentences, and even those passages rouse such a sense of the real horribleness of the affair that they preclude any titillation.

The weakness of the book lies, I feel, in the introduction of the "miracles," though, granting their intrusion, they are well handled. I believe that they do intrude, for we are not prepared for them by a sufficient portrayal of Sarah's saintly life. Her sacrifice—great as it was, and her conversion—deep as it was, aren't enough to give base to miraculous intervention. Perhaps Greene introduced them to avoid the charge of leaving this story as ambiguous at the end as many thought *The Heart of the Matter* was. At any rate, Mr. West is right when he says this is a more positive book. There is nothing ambiguous about it, either in the values it upholds, the deep and valid sympathy it evokes, or the place it deserves in the world of literature.   (December 15, 1951)

MOST ARTFUL DODGER

You may not know it, but there is a Society for the Prevention of Disparaging Remarks about Brooklyn. Its president reports that slurs against that noble borough dropped from 6,457 in 1941 to

2,623 in 1942. I venture to state that when *A Tree Grows in Brooklyn*, by Betty Smith, becomes well known, as it certainly will, slurs against Brooklyn will be greatly counterbalanced by encomia heaped upon her, or at least upon this one citizen, Betty Smith, and the family of which she writes.

For this is a remarkably fresh and warmly humane story. It is called a novel; it is rather the biography of Francie Nolan, from her twelfth to her sixteenth year. The first chapter opens with her taking her weekly collection of junk to Cheap Charlie's to collect her fabulous penny; the last chapter closes with her ready to move from the old neighborhood and start college. In between, adolescent dreams and impressions, escapades, dangers, and disappointments are set before us in a fresh simplicity of style and language that is truly good.

Francie is Irish, Catholic, and poor. Irish readers may not like the book, but they ought not forget that the slovenly characters in it are more than overbalanced by the warmhearted goodness and generosity that animate the others. The Catholic elements in the story are a little clumsily handled at times, with the consequent suspicion that the author is not quite sure whether the beliefs are motivated by faith or superstition. Emphasis on poverty—which, of course, cannot be avoided, for that is the environment the author has chosen—tends to stress the impression that poverty of itself is brutal. Francie was poor, her life was hard and "underprivileged," but she had a marvelous mother, a kind, companionable (if too frequently drunk) father, a warm, loyal family life—and lots of fun. If that be brutality, plenty of children could stand a bit of it.

One or two incidents in the story could well have been played down a little, as, for example, Francie's nearly disastrous experience with a pervert; but these frank passages and the vulgarity of expres.ion that crop up from time to time need not be a worry to sensible and mature readers.

These elements, of course, follow from the fact that the author chose to put her foot in this particular portion of the stream; granting that she writes of that type of life in that town at that time, the picture is authentic. Certainly we have in this alive book a vivid recapturing of childhood. Any reader who ever collected old newspapers in his youth under the impression that he would soon get rich thereby, who fell in love with vaudeville stars, who reached

seventh heaven with a penny bag of cake ends from the neighborhood bakery, will see his youth again, and nostalgically, in this
Brooklyn masterpiece.   (August 21, 1943)

BLESSED THE CLEAN OF HEART

Some criticism was leveled against Franz Werfel's *Embezzled
Heaven* because the heroine of that Catholic tale was so material-
minded. Such faultfinding, whatever were its grounds, will have no
place in *The Song of Bernadette*, for in this magnificent novel we
have an artist rising triumphantly to the goal toward which his
talents and former efforts have all along been secretly impelling
him—the writing of the life of a saint. Such a theme, handled by
such an author, makes this one of the great books of this or any
other year.

In his "Personal Preface," Mr. Werfel remarks that "in our epoch
an epic poem can take no form but that of a novel," but truly this
is more than a novel. It is read to a hidden accompaniment of deep
and profound music, because it treats so reverently the mystery of
grace, the supernatural explanation of suffering, the purity and
beauty and steely strength of utter childlikeness—all reflected in
the soul of the little girl of the Hautes Pyrenees, Bernadette
Soubirous, who was what our clever sociologists would call an "underprivileged" child, for really the only thing that lightened her
drab childhood was the fact that Our Lady appeared to her in the
grotto of Massabielle in her native town of Lourdes.

Bernadette's whole story is here, told graciously and unaffectedly
as she herself was unaffected. It is the story of her home life, hard
and poor, but not (as a "realist" might so easily have made it)
sordid; the story of a bureaucratic world, national and provincial,
whose phalanxes of strutting officials and pompous red tape re-
treated and snapped before the limpid "Yes, I really did see the
Lady" of the little girl; the story of France in turmoil, of the press
embarrassed, of the humble people shaken with enthusiasm, of the
Church cautious to approve the miraculous nature of the cures at
the spring, which followed the visions.

Franz Werfel nowhere states that he believes that the miracles
at Lourdes are miracles, and there is no reason why he ought to

inject his personal opinion into the narrative. But every implication in the book shows that he is, to say the very least, sympathetic to the possibility: the atheists who are silenced, the doctors who are convinced, the princes of the Church who finally approve—all of them shout out on almost every page that here in the south of France is truly a sacred spot which God has blessed to be the place of the outpourings of His Fatherliness through His Mother.

All the characters, and there are many, are superbly drawn. Bernadette, of course, is the soul of the book: her impregnable and utterly disarming simplicity and veracity shining like a sun. Others notably well done are the gigantic Dean Peyramale, that rugged man with the voice of thunder, who was at first convinced that he had to deal with either a neurotic or an impostor or both, but who became her staunchest friend, and Sister Marie Thérèse Vauzous, Bernadette's early teacher, whose all unconsciously proud soul is broken to peace when she sees the mystery of Christian suffering realized in the young nun Bernadette has become.

There is even a wisp of romance in the book, the extremely delicate love the young miller, Antoine Nicolau, so shyly and indirectly expresses just as Bernadette leaves for the convent.

In a book of such excellence, it is a shame to have to remark some defects. Mr. Werfel's lack of complete familiarity with our Catholic practices leads him into some minor errors, as when he refers to the young nun's putting the "consecrated wafers" into the ciborium. One scene, that of Bernadette's father in the tavern, where he is rather blasphemously twitted by his none too sober companions about now being a member of the Holy Family, is out of taste, if a faithful picture of how the events were taken by some low persons.

The book is to be, we are told, filmed. We can only greet that with a shudder. Bernadette herself could not describe the Lady. We do not want to see her on the screen. This book shows her where she can alone be seen, in and through a simple heart. Bernadette saw her thus, and the world still does, at Lourdes. (May 9, 1942)

"THE MAN ON A DONKEY"

"The book has been cast in the form of a chronicle," writes H. F. M. Prescott in her preliminary note. "This form, which requires space to develop itself, has been used in an attempt to introduce the reader into a world, rather than at first to present him with a narrative."

That second sentence is the key to the greatness of *The Man on a Donkey*. For this is a great novel—great in its conception, in its achievement, and worthy of comparison with any of the great historical novels of the past. It has already made literary history in England, where its appearance (in two volumes) occasioned such praise as "a great and shattering book," "a great theme treated magnificently," "a magnificent reconstruction of the living past." Its American edition will put to the blush what an English critic refers to as "the faked-up, costume stuff we usually get in historical fiction."

Indeed, it is hardly fair to call this book simply fiction. As the author indicates in a note, most of the characters are real, and many of their conversations and speeches are taken verbatim from the records. "In broad outline," she asserts, "the account which I have given of historical events is as correct as I have been able to make it, with two minor exceptions," which she is scrupulously fair in specifying. In addition, the whole feel for the times, for manners and modes of speech, for dress and cuisine, for the deeper psychological matter of how people thought and dreamed come through with a note of utter conviction. It is as though the author had actually lived in the England of 1509–37 and, by some alchemy of space-time, comes walking into our twentieth-century world to tell us of those ages. Better, she takes us across the centuries to live those years with her and Henry VIII and Thomas, Lord Darcy, and Gilbert Dawe and Robert Aske, so that we learn "to know them without knowing that we learn."

The chronicle concerns four main characters: Thomas, Lord Darcy; Julian Savage, gentlewoman; Robert Aske, squire; Gilbert Dawe, priest. In one way or another they are all caught up in the bewildering and convulsive times when Henry VIII began his dalliance with Anne Boleyn, broke with the Pope, declared himself supreme authority of the Church in England, and embarked on the ruthless course of suppressing the abbeys and monasteries. This confiscation caused the rising of the northern lords and commons and resulted in the Pilgrimage of Grace, an armed uprising that aimed to relieve the king of his noxious counselor, Thomas Cromwell, and so bring him to reconsider his actions. This pilgrimage is the culminating section of the book, which ends with the never-to-be-forgotten scene of the execution of Robert Aske, the great captain of the pilgrimage, hanged in chains above York Keep.

All the intellectual and emotional ferment of the times seethes and bubbles in these vivid pages. Gib Dawe, the priest, caught up in the "new learning," passionately and rabidly cons his newly Englished Scriptures to prove that Rome is the whore of Babylon, but never does his savage and distorted zeal come to know the meaning of love. Christabel Cowper, prioress, fighting to keep the King's favor and control of her convent, thinks she is serving God when in reality she is worshiping her own little authority. Thomas More, Chancellor, makes a brief appearance as he rebukes, with heroic gentleness, the lords who have condemned him to death for treason.

But the two most marvelously realized characters are Robert Aske and Lord Darcy. In them is personified the terrible confusion of the times. Good and brave men were wrestling in conscience with the question whether obedience to the King would mean betrayal of the Church and of God—how could a man disobey his legitimate sovereign and pretend that he was faithful to the King of Heaven? With groaning of spirit and in the face of the contempt of many, men like Darcy and Aske finally went to horrible deaths, secure at the last in the realization that their so-called "treason" was in truth the highest fealty both to the King and to God.

Throughout the narrative appears the figure of Malle, a poor serving-maid in Lady Cowper's convent. She is dim-witted, but sees at times the vision of The Man on a Donkey, who is Christ, who is love. Her enigmatic statements about her visions are a running commentary on God's providence and love that counterpoints the cruelty, the lust, the treachery, the faintheartedness, and the heroism of the times. As long as men like Aske die for God's honor and their own, Christ may indeed seem to be crucified again, but He triumphs.

I am painfully aware how inadequate is even this high praise. I can only repeat—this is a magnificent book. If I must add a topical note to urge those to read it who are not ordinarily attracted to historical novels, *The Man on a Donkey* is a vital and timely reminder that in today's world, too, Christ is dying only to triumph in the deaths of thousands of unknown (except to Him) Robert Askes.   (September 20, 1952)

ON SAYING "BOO!" TO GEESE

At the risk, perhaps, of sounding like a proper Bostonian, I want to raise a standard to which I think all critics ought to be willing and eager to repair. I'd like to start a movement or found an organization for the Cessation of Adulation Heaped on Authors (generally Young Authors) Because They Write in a Bizarre, Shocking, Grotesque, and Violent Style of Bizarre, Shocking, Grotesque, and Violent Things. Will my fellow critics, of both the secular and the religious press, care to come in?

If they do join, they will find themselves in good company. They will meet, for example, Mr. Edwin Waugh remarking: "Exaggeration, violence, and vulgarity are [literature's] deadliest banes; reticence, modesty, and shy beauty are its infallible qualities." Or they will hear more famous S. H. Butcher, in his *Aristotle's Theory of Poetry and the Fine Arts,* proclaiming: "The esthetic pleasure produced by any ideal imitation must be a sane and wholesome pleasure, which would approve itself to the better portion of the community." Or even still better-known Arnold Bennett would tell them (in his *Literary Taste*): "The pleasure derived from a classic is never a violent pleasure; it is subtle—it will wax in intensity. . . . The artistic pleasures of an uncultivated mind are generally violent. . . . The pleasure of a classic does not at all knock you down—rather, it steals over you."

These are but three of a veritable chorus of critics who have affirmed, down through the history of our literature, that it is the common, universal human values, and not the shock techniques, which have been the touchstone of excellence. The persistence of this critical tradition is not invalidated by the undoubted fact that there are recognized masterpieces of macabre writing—Edgar Allan

Poe's, for instance—but I doubt that anyone would deny that such work is automatically relegated to a lesser sphere of literary blessedness, perhaps almost to a limbo of letters.

And it is equally true that there are classics with violent and even distasteful themes—we have some of the great Russians and an Oedipus. But it will be found, I think, that these apparent exceptions but prove the rule; they are not violent for the sake of the violence, for beneath their fury and their immediate repulsion lies the common and universal human struggle, the all-pervading and supporting atmosphere of human morality.

However far afield a consideration of other literatures might lead us, I think it is demonstrably evident that in very much current American fiction the frenzied striving for the unusual, the shocking, the grotesque is dehumanizing the writing, stultifying the authors, and, it is to be feared, debauching the reader. And the evil, far from being checked, is not even noted by critics who award to neurotic exhibitionism the accolade of "genius" or "virtuosity."

This mild animadversion is prompted because I have just finished a magnificent story. Its subject matter is as explosive as any that can be handled in today's fiction—the tensions between Negroes and whites—and yet there is not the faintest whisper of shrill propaganda; it deals plainly with the lusts of the flesh, and yet there is not the slightest suggestiveness; it plumbs deep into human suffering and punishment without a hint of moralizing or of maudlin sentimentality. It is a fine, indeed a great book.

It is *Cry, the Beloved Country*, by Alan Paton. The scene is South Africa, the main character a magnificently conceived native Anglican minister, the theme a twofold one: the struggle of the natives, attracted from the land and their tribes to the huge mining towns like Johannesburg, for tolerable living and working conditions; and the decline of tribal life and customs, fostered by the white man who had nothing to give the natives in return. All this is superbly told in a rather stately style, which is presumably a fairly literal transcription of the Zulu idiom and which gives the poignant tale a somewhat Biblically patriarchal tone.

Kumalo, the hero, is summoned from his little church among his tribe to go down to the frightening big city to help his sister, who has fallen on evil ways, and to find his son, from whom his parents have not heard since he left to work in the mines. The boy runs away from a reform school and becomes involved in a killing, the victim being the son of the white farmer whose lands lie near Kumalo's church; the son himself had sacrificed a career of great promise to work for the betterment of the natives. The pastor's sister agrees to return home with him but runs off at the last minute, leaving the crushed and, he thinks, disgraced man to go back to his tribe with his sister's child and the pregnant young wife of his condemned son. Drought and poor farming are threatening the life of his tribe when no one else steps in to assist them but the father of the murdered son, who does it in remembrance of his own son's devotion to the natives.

But the story is pre-eminently one of individuals. There are no sweeping and grandiose statements about "the race problem." Jarvis, the white father, and Kumalo, the black one, are two men sorrowing for their sons, and the reader soon realizes that it matters not a tinker's dam what the color of their respective skins is. It is the human (and divine) values by which the two men live, the human dignity both portray, the sublimation of human suffering they achieve, which puts the black man and the white man shoulder to shoulder in the book and suggests by implication that the black and the white populations of South Africa and indeed of all the world can work shoulder to shoulder as well, if only every person will stop looking at the "race question" and start looking at the individual soul. This thought the book presents superbly. Though its very theme is race tension, in the inner workings and motivation of the characters the book shows utter unconsciousness of "race."

I wish there were space to quote many of the deeply moving passages of this most truly compassionate book. There is the scene in which Kumalo tells Jarvis that it was his son who had killed the white man's, or the scene in which Kumalo says farewell to his son, awaiting execution, or that which depicts the old pastor, back with his parish, leading prayers for his condemned son. But as I want to draw the comparison suggested at the start of this discussion, I must leave you to read these for yourself. I must remark, in passing from this truly noble novel, that there is one defect in it. It is marred by a page or so of some very shallow remarks on what law is and whence it derives its authority.

Let us turn now to two current American novels that are getting a lot of critical acclaim. I think that perhaps Father Alfred Barrett's review of *Raintree County* in *America*, with which I thoroughly agree, will serve to stress the point I am trying to make here, namely, that Mr. Lockridge has been at considerable and revolting pains to shock, to canonize the bizarre. But if there be some doubt that this is *Raintree County's* main and root defect, there is no doubt in the world, I am positive, that this is the crippling defect of the highly touted *Other Voices, Other Rooms,* by Truman Capote. Even the ad for the book, with its photo of the languorously reclining but burning-eyed adolescent, shrieks of Oscar Wilde and the mauve decade.

I can perhaps best impress you with this characteristic of the book by quoting passages which were suppressed in a review published by a very influential literary journal. Incidentally, could it have been that these passages were cut from the review because *Other Voices, Other Rooms* was advertised extensively in the journal? Anyway, here is what the reviewer actually wrote:

> The result is as nasty and repellent a tale as has ever graced a Southern plantation drawing-room table. Only it is highly doubtful that Southerners will take Mr. Capote very seriously, if at all —they will leave that to us more gullible Yankees.
>
> One [of his useful tricks] is that under his somewhat remarkable facility with words, what might otherwise be considered normal horrors and shocks become terrible enormities upon the senses.
>
> One has the strong suspicion that if one walked out into the dankest part of the woods and came to a big rock and lifted it up, there under the rock would be all the people Mr. Capote has put into his ridiculously gruesome little tale.

This reviewer's castigations (and I know the reviewer and applaud this criticism heartily) seem to me quite conclusive evidence that the elements for which the book has been so widely praised are the very ones which definitely rule out the work as a piece of genuine literature.

To a lesser extent, the same emphasis on exaggeration and the extraordinary is quite obviously considered by the author as the most significant part of his book—and accepted by the critics as such—in *The Years of the Pilgrimage,* by Kenneth S. Davis. In this book the violence is not so much physical (though there is plenty of that) as intellectual. The dominant character is the aesthete, Harcourt Stevens, who preaches through long and involved pages a philosophy of might makes right, of rabid anti-Christianity, of tyranny. True, this nihilism leads the character to ruin at the end, but I have the uneasy impression that the author thinks this is what is really important in his book, rather than the more human, universal motives that clash with and finally overcome this horrendous intellectual grotesquerie.

Indeed, this highlighting of the abnormal, though it perhaps has come to an angry head in such a book as *Other Voices, Other Rooms*, has long been festering in American fiction. It was mildly virulent in Mary Ward's *The Snake Pit*; it became more critical in such adolescent shockers as Sinclair Lewis's *Kingsblood Royal*; the patient was delirious by the time Katov's *Eagle at My Eyes* appeared. It accounts, of course, to a great extent for all the frantically sought-for variations by which fornication and adultery are paraded in meticulously chronicled detail.

The loud and the startling things are not always the significant things in life; they are rarely the important things in a novel. *Cry, the Beloved Country* is an Everest in the flat wastes of modern fiction precisely because it is not shrill about the riots, the broken heads, the sullen hatreds of race tensions, but rather delves deeply into the serenity of love, compassion, consideration, and devotion that can alone solve race tensions.

The literature of exaggeration may be inescapable today. We live in an age of exaggeration—millions of slave laborers in Russia, sky-blanketing fleets of war planes, supersonic flight. Who knows when we will return to the human level again and leave the apocalyptic? Literature can, I think, help in its relatively small way to lead us back, but it will first have to rediscover the truth about life as well as about itself—the truth that "the Lord is not in the wind, and after the wind an earthquake: the Lord is not in the earthquake. And after the earthquake a fire: the Lord is not in the fire, and after the fire a whistling of a gentle air."

And the Lord—of literature as of life—was and is in the gentle air.   (March 13, 1948)

ALAN PATON'S SECOND MASTERPIECE

One of the tiny triumphs in which I take some small if immodest pride is the fact that *America* was well in the vanguard of those who recognized the quality of Alan Paton's *Cry, the Beloved Country.* The book was originally published in February 1948. In the March 13, 1948 issue of *America* it was given an article-length review under the somewhat misleading title of "On Saying 'Boo!' to Geese." There we summed up our impressions of the book by saying, "It is a fine, indeed a great book."

Several more months were to pass before the general reading public began to realize what a fine book it really was. It then appeared on the best-seller lists and attracted the praise of critics in general. Since then it has been reprinted several times and has attained the stature of at least a minor classic, since it is now included in the Modern Standard Author Series (Scribner's).

It seems, however, that we won't be quite so vanguardish in recognizing the quality of Mr. Paton's second novel, *Too Late the Phalarope.* This book has already been hailed in publicity releases and preview encomia from critics as being even more impressive than *Cry, the Beloved Country.*

I believe the critics and the admen are right. First, it is a much more tautly drawn tale. Mr. Paton has tightened up his narrative technique and though his first novel was by no means sprawling, this one has some of the spare muscularity about it that characterizes Graham Greene's technique. Second, *Too Late the Phalarope* is simply plunged into an atmosphere of what the critics generally call compassion. Let this not be understood as meaning that the book is drippy with humanitarian sentiment. It is not. The compassion is strong and manly and manifests (as does Mr. Paton's current political activities against the racists in South Africa) a deeply felt realization of the moral plight, of the agony of soul of others, which is not content merely to sermonize but which strives to burst forth into action.

At first reading one would be inclined to think that here is just another version of the plot of Graham Greene's *The End of the Affair.* The story itself is simple. Pieter van Vlaanderen is a young police lieutenant in South Africa. He is a decorated veteran of the war, a famous Rugby player, respected and admired by white and colored alike in the community. In addition, he is happily married, with two children. On a certain night while making his rounds he surprises a young white boy who is in pursuit of an attractive mulatto girl. He is able to prevent anything untoward happening and asks the young man to come to him the next evening for a talk.

There, speaking as a friend, he lays before him the sordidness and danger of the whole situation. When the young man leaves, repentant and straightened out, the young lieutenant drops upon his knees and prays, "God have mercy upon him." But then he goes on—and here is the first hint of tragedy in the story—to pray, "God have mercy upon me."

The tragedy quickly and almost inevitably develops. Despite his happy marriage, something has been missing in it. The deep love he feels for his wife has not been fully and completely reciprocated, and as he broods more and more upon the situation, he finds himself with a great loathing and strange fascination drawn toward the Negro girl whom the young man had been pursuing. During the period when his wife and children are off on a short vacation he meets the young Negro girl clandestinely and has an affair with her.

The upshot of the whole matter is that the liaison is discovered; the young lieutenant is ruined and his family almost literally destroyed.

This is all told through the reminiscences of a maiden aunt who has loved Pieter as her own son and who had realized early in the tragic coil the agony he was going through. It is told in admirable style which catches with real skill the loneliness, the simplicity, the God-fearing reverence of one whose great cross in life was that she had never had a love of her own.

This may sound as though the story is a simple account of passion. It may even sound as though it is simply a sordid tale. Let me hasten to say, first of all, that there is a delicacy and chasteness of expression which immediately lifts the book above any suspicion of sensationalism. Let me add that there is a religious tone running through every step of the account which makes it a truly Christian approach to the problem of sin and sinner.

But the book is infinitely more than this. It is infinitely more than a mere tale of misguided passion. The great passion that emerges in the pages is the passion of Mr. Paton's own hatred of racial discrimination—which must be the passion of everyone who reads the book, even had he not entertained it before. Mr. Paton's whole thesis is that the criminal law in South Africa has succeeded for generations in making the Negro no more than an animal. It is, he says, "the iron law that no white man may touch a black woman nor may any white woman be touched by a black man. And to go against this law of a people of rock and stone, in a land of rock and stone, was to be broken and destroyed." This terrible philosophy, we are informed in the book, is enshrined in the South African Immorality Act of 1927.

If Pieter had had an affair with a white woman, he would, so far as the law is concerned, have been untouched by the horrible penalty which was inflicted upon him. But the mere fact that his offense had been with a Negro woman was enough to hurl him outside the pale of civilized life. It was enough to separate him from wife and children. It was enough to kill his stern, unbending father. All this means that under the law in South Africa the Negroes are looked upon simply as animals. Pieter was not punished for adultery. He was punished because he had overstepped racial boundaries, simply because he had "defiled" the sacred Afrikaans blood, sacred because (as they almost blasphemously thought and think) "as God had chosen them for a people, so did they choose Him for their God, cherishing their separateness that was now His Will."

This is admirably summed up in the response of the police captain whose duty it had been to break the lieutenant and to inform his family. When the captain had told the story to Pieter's father, the fierce old man struck the arm of his chair and said:

—I would shoot him like a dog. Then because no one spoke he said to the captain, wouldn't you?
And the captain said—No
—But he has offended against the race.
Then the captain said, trembling
—Meneer, as a policeman, I know an offense against the law and as a Christian I know an offense against God, but I do not know an offense against the race.

Too Late the Phalarope is one of those rare books which make a reader face in terms of suffering and agony and ideals a situation which he may know only theoretically. We have all read, I suppose, of the racial discriminations still prevalent in South Africa. But how remote and impersonal they seem to us in the news stories. Here they are driven home to us in terms of persons whom we get to know very well indeed as the tale progresses.

The book may in one sense be called propaganda but it is propaganda that is strong with deep and valid emotion. It is propaganda which does not merely uphold a thesis but which portrays human persons being crushed by a thesis. Mr. Paton deserves the gratitude of everyone who would make real to himself the injustice, the dehumanization, which is implicit in every act of racial discrimination, however slight it may be.   (August 29, 1953)

"ENCHANTING REVOLUTIONARY"

"The first thing you do in a strange town is to find the central café, take a table there, and then sit for a time and watch the world pass by." This was the advice once given by her father, an experienced traveler, to Sister Luke, the heroine of this magnificent novel, *The Nun's Story*, by Kathryn Hulme. It is safe to say that for many readers, even among Catholics, the world to which they will be given entrance by this book will be a strange world. It is also safe to say that the book provides a wonderfully central spot from which to watch the world—the world of nuns—pass by.

This is so because the story of Sister Luke, though it is most convincingly embellished with countless details of convent life, owes its strength to its comprehension of the real center of the religious life, the rules and spirit of the Order as means to achieving St. Paul's magnificent identification—"It is now not I that live, but Christ that lives within me"—and the expansion of that Christ-life to the world through the apostolic dynamism of the religious life.

The countless details of convent life by no means make this the story of a lot of "sweet little nuns." Here is that *rara avis*—a tale that does justice to the spiritual steel that runs like a central, sustaining girder through all the penances, devotions, quaint-seeming customs, and all the other externals of the female religious life. Above all, the book is a most moving incarnation (I was going to say "tribute," but the writing does not stand apart and watch; it lives with the subject) to the spirit of devotion and utter dedication. Some critics of the novel have paid what is apparently their highest possible compliment by saying that the dedication portrayed is reminiscent of the spirit of Albert Schweitzer. Actually the dedication is more sublime, as devotion to Christ and His work is more exalted than devotion to humanitarianism.

Sister Luke's dedication is to her rules and what they stand for and then to the sick, for she is a member of an (unnamed) order

devoted to nursing. After a period in service in her native land, she
realized her holy ambition to be sent to a mission hospital in the
Belgian Congo. Here, through her selflessness, her skill, her becoming all things to all men, she endears herself to the other nuns,
to the lay medical men, and to the natives. She has some really
spine-tingling and hair-raising adventures, which may sit uneasily
with the too-sensitive reader, but every one of them is stamped
with the seal of authenticity and heroism.

Invalided back home for a rest, she arrives just in time to witness
the brutalities of the Nazi occupation of her native Belgium. Despite her seventeen years of spiritual discipline, she discovers that
she cannot rise above feelings of profound hatred for the Nazis.
Convinced that she cannot be the nun the rules of her Order hold
as the ideal, she gets a dispensation from her vows, and the book
closes as she disappears into the Resistance movement, resolved to
serve God and her country as nurse rather than as nun.

Did she fail her vocation? Did she yield to a temporary discour-
agement? Had she ever seen with clear vision the ideal that was
before her for so many years in religion? These are questions that
we have to leave to herself and God; but the story of her struggles
to get close to the "Living Rule" the nuns are supposed to be, the
superb portraits of some of the nuns, the vivid descriptions of hospital work—all make this a religious novel of fine insight into the
meaning of a nun's life and a document that is economically, dra-
matically, and poignantly written.

A factual note may be in order. Miss Hulme worked for the UN
in an UNRRA camp in Austria after the war. There she met a
Belgian nurse, whose story she tells in this present book. Miss
Hulme became a Catholic, and if that step can be attributed to the
influence of the ex-nun, it was basically because, as Miss Hulme
says, "living with a practising Christian is a completely disarming
experience."

How much this practice of Christianity is rooted in the ex-nun-
nurse's convent years is beautifully stated toward the end of the
book:

. . . her nun's inner formation was a Gibraltar that would never
be leveled. . . . The ingrained habits of acting with charity and
justice, with selflessness and sincerity, were to stamp her always
with a certain strangeness and make her seem to future nursing

colleagues like some sort of enchanting revolutionary who prac-
tised a way of life quite new and unheard of. . . .

The enchanting revolutionary is now working as a nurse in California, where she brings to her daily tasks, Miss Hulme says, "some
kind of plus thing that nobody can put a finger on exactly—a caring
for the soul first, then for the body."   (September 15, 1956)

STORY ON THE NUN'S STORY

What with trying to keep afloat on the tide of books published
weekly, the need does not arise often, nor is the leisure at hand, to
re-evaluate a current best seller. Most books that attain that dizzy
pinnacle are simply not worth a second thought. We can be thank-
ful, for example, that few best sellers are as fetid and revolting as
the recent number one, *Peyton Place*. But it is rare that a best seller
is worth rereading to plumb a depth, catch a meaning, relive an
experience that the first reading suggested but did not satisfyingly
reveal.

Correspondence (some of it sharply critical of my original review) and analysis of other reviews show that there was more in
Kathryn Hulme's *The Nun's Story* than the first reading uncovered.
I would like to return to the book here and make some observations
on the reactions it has occasioned. I do so, if my readers will credit
me with sincerity, not to protest that my original estimate was un-
erringly correct and not in any sense to convince anyone who has
disliked the book that he has to change his opinion. I am, however,
somewhat concerned that so much dislike of the story has been
based on false premises and posited, regrettably enough, by reviewers in Catholic organs.

All that follows, then, is to be taken as a plea for more objectively
balanced reviewing and more charitable personal reactions to books
that arouse one's zeal for controversy. The duty of objective evaluations, whether by the professional critic or by the reader, who is
his own critic, was made much of by Pope Pius XII in his address
"On Literary Criticism." The late Pope stressed that "the personality of the author, his life, and his tendencies are not to be the
starting point of the critical study." The critic "must keep close to

the clear, objective meaning of the writing, since his strict function is to judge the work and not the author." Further, "When the objective meaning is doubtful . . . it is better to incline toward a favorable interpretation." These norms of prudence and charity will be seen to apply, I feel, to some of the published reactions to *The Nun's Story.*

I erred in two ways in my first evaluation of this amazing book. My first mistake was perhaps not a substantial error, but it gave rise to misconceptions that might easily have been avoided. I have consistently referred to the book as a novel. It is indeed novelistic in form: the dialogue is supplied and the action is in all probability fitted into a dynamic framework to advance the story element. But the book is obviously biographical in content and the author's claim that there is not a single trumped-up incident in the whole story is to be taken, it would seem, as the simple truth. By calling the book a novel, I may have given unconscious comfort to those who profess to believe that the "substantial truth" to which the book's blurbs refer is but a minimal basis for the sensational elements that are pure embroidery. One critic in a Catholic paper openly makes this charge and thereby imputes to the author the unworthy motive of deliberately gilding the lily of fact just to write a best seller.

My second false lead was one of emphasis. I find that I teetered on the edge of the very defect I shall have to reprobate in other reactions. My statement was:

> The book owes its strength to its comprehension of the real center of the religious life, the rules and spirit of the Order as means to achieving St. Paul's magnificent identification—"It is now not I that live, but Christ that lives within me"—and the expansion of that Christ-life to the world through the apostolic dynamism of the religious life.

This may have given the impression that I was canonizing the book as an adequate treatise on the religious life. This the book is not, nor does it pretend or intend to be. It is the story of one woman meeting her peculiar difficulties. She was not a "normal" nun, whatever that may be. She was not even "normal" among the sisters of her own Order, because she was the one who could not quite live up to the ideals she conceived to have been held up for her.

But how can it escape the attentive reader that it is precisely here that the tribute to the religious life in general enters the story? Sister Luke did not find peace; she did not solve the problem of strict obedience to her rule nor the apparent conflict of that virtue with her duties as a nurse. But hundreds, I suppose, of her sisters did. They have not followed Sister Luke back into the world. Presumably they have found the peace—and even the joy—which one nun yearned for. And, speaking of joy in the religious life, I cannot go along with those who have seen no joy in this book. They may find little in Sister Luke, to be sure, but what about "sturdy little" Sister William and her "tout pour Jésus," as she bustled about, emptying the bedpans and the sputum cups? What about the

> clear note of gladness in the salutation to the Virgin, a sort of breathlessness when the nuns chanted ". . . full of grace . . ." as for a grace discovered that morning for the first time by all two hundred of them?

This note of joy and peace re-echoes many a time in the book, but the reader is apt to miss it because the author has so admirably focused attention, as she must, on the nun who herself largely missed it.

The charge has been made that the book will do harm to prospective vocations. That is a judgment about a future contingency, and only the future can tell. Any sensible American girl will certainly not have to be told that this is a European Order, seen through the eyes of one who could not quite "make the grade." If the potential American postulant thinks that she is reading about an "average" American nun in an "average" American convent, she misunderstands the story. And yet, if the dedicated lives of the nuns, European or not, do not strike some spark of admiration and emulation in the reader who may be pondering a vocation, I would suspect some lack of generosity.

I have not read a single review in secular papers and journals which fails to remark that the critic has been profoundly impressed by the dedication and selflessness of the nuns of Sister Luke's order. I do not claim to have read all the reviews, but I have not met one reaction of shock at the physical penances, of distaste for the discipline and rigidity (perhaps foreign even to American Catholic sensibilities) of the life, nor the conclusion that a group of women in religious life must be a creepy assembly of frustrated neurotics.

In fact, the secular reception of *The Nun's Story* has been more sympathetic and more objective than many Catholic critiques. I do not think it is fair to assert that only morbid curiosity has impelled non-Catholics to run to read, and that the farther they are in their own lives from the ideals of religion, the more their curiosity is whetted. This charge has been made, but it seems to me unworthy of the Catholic press in which it has appeared.

What must be disclaimed in the strongest terms, if we are to claim that Catholic criticism is fulfilling its proper function, are the judgments on this book that have been warped by sentimentality and darkened by uncharitableness.

There is such a thing as "clericalness." It is the opposite of the anti-clerical attitude and refuses to acknowledge that there can possibly be any valid criticism, not only of religious institutions but of individual priests and religious as well. How dare anyone ever say that any nun (or priest) has ever failed to live up to the very highest standards?

This attitude I am alluding to is not one I am dreaming up. It has appeared in one Catholic paper and has been reprinted in others. It says: "We would be less shocked if our own mothers deserted us than we would be if it were proved our favorite nun or nuns had feet of clay." What is to be made of such gush and especially of the holier-than-thou attitude of what follows: "It is then a painful experience to read of one who did [have feet of clay]. Such a one is the poor convent-dweller described in *The Nun's Story.*"

How can it have escaped this reviewer that if Sister Luke was a "failure," she was a magnificent failure, who took away from her years in religion the "nun's formation" that "was a Gibraltar that would never be leveled, that the ingrained habits of acting with charity and justice, with selflessness and sincerity, were to stamp her always. . . ."

Even more to be excoriated is the utterly uncharitable imputation of base motives. This, fortunately, has not appeared in reviews, but some correspondence has revealed such uncharitable bias. One letter went so far as to claim that the book is a deliberate attempt to undermine the Church. Conscious of the fact that the author is a rather recent convert, the critic felt able to call into question even the sincerity of the conversion by saying, "Well, she may *call* herself a convert." [The sneering emphasis is not mine.]

So, perhaps this inadequate re-evaluation will serve some good purpose. We cannot here discuss objections to details in the book, such as the advice given to Sister Luke to fail deliberately in her exams. Shall we think it actually happened? Yes, unless you would sooner believe that your mother could desert you than that some nun sometime could have given misguided and misguiding counsel.

Far more important than the details, however, is how the book has been unfairly judged by segments of the American Catholic public and the reviewing profession. They expected the book to achieve something it never set out to do. Then, when they found that that imposed purpose was not accomplished, they seized on every detail that could be interpreted in a pejorative sense to bolster a viewpoint that was from the beginning either sentimental or uncharitable, or both.

No one, obviously, has to like this book. But one should not pass judgment, especially in an official capacity, merely out of personal like or dislike. One must keep an objective view. It is to establish such a view more clearly than was done in my original criticism that I have wearied one and all with this reconsideration.

(December 8, 1956)

Chapter Four

SLIGHTLY MINORITY OPINION
ON SOME "GREATS"

The critic cannot get by on the uncomplicated philosophy of the gentleman who did not like Doctor Fell:

> *I do not like thee, Doctor Fell;*
> *The reason why I cannot tell,*
> *But this I know and know full well:*
> *I do not like thee, Doctor Fell.*

If Doctor Fell happened to have been a highly respected medical practitioner (or was he just a Ph.D.?), widely admired by his colleagues and revered by a large number of patients, the one who did not like him was undoubtedly considered crabbed, churlish, and downright wrongheaded.

The novelists descanted upon in the following selections are among the most eminent on the American scene. Two of them, Sinclair Lewis and William Faulkner, are Nobel Prize winners; John O'Hara received the 1956 National Book Award, and so on. Praise, honors, critical acclaim, and best sellerdom have been the meed of these authors. They are, therefore, fully representative of our American culture, as they both mirror it and have been shaped by it. What does that culture look like in their pages?

It does not, first and foremost, look very much like a Christian culture, and perhaps in that the authors are faithful, non-distorting mirrors. But, second, our culture does not look very sturdy; there seems to be a certain hard-to-define flabbiness, even a self pity that runs through what many of these creative writers have to say about what Americans think of themselves. *Hemingway's* The Old Man and the Sea, *to be sure, does have some bone and muscle to it (but its hero, it is well to note, is hardly representative of American culture)—it is at least an affirmation of stoic fortitude, and some critics have read into it a profound spiritual symbolism.*

At any rate, here are some opinions that more or less sing outside the chorus of American criticism; the dissent is more acid in my treatment of Sinclair Lewis and John O'Hara than in my remarks on John Marquand, for example, but whether my minority opinion be a gentle demurrer or a loud protest, I trust I put forth sane reasons why I have not liked some literary Doctor Fells—or what has fallen from their pens.

HE-MAN WHIMPERING

The "great bronze god" of American fiction for so many years, Ernest Hemingway, has definitely lost his sheen in this utterly trivial book, *Across the River and into the Trees*. His name will still carry, of course, and some critical puffs (in addition to winds of wide popular acclaim) will fill somewhat the sagging sails, but I believe that the bark of Mr. Hemingway's genius is here like the famous painted ship upon the equally painted ocean.

A battered old professional soldier (he is all of fifty and filled with self-pity enough for a doddering ancient of eighty), takes a vacation in Venice to go duck shooting. There he meets a beautiful girl of eighteen or so. He spends his time with her mainly in talking, though there is enough furtive love-making to remind us that Hemingway is the author. And what does he talk about? The glories of duck shooting, the bouquets of various wines and champagnes, the merits of various cities, and above all, the stupidity of soldiers (particularly of all high commands, but especially of the British), the ignorance of war correspondents, and of his own exploits in battle.

That's all. After he has talked himself out, he dies on his way back to his outfit. The title, by the way, is taken from the statement attributed to Stonewall Jackson when he knew he was fatally wounded. It seems almost irreverent to lift the lovely words from the dying lips of a military leader we know to have been a very religious man and put them in the mouth of a disillusioned, cynical, and lecherous egotist.

Hemingway, to be sure, still has some of the old touches for which he was laudable. There is the sense of human fellowship, especially that of men under stress and agony. There is the bitter realization of the futility of war and an appreciation of the winning beauty that does dwell, even heartbreakingly, in material things. But all these traits are here subordinated to an unmanly atmosphere of griping and whining. The colonel is a beaten man from the start of the book, and he knows it—and so does the reader.

It's extremely interesting and instructive to compare the colonel in this book with the Ernest Hemingway who emerges in the classic "Profile" published in the *New Yorker*. If they are not kindred souls, I miss my guess. In that "Profile," by the way, it seems to me that Hemingway, despite all his bluster, was not at all confident that this book had come off. It seems that, in the very writing of it, he was laying the groundwork for excuses for the failure.

If this turns out to be his last book, he will surely have gone out, not with a bang, but a whimper.   (September 16, 1950)

"PATHETIC FALLACY"

The champ has staged a swell comeback—well, maybe not a complete comeback to the heavyweight title he lost in *Across the River and into the Trees,* but he has worked his way back into contention for the light-heavyweight title.

That is to say, Hemingway has here woven one of his better stories. *The Old Man and the Sea* is very simple, as most of his master stories are. It is concerned with a clear-cut struggle between a man and a giant fish. The man is simple and elemental, and so, obviously, is the fish—and there is not much to choose between them. The old fisherman, who has not made a catch for a long time, finally sails and rows out from Cuba further than any poor fisherman has and, after two days and nights of heartbreaking toil and courage, starts towing back to port the huge marlin he has hooked. On the return trip the catch is attacked by sharks and, despite the heroic efforts of the old man to preserve his prize, all he manages to haul up on the beach is the giant skeleton. He has won, has been defeated, but is triumphant even in defeat.

Hemingway has decked this plot skeleton with most of his old magic. There is, to coin a phrase, not a wasted word in the lean, tense, utterly functional narrative. There is the atmosphere of struggle even in the rhythm of his sentences. There is the extraordinary feel for the cleanness of the sea winds, the mysterious life under the waves, the lone majesty of the sunset. And there is, above all, the feeling of kinship between the two elemental creatures—fisherman and fish—each noble in his own way.

The trouble is—and here is why the champ is still in the light-heavyweight division—that the respective nobility tends to get blurred, and Hemingway is the one who does the blurring. It is extremely doubtful, I believe, that the fisherman would refer to the fish, which is likely just a fish to him, in the romantic and sentimental terms which the author puts into his mouth. Long ago, Ruskin used the term "pathetic fallacy" to describe the "undue attribution of personality to impersonal objects." It is this quality in this story, and indeed in most of Hemingway's work, that militates against true greatness. The form is superb; the content is really rather diluted.

The publisher's blurb, by the way, is nonsensical. It is claimed that Hemingway has looked "beyond conventional forms" and has "improvised in effect his own new mode," setting a "new pattern for generations of followers." What Hemingway here does, though he does it in his unique style, has been done before in our times—by Steinbeck in *The Pearl*, for example, and by Paul Horgan in *The Devil in the Desert*. (September 13, 1952)

HERO AS YO-YO

A middle-aged playwright engages in a long meditation on what's gone wrong with his life and why. He had been acclaimed a bright young genius when his first plays sparkled on Broadway, but now, he wryly admits to himself, he has lost the touch. More than that, he has also lost his shirt, or the lucre that buys his shirts, because of a disastrous flyer in making movies and a musical comedy from one of his plays. He is alarmingly near the financial rocks and, for the third time, on the marital shoals.

How did I ever get in this mess, he wonders through this long, witty, nostalgic, slightly acerb, and undoubtedly sad book, Marquand's *Women and Thomas Harrow*. It's sad because there are so many people like Thomas Harrow, decent, well-meaning, with some ideals (even if somewhat vague), who slide through life without ever facing up to moral decisions. Perhaps Tom Harrow's vacillation was deepened for the simple reason that, though he was clever, he was not really very intelligent. The intelligent reader can see disaster looming long before Tom Harrow gets even the faintest whiff of it.

It is obvious, for instance, that his first marriage (incidentally, to the only woman he really loved) is going to bog down. Wife Rhoda, a small-town girl, grows progressively more and more of a seeker for financial security; she has "a financial face," says a banker friend, and when Tom's dramatic touch gets less deft, she is ready to seek that security in another marriage. The real reason for the breakup, however, lies in the fact that the couple had never really understood one another and had certainly never made any moral decision that the "for worse" of marriage is just as much a part of the contract as the "for better."

We meet wife number three at the start of the book, and poor Tom has fared no better this time, either, for Emily is, to put it bluntly, developing into a shrew. Wife number two is barely mentioned. Despite the fact that marriage problems bulk so large in the story, the book is not at all explicitly concerned with sex.

What is it explicitly concerned with? That is a little hard to say. It is eminently readable but at the end one wonders what all the shooting has been about. Mr. Marquand does not like our century too much, and some of the finest set pieces in the book linger fondly over some of the supposed glories of the past. But, as in all Marquand's major books, there is an oblique commentary on moral crises. He is fond of Thomas Harrow, but he hardly accords him unqualified approval. Marquand passes judgment—gently, wryly, ironically—and so the book is, in the proper sense of the word, compassionate. But it is a little more tired than the earlier novels. Can it be that Marquand, too, has reached the point of no return?

(October 11, 1958)

TWO SOUTHERN TALES

Faulkner's novel, *Requiem for a Nun*, has been getting the reviewers and critics into a lather—and for some good reasons. It is
not top-drawer Faulkner and seems to justify the suspicion, entertained for some time, that he is beginning to take a sort of wry
pleasure in displaying a positive contempt for style. There are long,
meandering sentences, some running for three and four pages, involved parentheses within parentheses, rivulets, torrents, and tides
of purple-patchish prose, unbelievably anacoluthic dialogue, and a
needlessly involved story line.

Well, then, is there anything good to be said for *Requiem for a
Nun?* Yes, there is. For Faulkner still has the touch: he can evoke
a sense of the moil and turmoil, of the crowded and sweating
human efforts, of the slow lapse of time, and the frantic pace of
events that go into the carving of a little niche of civilization out
of the wilderness of America. And he can still probe—perhaps with
too many involutions and opacities here—the sullen and shy motives of the heart.

The historical panorama spreads out lushly in this tale in the
descriptions of The Courthouse, The Golden Dome, and The Jail,
which are rather like extended stage directions to the three "acts"
in which the story is cast. The story, briefly, concerns a Negro
woman of ill fame sentenced to die for killing a white child she had
been hired to nurse, and the attempts of the mother of the child to
have the confessed murderess acquitted because her own sense of
guilt over her past life leads her to believe that she had really put
the whole train of tragic consequences in action. There is a great
deal of muddy talk about the necessity of sacrifice and suffering,
but the reader who hasn't the patience to reread and ponder won't
come away with any very clear idea of what it all adds up to. Even
those who have the patience will wonder if it is worth expending on
one of Faulkner's less conspicuous efforts.

Caroline Gordon, author of *The Strange Children*, might have
seen more to commend in *Requiem for a Nun* than I did, for she is
an authority on Faulkner. At any rate, her own book is limpidity

itself in comparison. Not that it's an easily analyzed affair; it isn't, but the style is crystal clear and the import rather simple.

It is another of those "adults as seen through the eyes of youngsters" stories. This time the youngster is a little girl too advanced for her age, who overhears many things not at all for her good. Friends who visit her parents are having marital troubles—one finally elopes with the wife of his best friend—one of them, a recent convert to Catholicism, is a little too intense in his new fervor; all drink too much, and, as a bizarre background to the whole business, a revival meeting of local Holy Rollers provides some lurid religious atmosphere.

There is little exterior action; emphasis is exclusively on interior strains and stresses. Throughout the tale runs the symbolism of the little crucifix which the young girl rather innocently purloins for a time from the convert. Time and again, as the emotional storms and vacuums, which she dimly senses, swirl or yawn about her, she takes it from its hiding place and studies it—dimly sensing the meaning of it, too. Perhaps Miss Gordon means that until people like these modern, beautiful, and damned learn the meaning behind the little crucifix, they, too, will continue to be very strange children, indeed. (October 6, 1951)

WILLIAM FAULKNER'S A FABLE

A standard *Handbook to Literature* (by Thrall and Hibbard) has this to say of symbolism:

> The tendency of symbolism is to seize upon some aspect of an object and to dignify it with imaginative, fantastic, or esoteric qualities, that it may represent some philosophic, religious, spiritual, or social abstraction. When symbolism is employed for any of these purposes it tends to build up a ritualistic, mystic literature which is not clear to the outsider without a key to the special significances and imagined correspondences.

Mr. Faulkner's A *Fable*, on which he worked for nine years and which is claimed to be the crowning achievement of the 1950 Nobel Prize winner, is clearly a symbolical novel; it is just as clearly, save to those who dare not say boo to geese, a mystery, a riddle, an enigma, for which a key is sadly needed. Indeed, after a careful and laborious reading of the 437 pages, I have begun to suspect that there is no key or that if there is one lying around somewhere, it is hardly worth the search, for it would at best open only an empty box.

The story in outline is simple enough. During World War I, a French regiment in the front lines simply sits still in the trenches when ordered over the top. It is discovered that this "mutiny" (for which the commander of the regiment wants the whole kit and caboodle shot) was paralleled at the same time by like actions in the English, American, and German forces. It is further discovered that it was instigated by an obscure corporal, who, with twelve companions, had been mysteriously working behind the lines of all the armies. They had not exactly been inciting troops to mutiny, but rather convincing them somehow that wars are kept hurtling along their bloody course only by the professional pride and greed of politicians, soldiers, and industrialists, and can be brought to an end only by the realization of the common man that all men are brothers. The mutiny ends, the corporal is executed, the war continues.

But the corporal and all the other characters in the book, and the situations in which they are involved, are all symbols; they are supposed to adumbrate—to carry the thought on to—other characters and situations, namely, to Passion week, to Christ, and to many historical figures who appear in the whole story of Our Lord. Some of the symbolism is clear; thus there is a Judas among the corporal's followers, and a Peter, too, and their roles are in close parallel to those of the historical characters.

But beyond these two figures, it is pretty hard to make out what the symbolism is. The corporal is undoubtedly a Christ figure, but some elements in his life are so contradictory to all that we know of Christ that the symbolism breaks down utterly. Again, the commander in chief of the Allied armies is obviously God the Father (he refers to the corporal as his son) when he is not obviously Satan (he subjects the corporal to temptation on a high mountain).

This is all confusing enough, but when it is told in the famous Faulkner style, here involuted, convoluted, elliptical, breathless to exaggeration and exasperation, one is really faced with a formidable task in trying to find out what all the shooting is about. It must be admitted that Faulkner's torrents of words sometimes overwhelm one with a sense of grandeur and apocalyptic force, even when it is hard to hold on to the thread of thought.

What is the meaning of it all? Has Faulkner written a plea for pacifism? Is it rather an involved and confused statement of the solidarity of mankind, a tortuously conceived and fumblingly expressed approximation to the doctrine of the Mystical Body? I wish I could say, and I honestly believe that some of the critics who are hailing this as a monumental and already classic work wish deep down in their own hearts that they could say, too.

One thing is certain. Many a "Key to Faulkner's *Fable*" will be written. If any of them turns the lock, I doubt that a treasure will be found inside.

(August 21, 1954)

THE EMPEROR'S NEW (LITERARY) CLOTHES

Once upon a time, so the old story has it, some high-pressure boys from the garment-workers district duped an old emperor into believing that they had some wonderful material from which to make his new state robes. It was so fine and delicate that it could hardly be seen, so airy and light as to be practically ethereal, and yet so colorful and dazzling as to blind the eye and stun the imagination. He agreed to be decked out in this marvelous stuff. The designers and the tailors measured and mapped; they went through the motions of fitting and draping, and all the time they were covering his nudity with just nothing. All the attendants and courtiers, though, dared not open their mouths, so taken was the emperor with the thought that his new clothes would be such as no other potentate had ever boasted. Even all his subjects, when he appeared at the grand reception, were not bold enough to shatter his fond delusion. It was only at last one little boy who was indiscreet enough to pipe up to his mother: "But, mamma, he's naked!"

There has been recently in the literary world a modern acting out of this fable. I cannot make a complete accommodation of all the characters and elements of the old tale to the contemporary scene, but it will be close enough to belabor the obvious a little. We have, first off, if not an emperor, at least one who is quite high up in popular opinion among the hierarchy of contemporary literary greats; we have the book reviewers and critics who may take the place of the attendants and courtiers; we have the vast and gullible reading public to parallel the emperor's subjects. Who the smooth-talking salesman is in the modern application, I do not quite see —perhaps it is Mr. Steinbeck's literary agent, or his publisher, or quite likely his own misguided judgment.

For it is Steinbeck and his novel *The Wayward Bus* that recall the old Andersen story. To date there has been large and vociferous acclaim for the beauty of this new garment in which (presumably) Steinbeck has draped himself and his reputation. There have been relatively few small and ingenuous boys in the mob to raise their simple voices and shout: "But, good people, he's naked!" These have been a handful of reviewers, and I would like hereby to join their unimpressed, ungullible, and, perhaps, unpopular ranks.

For once again the great majority of bookmen have played the American reading public false. The reviewers have banded together for the huge swindle; the Book-of-the-Month Club has broadened its scope; word-of-mouth advertising blows up bigger and bigger the bubble gum of false reputation, and all the time Steinbeck, in this novel, has divested himself of the few garments that covered him, if not with glory, at least with some shreds of decency, and now stands embarrassingly naked—and few have dared to say it.

What does *The Wayward Bus* have to say? This: eight people gather in a wayside lunchroom out in California to take a rattling shuttle bus from one main Greyhound line to another. We are introduced to each character as he enters, and it does not take more than the first two pages to realize that they have one thing in common—they are all ridden, obsessed, warped by sex drives, urges, repressions. They finally board the bus, with this mephitic atmosphere crackling around them, to make the run which turns out to have some danger to it because of constant rains and the threat of washed-out bridges. At one point the driver deliberately bogs the bus down, pretends to go off for help only to seek shelter in a barn because he feels that one of the women will follow him for no good purpose.

Various other characters have by this time bared their souls to one another; the little waitress who loves Clark Gable in secret has revealed her silly desires to the glamorous Camille, an entertainer about whom more later; the Babbittish businessman, his amorous advances to Camille rebuffed, has literally physically attacked his own wife; a lecherous old goat of nearly eighty has suffered a stroke;

the disgustingly pimpled youth has ogled every female curve in the bus; the "pilgrimage" ends with the lights of the terminal in view, the passengers, we feel, drained to their passionate dregs, and the reader impelled (we hope, though we hope still more that there have not been any readers) to rinse his mouth out with ipecac to taste something sweet in comparison.

Now, lest someone may think that this caustic summary is dictated by nothing more than blue-nosed puritanism, let me say that it is not exactly because the book is so steeped in sex that I have such an aversion to it. It is conceivable—though I admit difficult and dangerous to bring off decently—that a book might be as single-minded in its study of that slippery subject and still impress the reviewer and reader as being a sincere and honest attempt to weigh the problem. There are very few areas of human interest that are automatically out of bounds for the serious writer. It may be agony for such a writer to tread all these areas circumspectly, reticently, decently, but that only proves that they are a keener challenge, a test of craftsmanship and sincere charity—toward both characters and readers—and not that the subject matter is taboo.

What I do have as a basis for my objection to *The Wayward Bus* is that Steinbeck has chosen to rest his study of these sex-mad people on grounds that are not at all short of dishonesty. My further gripe is that most of the reviewers have swallowed Steinbeck's disingenuous window dressing and have therefore revealed themselves as either sycophants or blind guides.

First of all, Steinbeck prefaces his story with three lines from the medieval morality play, *Everyman*:

I pray you all gyve audyence,
Here is matter with reverence,
By figure of a morall playe.

The inference, neatly hinted thus and promptly gobbled up by the reviewers, is that Steinbeck, because he says so, has actually written a modern morality.

This is subterfuge. I am not saying that Steinbeck may not have intended so to write; I am saying that the finished product is not a modern morality. It is not because there can be no morality play or story unless the immorality described or hinted at has as a counterfoil some moral standards which are also described or hinted at.

There must be some stated or implied source of reference; some true north must be fixed, else the immoral vagaries of character and action cannot be judged to be off the beam when there is no beam.

Now Steinbeck establishes no such fixed point. It is not for the novelist to state the Ten Commandments at the beginning of his story and then say: "See, this is what my characters are going to violate." But there has to be some place in the story, the sense, the impression that there has been a violation. This is not shown in action in this book.

We are told, to be sure, that the pimply youth alternates between periods of exhilaration in his impure desires and utter misery for his lapses, but we don't see it. Chicoy, the driver, had a statuette of the Virgin of Guadalupe over his windshield, and on the back of the bus the motto *El Gran Poder de Jesús* (the Great Power of Jesus) is still discernible under the superscribed "Sweetheart." But these are cheap and facile externalities and do not touch or affect the heart of the story.

Steinbeck has used quite cleverly a little sleight of hand and told us he is going to write a morality tale; then, having set us all vigilantly watching for the wrong thing, he has pulled out of the hat a pinchbeck bit of realism which, while detailing immorality, fails in the essential task any satire or moral tale has to do— obliquely suggesting standards, norms, principles which are tried and steadfast, though perhaps here and now flouted.

This is inevitable indeed in most of Steinbeck's work, but inescapably obvious in *The Wayward Bus*. This is so because his sympathies are sentimental and wrongly directed. Here is where most reviewers have gone wildly haywire: they have consistently lauded the author's sympathy and compassion, but it is precisely the distortion of these qualities which frustrates from the start any rational moral tone of the obvious allegory.

For there can be no compassion on the part of an author unless there is a passion (and that means suffering, conflict, fight, effort) on the part of the characters. It is here that Steinbeck fails. There is no tiny core or dim spark of resistance and struggle in these characters. The most flagrant example is his character of Camille. She is portrayed as a girl so charged with sex appeal that every man Jack or Juan of all the men she ever meets must preen himself, ogle her, desire her, and make nauseous passes at her. This is to stretch our credulity uncomfortably but, what is far worse, Steinbeck would have us believe that the poor, persecuted girl would much rather be let alone. Though her "entertainment" consists in parading her nudity at stag parties, she dreams of a quiet little home, preferably with a nice girl friend, away from the disgusting men who make her life a constant siege. This strains our credulity still more. But the real dishonesty of the whole picture lies in the fact that this oh-but-fundamentally-good girl deliberately makes the most of her seductiveness all through the book, in dress, if in nothing more.

This, I maintain, is to arouse sympathy on the wrong grounds; this is to drip sentiment for the sin and not to show forth compassion for the sinner. It is true that we cannot demand that Steinbeck write satire that is stinging and indignant; he is no Swift. But satire, even gentle and sympathetic satire, simply cannot be based on the sentimental twaddle that the poor creatures just cannot possibly help acting as they do.

Well, perhaps this is enough about the book. What is actually of more importance and more a source of indignation is that the reviewers, by and large, have been again hypnotized by the name of the author. Steinbeck, they seem to say, has written another book, and woe to our reputation for advanced thought, for devil-may-care liberalism if we do not praise it. One conspicuous exception was Orville Prescott in the daily New York *Times*, who is bold enough to say that perhaps, after all, Steinbeck is a one-book author (*Grapes of Wrath*) and that that book still tinges with a rosy hue the spectacles of reviewers of all his subsequent books. Had his name not appeared on this particular book jacket, the work would undoubtedly have received fairly damning notices and would not have set an all-time high in advance sales (95,000) and now be in the hands of hundreds of thousands of readers.

Some time ago, Ben Lucien Burman wrote a scathing attack in the *Saturday Review*, "Wanted: New Gods." I make bold to appropriate some of his phrases here:

We need a new set of gods, a new literary religion. For the present faith, a faith of petty and immature minds, contains the ferment of its own destruction. . . . Our standards are blurred, our perceptions blunted. . . . Authors have been reluctant to speak out against the stupidities of the realistic school . . . for fear that they would be classed with those enemies of all art, the Puritans.

And more of the same good sense. I charge that the reception given to the latest Steinbeck book adds further weight to Mr. Burman's indictment. I cannot charge that the reviewers have been insincere in their thumping of the Steinbeck drum, but they have either been insincere or they sadly need "a new set of gods."

Alas! poor Yorick Steinbeck—he may have been an emperor of American literature once; he is pretty bare now. And that whispering sound? Can it be the togas of the critics falling to the ground and leaving them shivering before a public which will one day, I hope, find its voice and shout out the long-suspected truth that the critics, too, are naked?   (March 22, 1947)

NOVELIST TO PHILOSOPHER?

What makes Steinbeck's huge novel, *East of Eden,* so strangely readable I just don't know. I suppose it is a sort of carry-over from Steinbeck's personal drive and dynamism, for *East of Eden* is certainly open to about all the charges in the critical calendar. It is a mishmash of sensitive appreciation of nature, admiration for the pioneering spirit, biographies of the author's own family, sincere but often phony philosophizing, melodrama, crudity, and tenderness.

Where Steinbeck's family is bid farewell in the story and fictitious characters are greeted is hard to say, but at any rate the main plot concerns the two sons of Cyrus Trask, Adam and Charles, and the two sons of Adam Trask, Aron and Caleb. The two sets of As and Cs are obviously intended to symbolize Cain and Abel and to epitomize in their lives the primordial struggle between good and evil, which Steinbeck (speaking through a Chinese character named Lee) purports to see prefigured in the Biblical account. A subplot, so to call it, is provided by the fortunes of the Hamilton family, who are relatives of Steinbeck.

It's impossible to attempt a summary of the book's action in a short review. Suffice it to say that all too much space is given to the "monster" mother of Aron and Caleb, who is one of the most infamous women of all literature and whose activities as mistress of a bordello after she has repudiated her twin sons and shot their father are related with a fullness out of all proportion to her place in the family chronicle. In addition to having created an unbelievable character, Steinbeck has trouble fitting her into his newly adopted moralizing tone.

What is vastly more important than the plot is precisely that sermonizing tone. It is an artistic blemish, to be sure, for the reader is baffled trying to keep Steinbeck the novelist apart from Steinbeck the propagandist, the panegyrist, the preacher, the prophet. But the very blemish marks a total change in Steinbeck the philosopher. As Reverend John S. Kennedy has pointed out in *Fifty Years of the American Novel*, Steinbeck had never been able to see the value and the dignity of the individual; man had some sort of worth only as he was part of the collectivity, of "Manself."

Here Steinbeck has changed his tune, though he pipes a little uncertainly. Now we hear that "the free, exploring mind of the individual human is the most valuable thing in the world." We are told that "there is only one story in the world . . . humans are caught . . . in a net of good and evil," and so on. Steinbeck is still not quite clear just what this good and evil are or how humans get caught in their net. A little streamlined psychiatric jargon is introduced to explain that wrongdoing is somehow a result of everyone's having been rejected sometime—Cain was, and so are the two Cains of this story. Such rejection results in anger and a rage to justify oneself, and that results in a deed that brings guilt—and this, it is implied, is the history of the race.

Steinbeck's change is to be praised, but he still has a long philosophical and religious way to go before he comes to the fundamental truth that we are "caught in the net" not because we have been rejected but because we did the rejecting, through original sin. I am not dragging in this concept of original sin; Steinbeck tries to wrestle with this concept in the philosophizing of his character, Lee. But it is a major, and perhaps a very promising, change that Steinbeck should now say: "Our species is the only creative species, and it has only one creative instrument, the individual mind and spirit of man . . . the group never invents anything."

East of Eden is not everybody's dish. Its frequent coarseness will repel many; its diffuseness will alienate others. But it is the work of

a born storyteller who seems to be realizing at last just where the
best stories must be found.   (October 4, 1952)

NEITHER HOT NOR COLD

Social satirists, it seems to me, fall into one of two classes—or fall
down completely. They can be sympathetically and ironically
amused at the foibles of the society they anatomize or they can be
acidly and savagely angry. Horace and Juvenal come to mind as
types; so do Swift and Trollope and, of contemporary writers,
Marquand and Sylvester. The characteristics may, of course, meld
and mesh in an author's total output or even in one book, but the
two elements must be present, either singly or conjointly, if a writer
is to be a satirist.

Now this I feel to be the precise point where Sinclair Lewis falls
short. I have never been able to see wherein he either sympathizes
with his characters or is heartily indignant with them—or, to be
more accurate, with the culture, civilization, and environment
wherein they move. The result has been that Lewis's novels have
had for me the imprint of a small mind; what ought to be the satirist's sympathy for ordinary people bogged down in the ordinariness
of life becomes the contempt that coined the earlier Mencken's
"boobocracy"; the vivid indignation that ought to roll and flash
about the forces that undermine decent society becomes a mere
scornful shrugging of the moral shoulder.

Mr. Lewis's work *Cass Timberlane* needs to be judged from this
approach, although I begin to think that it is an approach Lewis
would willingly have rid himself of. Can it be that he was talked
into considering himself a satirist when all he really wanted to be
was a straightforward storyteller? Did reviewers and professors see
a "social message" in so many of his early books that he later felt
he must always mount the pulpit?

This conjecture seems inescapably suggested by *Cass Timberlane*. As a story of the marriage between the middle-aged judge
and the almost twenty-year-younger Jinny, of the painful adjust-
ments, the initial success, the slow boredom, the near shipwreck,
and the final solution, it is quite a superior job, all the more so for
the utter barren waste of spirituality in the marriage which mirrors

with all too painful fidelity, I take it, the general marital atmosphere of modern paganism. But it is just at this point that Lewis's function as a satirist should have taken hold of the story and deepened its meaning. There are a few and rather unconvincing reflections on the degenerate state of marriage in the stratum of American life he treats; Cass Timberlane's horror at his young wife's adultery is genuine, but so is the casualness with which he earlier suggests to her that they postpone children for a good time. On such a basis there can be no just moral, satirical indignation; there is rather a cynical amusement, touched with a tinge of annoyance, that marriage is in a bad way, that there is little that can be done about it, that Cass and Jinny finally pulled it, barely breathing, from the wreckage only by a happy chance and will probably keep it gasping for a while longer by artificial respiration and not by any fresh winds of spiritual values.

Apart from this main story which—this major defect noted—is shrewd, extremely well managed in dialogue, and well paced, Lewis has interspersed little vignettes of other married couples in the city of Grand Republic. This he has done, it seems, to be able to justify the subtitle "A Novel of Husbands and Wives." And it is when he gets away from the neater, less demanding outlines of the main story into what we may call, for lack of a more exact term, the philosophy of marriage—a philosophy made up of examining these many case histories—that Lewis shows too clearly the smallness of mind that limits him. Some of the sketches, it must be admitted, are gems of characterization and cynical humor, but the tone of them all together is one big sneer. The few happily married couples are either morons or coarse louts; the people of education and refinement (even such as Grand Republic provides) are simply and habitually adulterers. And Mr. Lewis is neither indignant at the sin nor sympathetic toward the sinner; he is half scornfully, half tolerantly, amused.

Such amusement over the fussiness of do-gooders, as in Lewis's prior *Gideon Planish*, may be adequate; when let play over the deadly serious matter of marriage in the modern world, it is, to say the least, a betrayal of the functions a satirist is supposed to fill for the good of society. Little good will come to society from sniggers over rotten marriages, even though one sincere man, Cass Timberlane, manages to cauterize the incipient rottenness out of his own.

(October 6, 1945)

SAUK CENTER WAS HOME STILL

It was always a moot point—if an uncharitable suspicion—whether one reason Sinclair Lewis could capture so neatly and pillory so mercilessly the U.S. provincial mind was that he himself was the quintessence of that mentality. And since provincialism springs from or leads to some sort of isolationism, it is likewise debatable whether Lewis was not always a cultural isolationist. Whether he was politically an isolationist is hard to say, because politics rarely found place in the Lewis canon, save in the unsuccessful *It Can't Happen Here.*

At any rate, the captions that appeared on reviews of his post-humously published book, *World So Wide,* have been somewhat misleading on this point, I believe. They have been saying that for Lewis the United States, no matter how much he poked fun at its follies, was still home. I believe that Sauk Center was still home, because I don't believe that Lewis ever truly knew the United States, save in a caricature of his own making as the goldarnest, grandest and most glorious, cantankerous and perversely lovable of all the countries on God's green earth.

This tone is dominant in *World So Wide.* It is roughly the story of American innocents abroad, wide-eyed at "cultuah," suspicious of the devious Italians (Florence is the scene), somehow bright and shining and naïve jewels in a murky setting of an older and more cynical civilization.

The story is simple. Hayden Chart goes abroad to recuperate after the motor accident that killed his wife. He falls in love—somewhat superficially—with the beauty of Florence (he is a young architect), hobnobs with the American-expatriate set (among them Sam Dodsworth), is attracted by an American woman scholar. He learns of her fickleness when she has an affair with a brash, four-flushing American university professor who is going to streamline European history courses for Midwestern students, and finally is saved from too much Europeanization by marrying a breezy girl reporter from his home town.

The Lewis idiom is unchanged and reads now for all the world like foreigners trying to use U.S. slang—they are always about ten years behind time, though they think they are right on the ball when they proclaim "yes sir, she's the cat's pajamas." Lewis's Americanese is dated.

All in all, this is a sorry book at the end of a career that did make at least some aspects of U.S. life known to the world and to ourselves, and thereby managed to cauterize some of our more obvious excesses. The pathetic reflection *World So Wide* occasions is that here Lewis gives a hint that his talent might have been on the verge of taking a new turn. He was getting interested in a world so very much wider than Sauk Center. That interest might have taken on depth as well. But the end came too soon and Lewis, so innocent about many aspects of American life, remained, like his characters, an innocent abroad. (April 7, 1951)

A TERRACE BOUNDED BY CURBSTONES

Reviewers have been hard put to find some kind words to say about this most ambitious work of John O'Hara, *From the Terrace*. The author himself found it much easier to be gracious while settling the laurel on his far from modestly bowed head. In an interview published in the *Saturday Review*, he admitted that his writing "took an upward turn after *A Rage to Live* in 1948" and then confessed:

[*From the Terrace*] is the best thing I've ever done. The scope of it—fifty years of our country's most exciting history—is larger than anything I have tried before. Writing this novel demanded more wisdom, more patience, more craft—all of which comes from growing older. I thought about [the novel] for six years. It took me two years to write it. I feel that I completed what I set out to do.

There precisely lies the literary conundrum of the year—what did O'Hara set out to do? What he achieved may well have taxed his own patience, for the reader must exercise monumental patience to finish the almost nine hundred pages, but the work most certainly did not summon forth any deeper wisdom than a cynical and sophisticated snobbery. It is equally sure that, far from "taking an upward turn" with *A Rage to Live,* O'Hara's writing—or perhaps it would be more accurate to say his concept of motivation—has become more tired, ingrown, and boring.

Consider the gallery of characters in this elephantine book. Alfred Eaton, the "hero," comes from the small Pennsylvania town that O'Hara has anatomized in many of his books. Alfred rises—socially, financially—but as we follow him up the rungs of the ladder of material success, we also go leaden-footed with him into a slough of moral degeneration, and there is no motivated connection between the two processes. Thrown in are vignettes of the "fifty years of our most exciting history"—World Wars I and II, Wall Street in and after the depression, "high" society, all of which O'Hara comments on with his often-mentioned and still-admired naturalness of dialogue and fidelity to authentic details. But when the dialogue and details add up to nine hundred pages of trivia, even O'Hara's "marvelous ear" has become more than slightly cauliflowered.

Surrounding Eaton are dozens of characters, most of them much if not well married. Looking back on this array, I cannot recall, among the major characters, one couple that does not engage in the most casual adultery, each wife and husband knowing about and even expecting the infidelity. Within two minutes after almost any boy meets almost any girl, they are cheerfully planning where they will spend the night together. It's all done, too, with no callow embarrassment, no gaucherie, for O'Hara is always at great pains to tell us that these moral zombies are "ladies" and "gentlemen."

This is where the snobbishness of the book rears its puerile head. O'Hara is so fascinated with this world of phony values and culture that he seems to feel these rare creatures cannot be judged by the standards we lesser mortals are struggling to preserve in this age of moral conflict. And the lack of moral standards is dramatized on page after page with a wealth of slyly insinuated physical details that run the gamut of aberrations that one would find in Kraft-Ebbing.

O'Hara has protested that no one can justly pin on him the label of writing smut. I pinned that label on him in reviews of *A Rage to Live* and of *Ten North Frederick*. I pin it on him again for this book and with an even surer sense that I am passing a justified verdict.

(December 13, 1958)

MONUMENT TO HOLLOW MEN

What is wrong with James Gould Cozzens's *By Love Possessed*, I kept asking myself; what is the flaw that prevents this novel from being the great book it promises to be in its first pages? The answer struck me while I was seeing the film *Around the World in Eighty Days*. The light dawned during the Spanish sequence in the film—a sequence filled with color, movement, and a sense of the vitality of life. The basic flaw in Cozzens's much-hailed book is a mistrust of life, a distaste particularly for the animal aspects of human life. If Cozzens would agree with the definition that man is a rational animal, he would, I estimate, emphasize the "rational" and concede with reluctance the "animal."

I am singing outside the chorus when I suggest that this novel contains such a major flaw. Reviews have been uniformly laudatory; we are told in not a few that this is the greatest American novel in twenty-five years, and so on. And it must be admitted that there is a sense of mastery in the writing; it is cerebral, penetrating, and revealing. It is, however, a style that makes for slow reading, and some of the dialogue tends to be tediously long and impossibly chiseled. Not even the Man of Reason—whom Cozzens so admires —talks in such impeccable phrases as we meet here on every page.

The story revolves around dignified and cultured Arthur Winner, lawyer in a small New England town, and consists in his progressive education in how much double-dealing there is behind the supposed righteousness of many of the town's leading citizens. It is a growth in disillusionment and, if I catch Cozzens's comment running throughout the book, he believes that that is all anyone can ever expect to find at the root of human motivation.

The Catholic press will be quick to note that the longest diatribes are put in the mouth of a character who is waspishly anti-Catholic. Here, I feel, is a clear example of poor character drawing, for the man is a brilliant lawyer, yet he makes the tactical blunder of estimating his foe, the Church, as being stupid. Certainly one of the necessary qualifications of a good trial lawyer is to assess properly the mettle of his adversary. Mr. Cozzens may say, of course, that he is not anti-Catholic, but it is impossible to avoid the suspicion that the author heartily corroborates his character's attacks.

But the essential flaw lies deeper. Love is a snare; those who succumb to it are "possessed," that is, made mad. Life is to be held at arm's length, and life's processes of being born and dying have been arranged by a bungling and cruel Power. Mr. Cozzens would have patterned life differently if he had been in charge of the blueprints. All that can be done with the messy business as we now have it is to keep the mask of convention properly poised over the empty shell that houses deceit, chicanery, and extramarital affairs. Several passages of considerable length that relate these affairs are as insidious pieces of description as I have ever read, and their insidiousness is heightened by the almost poetic prose in which they are couched.

The book is a runaway best seller and will almost certainly get the annual National Book Award come March. It will be referred to as "monumental"—and it is, in scope and careful plotting. But it is a monument erected to the inglorious memory of hollow men who dwell in a wasteland.   (October 5, 1957)

Chapter Five

THE GREAT BOOKS, BEST SELLERS,
REVIEWERS

When the great books of our literature were written way back in the dim past, I suppose there were some who "reviewed" them, and I suppose further that many of the books turned out to be "best sellers": they were copied and recopied by the scribes, and Caesar may well have said to Brutus (before he spoke to him in less friendly fashion): "By the way, could you lend me your copy of Aristotle's Poetics? Mine hasn't yet been returned by Metellus, the cad—he promised to get it back in a week."

Books have been reviewed (discussed) and circulated as widely as possible (been best sellers) ever since they appeared in more convenient form than blocks of stone, which actually did make circulation hard, since none of the hieroglyphic stones was of the rolling type. But reviewing, as we know it today, is a recent boon for the public and frequently enough a blight as far as the author is concerned. And the best sellers of the astronomical figures did not flare in the literary skies much before the sputniks sputtered into the vastness of space.

The challenge that the great books of the past offer to today's reader obviously cannot be plumbed to the depths in the few selections that follow; nor can the critical problems posed by the best sellers and the critical stances and standards of the book-reviewing fraternity be adequately assessed. Here, however, are some thoughts that have occurred to me on the threefold subject. The great books will continue to be great, no matter what I have to say about the

*methods of their use. I wish I could say the same about all best
sellers and about the judgments of all reviewers—myself included.*

WHAT ABOUT GREAT BOOKS COURSES?

Homer, St. Augustine, Shakespeare, and their peers are in for a
mighty surprise if the little embryo hope nurtured in some American hearts becomes full-fledged reality. For there is a possibility
that the *Iliad,* the *Confessions,* and *Hamlet* will head the various
lists that now start with *Gentleman's Agreement* or *Kingsblood
Royal.* The classics, in other words, may become best sellers—O,
frabjous day!

How will this intellectual millennium come about? Through the
wide extension of courses in the world's "great books." Such courses
have been conducted all over the country for a number of years,
notably at the University of Chicago. So widespread has interest
grown that that university has just announced the formation of a
Great Books Foundation. This is a non-profit, independent organization with a board of eleven directors who will relieve the University of Chicago from responsibility for the courses. The first step
of the foundation will be to organize a training center in Chicago,
where six courses will be offered to prepare leaders to conduct discussion courses on the great books. These leaders, returning to their
communities, will then organize groups in their local libraries,
churches, schools, and other centers. That the work will meet with
impressive response is shown by the fact that last autumn an estimated 20,000 took part in such forums in seventeen American cities
and in Vancouver, B.C.

Mortimer Adler, one of the directors, has this to say about the
aims of the foundation and the courses:

The significance of the Great Books is their utility in universal
adult education. Democracy cannot function successfully without a liberally educated electorate. . . . To achieve the kind of
liberal education for which all schooling is at best a preparation,
adults must make every effort to keep their minds active by en-
gaging in self-education. . . . It is to serve them in this process
that the Great Books perform their essential educational func-

tion. . . . They are concerned with the relatively few basic ideas through the discussion of which men have gained insight, clarified their common problems, and directed their thinking in every field of subject matter.

Some comments on the Great Books plan seem to be in order. I do not by any means intend to belittle either the books themselves or the high ideals of the foundation, but there are dangers that threaten and precautions that ought to be taken.

First of all, the plan for discussion of these books, as outlined by the foundation, seems to hint that discussion for the mere sake of discussion is a cardinal means toward genuine adult education. This, of course, is an oversimplification; discussion has little educative value unless it ends in an approach, at the very least, to the truth. This ideal seems ruled out of the forums as they have up till now been conducted, because the leaders are not supposed to give any "answers," but simply to keep the ball rolling among the discussants. This, in turn, it seems to me, effectively negates any function of teaching on the part of the leaders, and how there can be real education without teaching is hard to see.

Second, the very choice of the Great Books themselves poses some nice problems. In the list to be used by the foundation (which will prepare cheap editions) are such sources of contention and misleading guides as Marcus Aurelius's *Meditations*, Machiavelli's *The Prince*, Descartes's works, Spinoza's *Ethics*, Locke's and Berkeley's philosophical works, Rousseau's *Social Contract*, Hegel's philosophical work, Marx's *Das Kapital*, James's *Principles of Psychology*, and most of Freud.

How can these books possibly be discussed—if the leader is not allowed and even enjoined to point out false directions, errors, misconceptions—without many of the participants having their thinking all mixed up or twisted, with a consequent democratic electorate that will be not liberally educated but generously confused? The fact that "great" books can be a very dangerous two-edged weapon is quite clearly shown by the sinister influence Marx's *Das Kapital* has had in our topsy-turvy world.

I do not suggest that Catholic educators wash their hands of this Great Books plan as part of their adult-education programs. Far from it, as I have seen the benefit derived from one conducted at Fordham University School of Adult Education this past year. I suggest, rather, that wherever possible, Catholic schools and colleges co-operate with the Great Books Foundation and with libraries and various cultural organizations for the purpose of bringing great books into the lives of as many as possible.

But such co-operation ought to be embarked upon with such wise provisos as those stipulated by Marquette University in agreeing to work with Milwaukee libraries and the foundation. The Reverend Gerard Smith, S.J., dean of the school of philosophy, states them as follows:

First, Marquette will select its own list of great books. Second, it will select its leaders from among the Marquette faculty, and pay them. Third, Marquette, while in agreement with the Great Books plan in so far as it is a method to get important issues aired, does not go along with the notion implied and sometimes expressed by its initiators, to the effect that "no questions are to be answered," that leaders were better for knowing less, that great problems were great because they were unsolvable, that truth was to be pursued but not reached, and so on. Marquette is interested in the plan as a means of raising and settling, when possible, the problems of men, quite as were the authors of the great books themselves.

It strikes me that the foundation would do well by the American public (15,000,000 can profit by the Great Books, it claims) if it were to examine this statement with a view to making it its own platform. Great books are indeed important, but straight-thinking teachers are more important still, and truth is the most important of all.   (June 28, 1947)

SIDE READING ON THE GREAT BOOKS: I

Since my brief article, "What about Great Books courses?," four reactions succeeded in engendering in me an idea. Let me tell you first of all what the idea is and then go back to discuss the four reactions.

The idea is this—and I hope you will feel, as I do, that it is a practical one. The Great Books courses, as planned by the Great Books Foundation, are bound to attract an ever-widening audience.

It was announced by the foundation that last autumn over 20,000 people took the courses; it is estimated that 15,000,000 Americans are of a caliber to profit by them. It follows, then, that a great number of Catholics are going to be attracted by the courses; I hope they will be, for this is the kind of cultural movement from which we ought not hold aloof but enter wholeheartedly—for what we can get from the courses, assuredly, but also for what we can contribute to them.

However, Catholics who attend these courses are, quite naturally, going to run into some difficulties. These, or some of them, will be pointed out later when I discuss the observations occasioned by my original article. Now, if there are difficulties ahead, why not forearm Catholics who will participate in the courses? The first thought that arose was to print the yearly lists of great books to be discussed under the foundation plans and to parallel these lists with suggested books that might be corrective (if needed) or, at least, supplemental reading. If, for example, St. Thomas More's *Utopia* were one of the great books, it would be suggested that R. W. Chambers's classic biography ought certainly be read as a preparation for intelligent discussion.

However, that idea I soon abandoned, for it adds to what is already a practical difficulty in these Great Books courses—the problem of getting the books under discussion actually read, let alone commentaries, even the most illuminating, on them.

Instead of that, why should not *America* provide in its columns a series of concise articles on the individual books to be discussed? I canvased a panel of experts, and I am happy to announce that every one of them was most willing and eager to contribute his particular competence toward the plan.

What is the purpose of our series? No one of the experts would proclaim his own personal infallibility—of that I am sure. But in every one of the great books under discussion there is a central core of thought, a theme, an essence, which must be laid bare in any intelligent discussion. If it is not discussed, the book will not be discussed. Moreover, many such an essence has a direct bearing on matters of high personal consequence—some aspect of private morality or social justice is often the theme, and on that it is imperative that the discussants have first of all clear perceptions and, further, arrive at sound conclusions. Each of the articles, therefore, will aim primarily at a clear exposition of what is the actual nub of the book: what is the topic sentence of the book, as it were; what is the author talking about; what is the problem he poses?

Further, each article will try to progress beyond that to suggest an answer, not in the sense of imposing an authoritarian solution but in the sense of indicating to what end a logical and objective discussion ought to tend.

With such an article read and digested, and with its suggestions in mind as guideposts, we hope that Catholics may co-operate in the Great Books discussions more intelligently, more helpfully, and, by their participation, help lift the discussions above a level of in-direction and inconclusiveness which is an inherent plague to such modes of learning.

I realize fully that this preliminary help *America* wishes to give will not be welcomed in some quarters. Some proponents of the Great Books courses will protest that this is the very thing the genius of the courses seeks to avoid—those who read our series of articles will come to the discussions with some ideas already formed or at least shaping up, while the ideal of the discussions is, objectors will claim, that ideas be formed only after the "democratic" give and take of talking things over. Well, I suppose that is a funda-mental divergence of opinion that will never be bridged; I would only like to remark that if the opinion-after-discussion-only school is entirely correct then the great books ought not even be read pri-vately; they ought to be read in common before their common discussion, for even in a cursory private reading any normal reader begins to have opinions of his own. In any case, the discuss-ant will come to the meeting with some preconceived (prior, that is, to the discussion) ideas; if so, what is wrong with having those ideas based on someone's solid scholarship rather than on perhaps unconscious prejudice?

So much for the idea behind the forthcoming series. Let me tell you now the developments that suggested it.

First of all, there is, in the whole conception of the Great Books Foundation, not a little confusion of direction and, worse, of ulti-mate purpose. The first trouble is not overwhelming, perhaps; it is lamentable in a project of such potential promise to the well-being of American culture that the goal has not been clearly thought out.

The confusion of direction is indicated by a correspondent who writes me as follows:

I was up in Chicago the other day and had a couple of good sessions with the men who run the Great Books Foundation. Incidentally, they had read and digested the remarks in *America* and, what is more, admitted their validity. They also said . . . that they start all their courses with the statement that there is such a thing as objective truth, that it can be arrived at, that some of the books reach it and some do not. But even though they (the leaders) know what is right and what is wrong, they will not reveal it to the people taking the course. Their reason is that in this way they stultify thought and that, if they were dictatorial (awful word) in their philosophical thinking, they would be accused of being special pleaders for Adler's brand of scholastic philosophy. It doesn't make too much sense, but that's what they say.

Another correspondent objected to the *America* article, among other reasons, because it suggested that discussion leaders, like other teachers (for they are actually teachers, no matter what you call them), have the duty of teaching the truth. Says my correspondent:

We don't attempt to "teach" him "truth." We can't. And neither can anyone, for truth is conformity between the mind and the object, and no one can teach conformity. That can only be imposed upon the mind by the object or by authority—and in these matters it is better done by the former. The best we or anyone else can do is to supply the tools and prepare the conditions whereby the student himself can bring about this conformity between his mind and the object.

This correspondent does not identify his position in the Great Books Foundation, but he speaks as one of some authority. It is disturbing, accordingly, to find such confusion of thought on a fundamental question. For truth can be taught, precisely as the truth of things, the objective truth, the ontological order, is clearly revealed to the questing mind. Once that mind sees the objective thing clearly, unclouded by prejudice or passion, the natural bent of the human mind is to assent. What cannot be taught is the capacity of the mind to conform; my correspondent, in saying flatly that truth cannot be taught, is confusing the ontological order with the logical and, in the logical order, capacity with exercise.

More disturbing, however, than this confusion of means is the nebulousness of the goal which the guiding spirits of the Great Books Foundation, the leaders of this vast mass movement toward culture, set before them. It will obviously not be possible to delineate fully the proper goals of a liberal education in the narrow confines of this and a succeeding article. After all, books and libraries have been written on the subject. I do think, however, that some reflections are called for by the very statements which outline the objectives of the course.

Most of these statements are contained in the *vade mecum* of those who will be trained to lead the discussion groups. It is the *Manual for Discussion Leaders*, by Mortimer J. Adler, subtitled a "Preliminary Draft for Use in Great Books Community Groups." In the introduction Mr. Adler has a very neat summary of the purposes of the courses. "Great books community groups are formed," he states,

> . . . for the purpose of carrying on adult liberal education. . . . Liberal education can be defined most simply as the education of man as man. . . . This definition, first of all, excludes physical education in the broadest sense of that term—the education of man as an animal. . . . The definition, in the second place, excludes religious education—the education of man as a spiritual being. . . . Thirdly, the definition implies that liberal education has little to do with [vocational or professional training]. . . . Liberal education has to do with the development of man in his distinctively human dimension. . . . Since every man is both an individual and a member of society, his education as a man must include these two aspects of his nature. . . . That is to say, liberal education ends at producing, first, the good man, and, second, the good citizen.

Here, verily, is a mystery. Mr. Adler and the hundreds who will use his handbook essay to educate man as men and then proceed to exclude (not merely to prescind from) two aspects of man's nature that are essential to man and to a study of him as man.

For man is an *animal rationale* and, if he is to be educated as man, both aspects of his nature need education. It is quite true that there is an "education" which would train man merely as an animal; but there is also possible an education—and it is not only possible, but necessary—which rationally trains the animal part of man. It is necessary because otherwise man is educated as though he were pure intellect and will, which he is not. Liberal education, then, though by its charter it cannot educate man as an animal, cannot ignore the animal aspects of man, in so far as they fall under the supremacy of the reason. What else is the idea of temperance, for example, concerned with, if not with man's specifically human (reason and will) activity in the proper control of (among other things) his animal instincts and passions?

This point, however, while indicative of confusion as to aims, may be conceded as minor. But what when we hear that the education of man as man excludes religious education? For Mr. Adler must (I hope) realize the absolute truth of the tenet in philosophy which asserts that man is essentially a being with relationships to self, to others, and to his first cause, God. We may waive for the time being any discussion of whether man as man is a being who has essential relationships to a *revealed* God (and to the whole sweep of supernatural religion); but there can be no doubt that the study of man as man must necessarily include at least his relationship to natural religion. If man as man is not related to a whence and a whither, I am not studying him as man but merely as a casual piece of flotsam on a mere tidal sequence of events.

All the more astonishing is it to have Mr. Adler go on from these dubious premises to the surprising conclusion that, having dropped man's animal activities and religious aspirations, this shadowy creature is to be educated to good citizenship. Certainly Mr. Adler must know that both individual and social virtues postulate a norm, a law; a law means a lawgiver, and I am right back at the question which the Great Books Foundation excludes: have I an individual and/or a social obligation to obey laws of conduct? Whose laws are they? Can it be that God is creeping back into the courses whose charter has somewhat pontifically excluded Him?

How have the siren voices of such confused purposes lured educators of high caliber, some of them, indeed, men well versed in scholastic philosophy? It may be a hardy statement to make, but I am convinced that, perhaps all unconsciously, the virus of secularism is at the root of such educational thinking. It is a secularized liberal education that is being held up as the goal of the Great Books courses. It is not even a hardy pagan liberal education—the old ideal of *mens sana in corpore sano*. The *corpus sanum* is too, too animal—away with it. Nor is it a Christian liberal education;

religion is no part of man; it's only a veneer and man can be totally human without it, perhaps even more human.

This frigid atmosphere of secularism, which, if I read the manifestoes properly, invests the very inauguration of the Great Books Foundation, actually does find its way into the discussion groups. But this further aspect is something I shall treat next week. For the present, and in ending, let me say that this is not a bit of special Papist pleading. When I say that man's highest possible human activities—namely, the examination by his intellect of his relationship to God and the execution of those activities by his will (and, under his will, by his poor animal body)—are preeminently his activities as man; I am not wooing anybody Romeward. I am simply saying that the objective truth about man is that he is essentially a religious being, because he is essentially a creature.

It's rather puzzling that Mr. Adler and many trained by him and his writings on the great books should think otherwise. For many, indeed, of the great books we are urged to read toward gaining a truly liberal education speak out unmistakably and even gloriously to the effect that man as man can only be liberally educated when he is *liber*, free—and the only true freedom man can have is the freedom of the children of God.   (September 20, 1947)

SIDE READING ON THE GREAT BOOKS: II

The strange confusion in the ultimate purposes of the "liberal" education proposed by the Great Books discussion groups under the Great Books Foundation plan, which I discussed earlier and which I attributed to a perhaps unconscious bias toward a secularistic liberalism, is nowhere more startlingly manifest than in the very handbook used in the training of discussion leaders.

Chapter 1 of Part II in that manual is entitled "A Typical Seminar" and consists of the transcription of an actual discussion with two leaders who are guiding their group through the mazes of St. Augustine's *Confessions*. A careful reading of the give-and-take of question and answer reveals a fairly high level of consistency, a good sense of direction in the discussion, and, unexpectedly enough, considering the fact that discussion leaders are not sup-

posed to "teach" the "truth," the arrival at some quite definite conclusions.

But—and this is really ironical if you will remember that this
type of liberal education, according to the same manual, excludes
education of man as a religious being—the one most definite conclusion this particular group of participants arrives at is that this
is a great book precisely and exactly because it is a penetrating
revelation of man's essentially religious nature. The group has
reached, after many backings and fillings, the stage of discussing the
relationship between faith and reason. This leads to whether or not
Augustine was happier after he had been given faith; the discussion
then runs:

Leader 2: But what had entered him here that made the
    difference?
Miss L: It was the peace that he found.
Leader 2: But what is the other word that we use?
Miss L: Who?
Leader 1: Consider Augustine after conversion. Before, he might
    have been happy, but after conversion? What is the relation-
    ship between the end happiness and the other end?
Miss L: Faith or supernatural happiness.
Leader 1: That's right, the supernatural element, and therefore
    the other takes a back place.
Leader 2: Is the love of God higher than happiness?
Miss L: Yes. That's supernatural happiness.
Leader 2: Why is this a great book?
Miss L: Because of the fact that it deals with the super-
    natural. . . .
Leader 2: Because it shows how one man arrived at faith, isn't
    that right?
Miss L: Yes.
Leader 2: Now we have taken something out of the pagan phi-
    losophy and put something on top of it.

And what has been "put on top" is something that makes these
discussion leaders, chosen as exemplars of how to conduct a typical discussion, untrue to the very "liberal" education outlined in the
first chapter of their handbook. For they have proved that you
cannot discuss man without talking about free will, aspiration,
hope, faith, the supernatural—in a word, God.

However, I do not want to pursue this confusion of final purpose any further. It may happily be that actual discussions will avoid the secularism of the announced theory of education on which the foundation plan rests. Cold theory often breaks down before warmer, human application—just as many a doctor, I suppose (and thank God), might have instincts sound enough to forestall him from administering the euthanasia he is ready to advocate in the abstract. But it is dangerous to have to depend on mere instinct.

However, not even that unstable security can, in practice, be counted on. If the theory of education behind this type of Great Books discussion is secularistic, and if that theory is drummed hard enough and often enough into the discussion leaders, it is to be anticipated that the natural bent of human inquiry, which is to search out ultimates, will be warped into actual discussions which are themselves tinged with secularism.

This is what I hinted at in the end of the earlier article. I know from some who have taken the leadership training that they have been alarmed at the atmosphere of irreligion they have had to encounter. Mind, they did not say, and I am far from charging, that any of their discussions were anti-Catholic, bigoted, sneering. It was only (but what a sad "only") that some of the participants and leaders seemed so steeped in an utter incomprehension of spiritual values that they were apparently incapable of grasping anything of spiritual import.

In one group, St. Augustine's *Confessions*, again, was being discussed, and I am informed that when the mention of "sin" occurred, there were obvious giggles; the discussion then proceeded to talk sin out of the window in glib terms of "complexes," "neuroses," "nervous disorders," and what not.

Now, please, I am not leveling the charge of impiety at the Great Books Foundation leaders and all their works and pomps. I am ready to grant sunnily that most discussion leaders would set and maintain a higher tone than that. But there will be hundreds of groups swinging into action this fall; in the metropolitan area of New York alone, some one hundred twenty to one hundred thirty leaders have now finished their preparation and early in October they will be leading local groups in the study of the great books. What if only ten or five of these leaders have been trained by a master leader who has managed to ingrain in them pretty ineradicably that in order to get a "liberal" education you have to exclude, and keep excluded firmly and unswervingly, any reference to man's relations to God? How else, under such a charter, can the mention of sin do otherwise than raise secularist contempt?

That the Great Books Foundation does not want or welcome any such end result is warranted by the caliber of the public figures who head its activities. But I say that if their theory of liberal education is carried out willy-nilly, such a result follows from the nature of the case. If their theories are more honored in the breach than in the observance, a truer liberal education may result *per accidens*—but that does not invalidate, it confirms, my criticism of the fundamental confusion that dogs the ideals of educating for good citizenship, for democracy, which the whole grandiose, gigantic scheme professes.

Hence the series of articles on the individual great books which will begin in *America* next week. We do not wish to take over the Great Books Foundation; we do not want to put the plan and its operation under anathema (we couldn't if we would). We only want to put back into the discussion of the specific book an element which the foundation has explicitly ruled out, and we promise our readers not to drag that in by the heels.

(September 27, 1947)

These two articles on the Great Books were introductory to a series in which the Great Books selected for the first year's discussions were analyzed, each by an expert in the field. These articles, which appeared in America *from October 4, 1947, to March 20, 1948, were published as* Volume One *in* The Great Books: A Christian Appraisal *(Devin-Adair, 1947). This was followed by three more volumes under the same title (1950, '51, '52), all edited by the present writer.*

BEST-SELLER FEVER

Slogging their way on foot through the forest of Mount Castre near La Haye du Puits and Carentan in Normandy, the tall, drawling GIs from Oklahoma and Texas, the New York *Times'* correspondent remarks, "did not know on what historic ground they were treading." Oklahoma and Texas, take no umbrage at the seeming slur; foot soldiers, tank men, paratroopers from New York or Massachusetts or any other state would very likely not have known, either, but they can all thank their stars that someone knew, for many a GI is now alive who might otherwise be lying in a Norman grave.

Who knew what? Well, the Army Intelligence knew that Caesar's legions had once, some 2,000 years ago, fortified the mount. They reared a fortress of masonry and defense rings of trenches and linked parts of the fortifications with tunnels. From the ruins of that ancient fort, the Germans peered out on D-Day and saw the Allies swarming up the beaches; from it they menaced and harassed our troops in their fight for La Haye du Puits. Our Intelligence knew all this; they had read up on the history of the place; they located the old tunnels and sealed them with demolition charges. What potential traps there might have been there in Caesar's fort were circumvented by the fact that some men in a twentieth-century mechanized army had read about the short swords and hollow squares that schoolboys agonize over in *De Bello Gallico*.

This is rather a long way round to calling your attention to a remarkable brochure published by the Enoch Pratt Free Library of Baltimore. It is a statement prepared for the Modern Language Association of America by a special committee of its Commission on Trends in Education. A group of educators collaborated in its preparation, but the body of the text is the work of Professor Howard F. Lowry of Princeton University, and to him go our hearty thanks and appreciation for the clear and cogent reasons he has given for a supreme place for literature in education. In this day of technology, when curricula must of necessity emphasize the physical sciences to the detriment of the cultural disciplines, the statement is a heartening sign that educational circles are preparing for a rebirth and deepening of the liberal-arts courses after the end of the war.

Now, one of the advantages that a study of literature has to offer, the brochure points out, is "increased experience of the past." This knowledge of the past is in itself a good; it gives that sense of perspective and balance that results, if in nothing else, in intellectual humility. "Any assumption," the statement reads, "that the past has no meaning for the student is to say that this century will in turn be worthless in the next; this decade in the next; and this year next year."

Apart from this intrinsic value, there is another that the report does not insist upon, perhaps because it is a little too utilitarian for the high tone in which the statement is conceived and uttered. Utilitarian or not, it is important, and if you will reread the first two paragraphs here, you will see the bearing. A knowledge of the past can aid our practical actions in the present; because some Intelligence officers (and intelligent ones, too, let us add) were wise enough to do a little browsing in Caesar's exploits, the American GIs from Texas and Oklahoma knew how cautiously to tread. Because one has known Oliver Twist and Shylock, let us say, his practical life today in its attitudes and reactions to labor and interracial problems will be deeper, fuller, and more humane than if he knew those problems only from statistical reports.

Knowledge of the past, then, through literature, is a compass for the present. How many contemporary American readers use that compass? It is, of course, impossible to say with accuracy, but a report has been issued that throws a little light on the puzzle. A New Jersey town of some 40,000 population has installed a tabulating machine in the public library, and this mechanical brain has done some thinking that makes us ponder. It seems that a one-week sample reveals that fifteen per cent of the books borrowed were published in 1944, forty per cent in 1943 or 1944, sixty-five per cent in 1940 or later. Eighty-seven per cent of all books borrowed by adults had been published since 1930.

In other words, this sampling of the reading habits of Americans shows that they are little interested in the great books of the past. As an editorial on the report in *Publishers' Weekly* wryly remarks: "In our world today children are the only readers who keep a balance in their reading. Perhaps adults might understand current events better if they made more effort to read the great books of the past."

What is needed, and particularly among Catholic readers, for their whole heritage from the past and their value of time and its spiritual opportunities demand it of them, is a certain intellectual aristocracy—call it snobbishness if you will. The Modern Language Association brochure we have been praising so highly makes a great point, as it must these days, of the advantages to democracy in having literary studies take their proper place in the postwar curriculum. What it is actually calling for is a widening of what used to be, in days gone by, the privilege of the aristocracy—the study of letters, the reading of good books—so that it becomes the heritage of constantly more and more of the people. But as always in the broadening of culture, care must be had that it is not, like rationed butter, spread thin to go farther.

It will be spread thin if increasing interest in books and reading confines itself to the current output. A steady diet of best sellers will not encompass the four results the brochure specifies as the fruit of a study of literature: to increase the experience of man in human understanding, in a knowledge of other countries, in quality, and in a sense of the past. These best sellers cannot do it, because the vast majority of them are simply books of no permanent worth.

Several years ago, a prominent book lecturer of New England performed an interesting experiment. In 1934 he had reviewed twelve books; six years later he still regarded four of those books as being of permanent interest and worth keeping. They were *The Flowering of New England*, by Van Wyck Brooks; *The People, Yes*, by Carl Sandburg; *Green Laurels*, by Donald Culross Peattie; *An American Doctor's Odyssey*, by Victor Heiser. Now, it is a very good year that can produce four really valuable books, but even in that good year, the best sellers come off shabbily indeed, because, of the four books chosen, only one was actually in the best-seller class. One best seller out of twelve judged a valuable book means that ninety-two per cent of the really popular books are of no permanent interest.

If this be true, then reading that is exclusively confined to the current output, whether of fiction or non-fiction, is by no means that study of literature which is calculated to make more keen our appreciation of quality. As far back as 1924, Hilaire Belloc noted the fatal propensity of the American popular book to dull the fine edge of literary appreciation. The singular vice of the American reading scene, he said in his book *The Contrast*, was the vice of "uncritical exaltation." Among us, "a book 'takes' exactly as fire 'takes' in dry gorse."

This, I take it, is one reason why the lists of our best sellers show books of such totally divergent quality jostling one another. How can the ten best sellers include near masterpieces like *The Song of Bernadette*, good but not really great novels like *So Little Time*, and definitely second-rate stuff like *What Became of Anna Bolton*? Is it that the general reading public just does not know what a good book is? I am quite sure that Christopher Morley, in his personal enthusiasm for C. S. Lewis's *Screwtape Letters*, would have chosen it as a Book-of-the-Month Club selection; apparently he or his fellow judges feared that the American public could not rise to it.

So does the fever to keep constantly abreast of the latest subtly undermine the ability to appreciate the best and concentrate upon the ephemeral those energies that ought, in part at least, to be spent upon the permanent. The Modern Language Association report that we have been recommending tells the sad tale of the young girl who asked the professor if he had read the latest best seller; when he said no, she cried: "Oh, but you must, and hurry, because it's just out." "Young lady," he admonished, "have you read the *Divine Comedy?*" And when she said no, he cried: "Oh, but you must, and hurry, because it's been out for over six hundred years."

An appreciation of the past, of course, can be got from some small section of the current books; I know of no better analysis of the skeptical, blasé mind of the French Enlightenment, for example, than that given in the character of Lafitte in *The Song of Bernadette*. But by and large, a diet of the current best sellers will teach the reader little or nothing of the past, and so will leave him in ignorance of the true meaning of the present.

Playgoers must have remarked the revelation it is to attend a Shakespearean play after many modern ones. If nothing else thrills one, the marvelousness of the language will—its fullness and sweep and majesty, in contrast with the piping and staccato colloquialism of modern dramatic dialogue. So, after the thinness of plot and character in so, so many of the best sellers, the depths of the great books will come as a revelation to those who will renew—if they do not have to make for the first time—the acquaintance.

Those of my readers who are teachers, those who are interested in making their reading worth-while as well as a delight, will do well to get a copy of the brochure that has occasioned this article. Its perusal will perhaps convince those who need the corrective, and strengthen those who are convinced already, that reading in the great books of the world is a supreme bulwark against that "triumph of quantity over quality," the perfect symbol of which Irving Babbitt saw in "an American of the present day reading his Sunday newspaper in a state of lazy collapse." For the purposes of this article, suppose you substitute "this week's and the next's and the next's best seller" for "Sunday newspaper."

(July 29, 1944)

CATHOLIC BEST SELLERS

A delicate task is crying to be done; I must confess that I have fought shy of it for too long, for I know how delicate it is and I fear that some sensibilities are going to be ruffled, but I honestly feel that it is a question that has to be faced and discussed with some frankness. It is the problem, and our attitude toward it, of the quality of some recent Catholic novels and the acclaim they have been accorded.

This problem has become more acute in recent months through the wide popularity attained by two of these novels, Father Raymond's *Three Religious Rebels* and Father Murphy's *The Scarlet Lily*. A glance at *America's* Book-Log will show that both books stand high in popularity among Catholic readers, *The Scarlet Lily* reaching, in the last edition of that report, the highest total votes of any book ever to make the first ten. It is in the face of this popularity that the problem for the reviewer arises: we have been working and praying in the Catholic press for more widespread reading of Catholic books; here come two books that are widely read, and this reviewer, at any rate, feels that he must in honesty quite definitely rate both books as inferior.

This, of course, is not an enviable position; it will displease many who mistakenly feel that they simply have to like any book written by a Catholic on a Catholic theme; it will strike others as snobbish and ultraperfectionist; still others will be confused because they fail to distinguish between the devotional good that the books may do and their merit as works of literary craftsmanship.

Let me first discuss at some length the two books and then try to embark on some of the wider reasons for my distinctions and strictures. *Three Religious Rebels* consists of the fictionalized portrayal of three saints who were forerunners of the Trappist Order. Each of them felt the call to a stricter monastic life, and the book recalls their ideals, their difficulties, the degree of their realization of the goal. The theme that Father Raymond has chosen is a profound and noble one; the times of which he writes were stirring in their pageantry, but the novel which results is strangely stiff and unmoving and combines, with the stiffness, an overabundance of sermonizing, which does not spring from the inner source of the characterization but is overlaid upon the story.

The characters, despite the vividness of the times and the deep reality of their achievements, are bloodless creatures. Perhaps one fundamental reason for this is that they constantly talk about the nobility of their ideals; they refer over and again to "the chivalry of Christ," to the ideal monk as being "the knight of the spirit," and other similar trappings of medieval chivalric romance—but we do not see this; we do not feel it in the scene as it unrolls. The main defect of the book lies, I feel sure, in this inadequate grasp of character in action. An illuminating contrast that will reveal this defect much better than pages of criticism would be to compare the grasp of character shown in the person of the monk in Thomas Kernan's *Now with the Morning Star* with the three saintly heroes of *Three Religious Rebels*.

Father Murphy's *The Scarlet Lily* is a current prize-winning Catholic novel, whose story is the life of Saint Mary Magdalene. We may grant at the outset that the author has essayed a much harder task than did Father Raymond, mainly because of the paucity of material on which he had to work. As a story, it has much more continuity and unity than the first book, which is, of its nature, tripartite. But my main difficulty with *The Scarlet Lily* is fundamentally the same—the character of Magdalene is not realized; it does not come alive; I have not met a person in all the pages of the book. Again, this springs from the fact that Magdalene tells us in the book, over and over again, that her life was blighted when her beloved little brother was slain in the Massacre of the Innocents; she informs us that she is bitter, that she has conceived a hatred for the Man who was the innocent occasion of the slaughter. She tells, she informs—she does not show us.

Heightening this unreality of the main character is the unfortunate cast and tone of the language that Father Murphy has chosen as his vehicle. I feel quite sure that Father Murphy has read Shakespeare well and widely, for I find throughout the story a fondness for the lush Renaissance language which is perfect for the romantic accents of impassioned young love, as in *Romeo and Juliet*, but which seems to me strangely discordant in the mouths of Magdalene or Our Lady, and above all on the lips of Our Lord. Please, I am not by any means saying that there is the slightest trace of irreverence in this; I do think that Father Murphy has unconsciously been betrayed into an impossible confusion between historically disparate modes and accents of speech. And this confusion results in what I can call nothing less than excessive sentimentality.

There are three main reasons why I think this stringent criticism is necessary. First of all, it is my honest and, I hope, totally unprejudiced opinion. That is exactly what I would have said about the books, had they been on non-Catholic themes by non-Catholic authors and manifested the same defects. The mere fact that the authors produced "Catholic literature" is no reason for them to escape criticism first and foremost on literary grounds. Had they chosen to write books of meditation or historical vignettes with homiletic asides, then they would not have invited judgment on a basis of literary norms; but they chose to write novels, to use characterization and story, plot and dialogue; therefore, their works are to be judged as any other novel would be; they have set themselves in competition, and *The Song of Bernadette* shows that the competition is indeed strong.

My second reason is more important, I think. It is this: neither of these books, as literary art, comes up to the standard of excellence that our Catholic intelligence and culture have the right to expect. The whole Catholic concept of life rises gloriously to the aspiration after perfection; we are justly indignant at slipshod sermons, at outmoded methods of teaching; religious art and architecture are reminded constantly that the second-rate, the imitative, is not worthy of God's service. Is it to be in literature alone that we will throw our caps in the air and cheer passionately over performances that do not come up to what we have a right to expect? Once again, remember that we have to distinguish between the spiritual good that these two books will most certainly do (and for that we are all grateful) and their standing as novels, as works of art.

My third reason is more apologetic than literary. I am holding my breath until the unhappy day when some smart and capable secular critic feels that Catholic books like these ought to get his attention. With little effort he will be able to make them look ridiculous, with the consequent implication that if Catholics wholesale, and Catholic critics and reviewers in particular, heap praise on them, then Catholics must be a very stupid and undiscerning lot, indeed. Mr. Edmund Wilson, a most capable critic, did something similar to that in the *New Yorker* recently on *The Robe*. He revealed the literary inadequacy of the novel and commented on the herd-mindedness of its millions of readers. The Catholic reading public may be just as herd-minded; if so, it is a condition that we have to combat by reminding them and ourselves in season and out of season that we cannot be that way. Our ideals of perfection forbid it—and those ideals of perfection ought to be just as operative in literature as they are in any art, in any field of endeavor that can be ennobled and deepened by consecration to God.

I admire and stand in no little awe at the courage of the two authors; I applaud the initiative of their publishers; more than critics who are something like Joyce Kilmer's poets who only make poems, they are making the trees—they are actually embarking on the writing that will, some day, be the fitting vehicle for Catholic profundity and truth, once the form is worthy of the content. But, until that day is a great deal nearer than at present, it still is the unwanted, and perhaps ungracious, task of the critic to point out that the trees now springing up on the American Catholic landscape are yet shrubs. It is the critic's task because he does not want either the authors to think that the growth of their fostering tops the surrounding forest, or readers to think that they really know trees, when apparently they are mistaking saplings for sequoias.

There is no reason written in the stars why American Catholic authors are not capable of writing a *Perelandra*, a *Bernadette*, a *Labyrinthine Ways*, a *Kristin* trilogy. The reason is not written in the stars; it may be written in the approach of authors and in the taste of readers; if so, it is a writing that needs the ruthless use of an eraser. The word that will have to be rubbed out first and vigorously is "devotion." It is the author's prime, inescapable job, once he steps out of the field of devotional writing, once he attempts a literary approach, to tell the story grippingly, thrillingly, deeply, vividly—what labels you will—but with the devotion welling inescapably and naturally from the "innards" of the story. To be devotional first, and novelistically capable only second or third, is to abdicate any claim to have produced Catholic literature.

The delicate task is done—how delicately is perhaps a moot question. By all means, read the two books under discussion; their authorship, their purpose, their characters will give food for thought and meditation and will perhaps deepen your Catholic life. Only, do not, as I fear many have done, finish them with an ejaculation of thanks that, at last, Catholic literary achievement is edging quite close to the top. No, we have a long way still to go—and I would not have so brashly ventured these strictures unless I felt that the two authors would agree with me. They, too, you see, know that for the aims we have in view, anything short of the best belittles, in its field, the Church's ideal, which is, in Louise Imogen Guiney's words, a "passion for perfection."   (January 27, 1945)

Chapter Six

BOOKS AS CULTURAL AMBASSADORS

Whenever two people get embroiled in a heated argument, there is always some hope that the differences may be composed if only one of the litigants can control his hotheadedness long enough to listen a bit, nod thoughtfully, and mutter: "Well, I see what you mean." Seeing what someone means may never, it is true, bring me to think highly of him, and much less to love him, but it is a safe bet that I will never come to love unless I first "see what you mean."

Understanding, then, is most often a first step toward external co-operation and toward that deeper co-operation that springs from the heart, which is charity or love. It is also lamentably true that one kind of understanding can and even ought to lead to clear-sighted and rational detestation. I understand quite well what the program of communism is—and I hate it; which is not the same as saying that I hate individual Communists.

But certainly among the nations and cultures of the Free World there is common denominator enough of respect for the dignity of man, the God-given glory of freedom, the imperative necessity for co-operation for peace, for us to find understanding of one another a prerequisite for charity and love.

What have books to say, in their degree, in fostering such an understanding and such a love? What impression have American books made abroad? Have we sold ourselves short? Have we lent color to the fable, widely believed abroad and deftly played up in anti-American propaganda, that we are a crude and materialistic nation? Can we tell the true story about ourselves—proudly yet *modestly? Or are our book ambassadors unkempt and unshaven gate crashers on the international "I see what you mean" party?*

SOME CULTURAL THOUGHT TAKING

We wouldn't like to begin standing in awe of the laboring mountains only to be embarrassed later with the necessity of hailing a ridiculous mouse, but there do seem to be signs of something new a-borning in certain groups whose only passion—so those think in particular who love to see the United States as disgustingly materialistic—is to pant in pursuit of the almighty dollar. From several quarters the rumor is abroad that not a few United States businessmen, big-time operators in various fields, are beginning to see a great light which beams out the message that this nation is strong because of more than its standard of living, more than its material comforts and advantages, and that it has more than these to talk about to the outside world, and even to exchange with that world.

Here is one wave of the rumor. Within the past year there have been at least two books which have discussed the place of big business in American life in terms of business's growing sense of social responsibility. David Lilienthal in *Big Business* and J. A. Morris in *Those Rockefeller Brothers* underline that thought. And the latest volume of a series on Ethics and Economic Life, prepared by the Federal Council of Churches, is devoted entirely to "The Social Responsibilities of the Businessman."

Even more arresting, perhaps, was a key speech made at White Sulphur Springs, W. Va., to the annual convention of the American Association of Advertising Agencies, by Dr. Vergil D. Reed, a vice president of the J. Walter Thompson Company. Dr. Reed pointed out something that advertising men have never sold well— particularly abroad: "Our present cultural level and the ease with which it can be lifted." Appreciation of good music, he indicated as an example, had risen to such a point that paid admissions to concert halls exceed the gate receipts of baseball games by $5,000,000 a year; the number of museums has grown from six hundred to 2,500 in a quarter century.

Yet advertising men have not told that story. It is time, Dr. Reed

challenged, for them to realize that, in the role of world leadership
in which this country is now cast, success

> will depend largely upon a proper balance between material and
> nonmaterial values. . . . Ideas and not commodities, under-
> standing and not dollars, culture and not boastful materialism
> must be our means of leading.

As though to corroborate such sane and welcome thinking, a
series of four articles in *This Week* magazine on "Crisis in Our
American Way of Life" was devoted largely to cultural problems,
such as those being fronted by schools and colleges, libraries and
museums. The standard of living was not viewed in the series as
the touchstone of our nation's well-being.

Finally, Hollywood is being drawn into a new interest in culture.
This time it is not precisely any change of thought in Hollywood
which has done the trick. It is outside pressure. The State Department has relayed to Hollywood protests from seven foreign countries against excessive brutality in American films, especially against
brutality portrayed in the physical manhandling of women. Accordingly, word has gone out to the studios that such scenes must be
toned down. It's regrettable that Hollywood itself did not spot the
evil; but even so, the belated and imposed realization shows that
the importance of cultural values in international relations is beginning to get some of the consideration it deserves.

Some United States leaders are thinking that "culture and not
boastful materialism" is our most valuable possession and export.
The problem is to convince our friends abroad that most Americans
say a hearty "yea" to such thinking.   (May 16, 1953)

"CULTURAL CIRCULATION"

The London *Times Literary Supplement* commented provocatively
on the budget reduction under which the British Council had to
work during the year ending March 31—a reduction of 8.1 per cent.
The British Council supervises cultural-information work in foreign
countries as a supplement to the general information that is taken
care of by the various British information services abroad.

Expressing regret that such a budget reduction was necessary,

the *Supplement* placed great emphasis on the positive value of
international "cultural circulation," a value, it strikes us, that might
well be more deeply imbedded in the minds of those in charge of
United States information services abroad.

In speaking, for instance, of the council's report, "Work in
Europe," the editors observed:

> As it happens, we have at the moment much to give, since as
> the balance stands at present we are among the most vital and
> creative of the European nations today, in the arts, in letters and
> inventions and in technical and political experiment. This is
> hardly modesty, but it is truth and we shall do well to recognize
> it. We had better realize also, first, that our national health de-
> pends on trade in ideas as well as in goods, and on a brisk, many-
> sided trade at that, and secondly, that what a recent writer in the
> *Economist* said of Italy is true of Europe as a whole: "No policy
> based merely on the cold-blooded interchange of purely economic
> and military aid is any longer sufficient." Europe's needs are not
> only material.

The spirit that animated these words, the *Supplement* continues,
is as well the spirit behind a speech of Dag Hammarskjöld,
Secretary-General of the United Nations, at a UN concert in New
York:

> In our preoccupation with the outward forms, the established
> procedure, the publicity, and the immediate issues which attract
> our attention from day to day, we may tend to forget that at the
> very basis of this organization there is the will of all peoples to
> create a world of harmony.

Such a world of harmony may seem now like a chimera glimmer-
ing on a far horizon, but it, rather than a world of military strength
or economic well-being, is the real one world the United Nations
has as its goal. A militarily strong and economically sound free world
may now be first in the order of execution, but it can never be first
in the order of intention.

Cultural circulation—the exchange of ideas, of literature and the
arts, of science and techniques—is a first step toward international
harmony. Hence the importance of such organizations as the various
national information services in foreign lands. Budgets, of course,
have to be trimmed from sheer necessity, but when funds have to

be sliced from cultural circulation in order to further military and economic ends, "It is an error," the *Supplement* dryly remarks, "to suppose there is no loss."

The world, it would seem, is awakening to a great craving for spiritual and cultural goods. Our policy planners would do well to keep firmly in mind how best we can do our share in supplying them.   (December 12, 1953)

SELLING DEMOCRACY TO THE EAST

"Cultural exports" from the United States to the rest of the free world have engaged the interest and concern of this review on many an occasion. We've expressed the fear that all too much of the propaganda that tells the free world of the "American way of life" couches that message in loud terms of material living standards while whispering in very mealymouthed tones about the spiritual and cultural values that really make the American way of life, of which the mere material advantages are but a by-product.

But the professional propagandists and the "realistic" diplomats do not seem to have shared our misgivings that the U.S. approach —to the East in particular—has been employing the wrong tone of voice. "Why, everybody knows," they say, "that the standards of living in India and China are terrible. So what better approach could there be than to tell these masses that if they adopt our way of life, they too can make more money, have better homes, be healthier, and so on? These are the practical things they want to hear about. All this cultural and spiritual stuff is kind of hazy to people who are hungry."

That's what the hardheaded American may think. The important point, however, is: that is not the way the people in India and China think. And we don't make that statement from any ivory tower; we make it because easterners themselves make it. Speaking at a Communion breakfast in New York, the Most Reverend Leonard Raymond, Bishop of Allahabad, India, said:

The Voice of America most often adopts the attitude that material wealth alone is proof of a superior culture; if you have TV and motor cars then you are definitely superior. In face of

the deep spirituality of the East such silly self-assurance makes a
very poor appeal.

He went on to say that "there are two other factors working in
India that do little good to America." They are Hollywood and
book covers.

I do not contend that [Hollywood] films are reprehensible but
I do say they represent an America wholly artificial, frivolous,
materialistic, and repulsive—a picture of living that is unnatural.
. . . Is this what America claims to provide against the materialistic philosophy of communism?

Admitting that he himself has not seen much U.S. pornographic
literature in India, the bishop pointed out that the Communists,
nevertheless, constantly charge us with pornography and "have real
cause for their complaint," because of the thousands of good books
which are sent to India from the United States "with the most
repulsive and repugnant covers. Again and again I have read Communists' articles in the local papers: 'Is this the culture that America
is going to supply in place of communism?' "
The pity of it is, the bishop stated, that it need not be so. He
expressed himself agreeably surprised at the depth of spiritual life
in America, especially among Catholics. If a picture of that were
exported to the East, we would have an inestimable propaganda
advantage. "I cannot understand," he admitted, "why America cannot be true to her own spirit, to the spirit of her founding fathers,
and to the obvious spirit of the large mass of her people."
It may not be a fact, as Senator Taft recently charged, that the
Voice of America is riddled with "fellow travelers," but it seems
discouragingly true that most of our propagandists have not yet
learned to speak the message that vast masses in the East crave
to hear.   (March 28, 1953)

OUR TROUBLE IN GETTING ALONG
INTERNATIONALLY

Cries from some quarters of "exaggerated," "oversimplified," "one-
sided," and, inevitably, "isolationist" will greet *The Ugly American*,

by William J. Lederer and Eugene Burdick. More than that, it seems likely that it will receive repudiation from some official source, for it is a hard-hitting, scathing, alarming assessment of how the United States all too frequently bungles the vast, complex, and tremendously important business of foreign relations, diplomatic, cultural, and economic. If the book is exaggerated and gloomy, it nevertheless poses some questions on whose solution depends the success or failure of our relations with the non-committed countries, especially in Asia.

The book is presented in the form of fiction, but the authors, who have had experience in the East, state in "A Factual Epilogue" that every instance they depict is based on fact. And what do they present? In a series of more or less connected episodes they dramatize the widespread inability of our diplomats, our economic mission heads, our information agencies to come to an understanding of the people with whom they deal and with the needs of the particular countries. This cultural block arises, first, because of a language barrier. The authors quote James Reston of the New York *Times* (March 18, 1958) as saying that, although "the most important element in a good Foreign Service officer is the faculty of communication, fifty per cent of the entire Foreign Service officer corps do not have a speaking knowledge of any foreign language; seventy per cent of the new men coming into the service are in the same state."

Further, even when language is not a prime barrier, many of our representatives abroad know nothing of the history or customs of the people with whom they are supposed to communicate. This leads frequently to grandiose economic projects, when what is needed in a particular country is often something simpler, which the natives will be able to manage when United States aid may come to an end.

Perhaps an even greater barrier to understanding is the tendency of Americans to live in close-knit groups and in entirely American style—with fin-tail cars, swimming pools, deepfreezers, and so on—which tends to alienate them from the people and buttress the feeling that America is, as the Reds preach constantly, a materialistic country bent only on exploiting the "underprivileged" countries.

Some of the episodes that make vivid these and similar problems are funny, some tragic. However, a sense of balance is given to the alarming picture by the stories of some Americans, diplomats and others, who do get down to grass roots in their dealings with the native populations. In this connection, let it be strongly said that the book is not against foreign economic aid, though it probably will be quoted as though it were. It sees the great need for such aid, but pleads for more practical application to the actual needs of a people.

The crucial problem raised, however, goes much deeper. The authors give many instances in which Russian diplomats and technical advisors are well trained in the language before they come to a foreign country, live as simply as the people do, mix with the populace, go along with strange customs, and, in general, beat us to the public-relations punch time and again. The Red emissaries, in other words, seem to have a sense of sacrifice, of dedication, that we have not to date matched.

What is wrong? We have not presented and do not present, say the authors, foreign service to our young people as anything of a challenge:

> The most recent recruiting pamphlet issued by the State Department (*Career Opportunities*, December 1956 Edition) describes salaries, living conditions, perquisites, and benefits. It shows young people boarding a sleek airplane, headed for their first assignment. It shows Americans shopping in the bazaar at Isfahan, Iran. But it does not have a single word which indicates the work will be demanding, not a single word to indicate that we are locked in a quiet struggle around the world and that recruits will be a part of that struggle. It is a pamphlet designed to attract mediocrities. We believe it is successful.

Many an official in Washington and many a private citizen will squirm resentfully or fearfully while reading this shocker. It is meant to shock—and perhaps deals too simple-mindedly with some large economic and cultural problems, but it can't be too shocking if it rouses us—educators, Foreign Service officials, and ordinary citizens—to a realization that a spirit of self-sacrifice, a real missionary spirit (call it the spirit of '76 if you like) must be recaptured if we are to win this Asian front in the cold war. (October 4, 1958)

U.S. CULTURAL BLOCKS TO WORLD UNITY

America's columns have from time to time called attention to the incontrovertible fact that in the cold war one of the hottest fronts is the cultural front. The fact is, indeed, incontrovertible, but it is too often passed over with a shrug by those who still think that dollars and cents, armaments and tractors are all we have to offer our allies, who, with us, are sincerely devoted to the principle that all the free nations of the world must work in harmony to front and repulse the threat of world communism.

It has probably been thought in some circles that our occasional emphasis on this matter has itself been distorted. What difference in the world does it make, the objection might run, whether India or the Philippines or France or Turkey like our American ways and manners, so long as they remain true allies in the political and military arenas? Paris may feel that American economic and military aid is subjecting *la belle France* to the subtle imperialism of "cocacolonization," but does that weigh very heavily in the international balance? Can this business of a national culture—or the lack of it—be of much concern save to a coterie of "one worlders?"

This very subject was considered in a long editorial in the influential London *Times Literary Supplement*. The writer began by observing that "the present division between East and West has had at least the one fortunate result of strengthening and multiplying the cultural ties between England and America."

One example of this, says the editorial, is the attention given in serious reviews to American novels and books in general, which are lauded for the "freshness and originality" they show to exist in "an allied culture." The favorable reception the *New Yorker* gets universally in England "is a spontaneous approval for the kind of wit and sophistication in which the Americans excel." It is obvious, then, the editorial continues, that "everything reasonable should be done to encourage this interchange, both for its invigorating effect on English letters and for its promotion of common political action."

The segment of the English citizenry which depends on the

Times for guidance in such matters is being told, accordingly, that cultural intercourse between nations does have something to do with friendly, familiar feeling, with community of interest, and hence with common political achievements. It is certainly probable that there is an equal number of United States citizens who think in like manner. Neither the group on this side of the Atlantic nor the group on the other can simply be brushed off by being called a bunch of long-haired dilettantes. They are people who take both literature and politics seriously.

But all is not well in this much-to-be-desired cultural traffic from the shores of the United States, says the *Times* regretfully. "It would be unwise," the journal goes on, "to dismiss as unfounded the arguments of those who contend that much of what America wishes to offer us under the disguise of 'culture' is not only worthless but unwholesome." Such contentions have generally centered around the American film, "the only debatable influence to which we have yet been consistently subjected"; but now the ground has shifted (with all the imperceptibility of a California earthquake) to a full-dress discussion on the effect of "American-type" comics.

This discussion is no mere drawing-room type of chitchat among our English cousins. It occasions the editorial in the *Times*; it has provided matter for many columns of comments in the London *Bookseller*. And it has occupied the attention of no less a body than the House of Commons.

The member who introduced the debate, Maurice Edelman, started by saying that he was not pleading for government censorship, but that he was acutely conscious that something had to be done to dry up the distribution of "this type of sadistic pornography," of which more than 30,000,000 copies are circulated annually—a figure that threatens to bloom into 400,000,000 or more a year as unscrupulous businessmen scent the profits. Mr. Edelman was seconded by another member who, standing on more idealistic ground, said that "unless we are more careful about this matter, it seems to me that the cheap and the sensational will push the finer literature out of the minds and experience of our children." This was all the truer, a third member agreed, because such "American-style" comics are to be had in "all kinds of peculiar places" to which parents and teachers would probably not know their children had access.

The debate thus sketchily outlined did not get very far in the

House of Commons, as Sir Hugh Lucas-Tooth, Joint Undersecretary of State for the Home Department, rather hush-hushed it all with some inconclusive remarks about not exaggerating and about the responsibility of parents and teachers. This seeming evasion by Sir Hugh drew a letter to the London *Times* from a grammar-school headmaster, who charged that the undersecretary "would have difficulty in convincing any body of teachers of the truth of [his] statement" that there was no real evidence of a direct connection between the present high level of juvenile crime and the prevalence of the "American-style" comics.

After adverting to this parliamentary exchange, the *Literary Supplement* editorial goes on to cite another instance where "American commercialism" is not smoothing the way for international co-operation. It quotes extensively from a booklet, *The Strategy of Culture*, by Professor Harold A. Innis, a Canadian, who claims that

> we Canadians are indeed fighting for our lives. The pernicious influence of American advertising, reflected especially in the periodical press, and the powerful, persistent impact of commercialism have been evident in all the ramifications of Canadian life.

As a specific instance, Professor Innis singles out the American magazines, which, "by swamping the market, have forced Canadian publications to imitate them in format, style, and content and have compelled Canadian writers to adapt themselves to American standards."

Professor Innis seems to be a little rough on "American commercialism," to be sure, and the *Times Literary Supplement* tries to redress the balance a bit by pointing out that commercialism is not confined to Americans and American business enterprises. The same fairness was in evidence in the debates on the comics in the House of Commons and in the columns of the London *Bookseller*. Everyone concerned was at considerable pains to point out that the vast majority of the comics read in England were not of American publication. Indeed, British import regulations now ban the introduction of such periodicals from the United States—strictly for economic reasons. Most of these "terrible magazines" are produced right in England or come in from the continent.

But the point is not whether comics and commercialism originate in the United States. The point for serious American consideration and action—where it is possible—is that most of the Western world is coming to pin an unflattering tag on us, perhaps with a certain mixture of reluctance and satisfaction. If that world does it from mixed motives, imagine the unadulterated joy with which the Communist world, for its own nefarious purposes, will affix that same label on the United States.

And what is the label? It is that most of the art and literature that are characterized by brutality on the one side and sentimentality on the other, by grossly materialistic values, by sly or open pornography, are inspired by our United States culture, if not directly produced by it. We now have the world referring to the "American-style" comic; we have the "A-S" pocketbook, the "A-S" war novel. Commercialism is "American." So, as it happens, is "know-how." Can we blame the peoples of, say, India, where religious culture is age old and deep rooted, if they look askance at "know-how" because they fear that it will bring in its train "American" materialism?

There is no doubt, of course, that the brush tarring the United States for these decadent cultural trends is a brush wielded too often by the hand of a jealous nationalism. But the uncomfortable feeling will not subside that, since we are so generally charged with having at least conjured up this embarrassing genie, we must have had some considerable part in his creation.

What can be done about it? We don't want any direct United States Government interference. We don't want any administration to "ban" the export of American realism, American "commercialism," though we do think that such an agency of our government as the Cultural Division of the State Department could well proffer some friendly advice to all purveyors of cultural materials.

What is needed most, perhaps, is the unflagging and self-sacrificing work of private individuals and groups who will make it their patriotic business to see that the real American culture is properly represented on the world scene. That was actually done when the Boston Symphony Orchestra was given standing ovations in Paris, Brussels, London, and elsewhere. Writing in the New York *Times*, music critic Olin Downes remarked how much these splendid concerts had done to convince Europeans that Americans are not—as Communist propaganda would have it—at just about the cultural level of emitting war whoops as they emerge from the forests. And speaking of the many young American artists who had won friendly acclaim at various festivals (Zurich, Brussels, Florence, and elsewhere), he observed that it was doubtful that the Voice of America "has spoken anywhere more eloquently" to the peoples of Europe than did these young cultural ambassadors.

As a matter of fact, there is an organization now functioning which could well look into this business of giving some friendly hints to those who portray American culture for foreign consumption. There is an American delegation on UNESCO (UN Educational, Scientific, and Cultural Organization). One of UNESCO's jobs is exactly that of stimulating and improving cultural relationships among nations. If the United States delegation would officially signify its willingness to co-operate with Hollywood and with United States publishers, with a view to exporting the most representative products—not the sleaziest—of United States culture, the rest of the world might become gradually disabused of the impression that all too many decadent cultural trends are "American-style."   (September 6, 1952)

LITERARY ENVOYS IN TIME OF CRISIS

"Does Europe welcome American leadership?" asked Raymond Aron, French historian and essayist, in a past issue of the *Saturday Review*, devoted to the spacious subject of "America and the Mind of Europe." Mr. Aron's article impressed me as the most thoughtful and challenging of the handful included. It is the most sympathetic and at the same time the most critical. We welcome, needless to say, the sympathy for American ideals and aims in world leadership; it is likely that we will be a little more than inclined to shrug off the criticism. Yet it is criticism that we dearly need to hearken to with humility and not a little soul searching.

Mr. Aron's sympathy is forthright and concisely stated. In brief, he is "entirely convinced that for an anti-Stalinist there is no escape from the acceptance of American leadership. . . . Europe can rebuild its society and insure its political and cultural independence only within the framework of an Atlantic Community in which, inevitably, the United States must hold first rank." Mr. Aron, moreover, is not merely resigned to this fact; he welcomes it.

But not all Europeans, he hastens to add, are of this mind. Some groups, such as the Existentialists, deny the fact or the need of American leadership and would retreat into an unreal "neutrality." Others, and they are probably the great majority of Europeans, would agree to the fact and the necessity, but with great reluctance. And the nub of the reluctance—which ought to sting us to awareness—lies in this: "There is no such thing as lasting leadership imposed against the will of the led."

Why are many Europeans reluctant to accept United States leadership? Mr. Aron treats at some length the distrust widely harbored for capitalism as it exists in the United States, but I don't care to dwell on that angle in this discussion. I would like to focus attention on the cultural alarm set off in many European minds when they are told that the United States is to lead. "Fears are already expressed," says our analyst, "that a militarily and economically dominant America may bring in its wake ideas and institutions unwelcome to the peoples of the European continent."

This reaction is explained in part, runs the argument, by the psychological reason that the at-present humiliated European needs to "cling to his self-respect in the face of the non-European whose aid he is forced to seek; he does so by recalling his centuries of cultural pre-eminence, to which his transatlantic rescuer cannot lay claim." And this psychological reaction receives "palpable and visible" reinforcement "in the fact that you have actually been sending us, together with the best that you produce, an appreciable quantity of gimcrack articles for which your own cultivated citizens manifest no great taste."

And what are some of those culturally inferior and stultifying products which bolster the European distaste to submit to American leadership? Hear this:

> Let it suffice to say that the European branches of your advertising firms, the European circulation of your mass-produced magazines, the taste acquired by millions of Europeans for your comics, your movies, your capsule-culture journalism and crime stories have quite sincerely frightened the European intelligentsia and been taken by them as a threat to serious thinking and disinterested art.

Mr. Aron goes on to single out Coca-Cola, offered as a substitute for the earthen cellar, and other vagaries as further reasons for

Europeans being "properly alarmed" at the prospect of the United States assuming the cultural leadership of the free world.

Now it would be futile and fatuous for us to yield to impatience and say that Europeans ought not be so sensitive and humorless. The point is, if Mr. Aron's diagnosis be correct, that they *are* so sensitive—and understandably so. Nor is it germane for us to claim that the cultural products we export to Europe are, as a matter of fact, not so inferior after all. The point again is that Europeans are convinced that they are bad. We may, for example, defend our comic books as a legitimate expression of one level of United States cultural life, but the average European is not interested in those distinctions—he is apt to read the comic books with so simple an eye that he believes they do portray the general level of our culture.

This is, of course, a thorny problem. And it is nowhere more thorny than in the field of literature. Shall the American writer be restricted as to what aspects of our life he may portray? If so, who is to do the restricting? Would not this open the floodgates to intolerable censorship and thought control? Are United States publishers to be told what books, magazines, and comics they may or may not sell abroad?

Another thorn is the whole problem of the proper reception of literary themes. No intelligent reader, sensitive European or other, should yield to the silly temptation of making baseless generalizations. Superman, Dick Tracy, slick-magazine heroines are not average, representative Americans, but when the European reader meets such characters day in and day out, and by the hundreds, can we blame him if he begins to think that all Americans are thus and so?

This, I believe, is a judgment that must be laid at the door of the late Sinclair Lewis. There is no doubt but that his mordant pen laid bare many of the bigotries and provincialisms of a segment of United States life and pricked us into awareness of the smugness and narrow-mindedness of Babbittry in all its forms. If his satire often degenerated into the ill-mannered snigger that just as surely betrayed his own smugness ("I thank thee, Lord, that I am not as the rest of men"), he still did us a service. But what impression would an average, not too deeply reflecting European get of United States life from a steady reading of Lewis? Was Lewis, then, to have been condemned because he wrote novels that could have been read in such distorting fashion?

Whatever the theoretical answer to such questions in normal times, I believe one solution stands out quite clearly now at a time when Western civilization is bracing itself to withstand the greatest threat to its continuance. That solution, I hold, lies not in the individual artist but in the publishers and distributors of his art.

This, it seems to me, is true because publishers and distributors are more directly in contact with the public and public service— and therefore are faced more clearly with public responsibility— than is the author. The author has his public responsibility, too, of course, but in today's world of mass distribution it is those who direct the distribution who have the greatest share in producing the impression, good or bad, that literary products (comics, pocket-sized books, and the like included under the convenient term) make on the reader.

Publishers and distributors, then, do have a role to play in the shaping of United States foreign policy. On their work depends to no small extent the reception that is being given, and will continue to be given, to our cultural leadership. Nor does this mean that every book, every magazine that is exported for foreign consumption will have to be peopled with American characters that are superbly cultured, admirably pious, and astonishingly manly. We don't even succeed in getting those qualities in the flesh-and-blood ambassadors we send abroad, so we cannot consistently demand them in the literary envoys who represent the United States.

But we do not, I hope, dispatch to the chancelleries of Europe as representatives of the United States men who are uncouth, vulgar, dishonest, lecherous, and physically repulsive. We try to send, I suppose, men who are good, if not flawless, specimens of United States culture and education, of Christian gentlemanliness, if not of Christian piety.

Should not the books that go abroad as envoys portray, by and large, American life in much the same colors? Authors have the right—sometimes, perhaps, the duty—to criticize our social shortcomings and sins, and, indeed, it is one of the proofs of our democracy that we can so criticize. But under today's world conditions, it may well be posed as a question for their sincere consideration whether publishers and distributors have the unfettered right to spread that criticism into circles where it can so readily be used as ammunition for those who, says Mr. Aron, "profess to see in the Atlantic Pact the opening wedge which will allow European cultures to be flooded by an inferior, mass-produced American culture."

This plea, not by any means for suppression of freedom of expression but for a more responsible exercise of it in the areas where it touches on international policy, will not go down easily with publishers and distributors who look only to the profits of their export trade. Those who do realize the importance of the cultural impact of their exports may gain some added heart to face the publishers' international responsibilities in today's death-grip world in terms of the following manifesto. It graces the foyer of one of the most influential publishing houses in the country today.

An honest Stationer (or Publisher) is he, that exercizeth his Mystery (whether it be in printing, bynding or selling of Books) with more respect to the glory of God & the public advantage than to his own Commodity & is both an ornament & a profitable member in the whole Commonwealth. . . . If he be a Printer he makes conscience to exemplify his Copy fayrely & truly. If he be a Bookbynder, he is no meere Book-seller (that is) one who selleth meerely ynck & paper bundled up together for his own advantage only: but he is a Chapman of Arts, of wisdome, & of much experience for a little money. . . . The reputation of Schollers is as deare unto him as his own: For, he acknowledgeth that from them his Mystery had both beginning and means of continuance. He heartely loves & seekes the Prosperity of his own Corporation: Yet he would not injure the Universityes to advantage it. In a word, he is such a man that the State ought to cherish him; Schollers to love him, good Customers to frequent his Shopp: and the whole Company of Stationers to pray for him.

George Withers, 1625

George Withers doesn't, it is true, advert to publishers' responsibility for impressions created abroad, but surely his exhortation that they exercise their trade "to the glory of God and the public advantage," and be "profitable members in the whole Commonwealth" would include a realization that understanding and cooperation among at least the free nations of the world today can be to some degree blocked by dissemination abroad of caricatures of American culture.

A good dose of self-imposed restraint would go far toward convincing Europeans that American culture is not some degenerate fag-end of Western civilization.   (January 27, 1951)

PART TWO

Other Cultural Leaven

Chapter One

THE COMIC BOOKS AND
JUVENILE READING

There is many a sage saying about bent trees and growing trees, about acorns and oaks. These may seem naïve figures of speech under which to approach the whole problem of young people and their reading in these days of advanced child psychology, but the plain common sense of the metaphors commends them to a middle-aged commentator on the American cultural scene.

It must be said at the outset that at present writing the problems posed by the comic books at the time the original articles appeared in America have somewhat subsided. Ever since the comic-book industry took a deep breath and tried to lift itself—hardly by its own bootstraps, but hoisted on a wave of public indignation—above the sensational exploitation of horror, crime, and sex, things have been a little easier in many an American home. But the problem that was so luridly dramatized by the comic books is still, in one shape or another, darkening our cultural doorstep. There is still enough and to spare of suggestive—or, if not quite that, at least worthless—reading material lurking around to entice the young reader.

It is with this thought in the background that I include in this section some modest, I trust, suggestions about the value and the joys of family reading. My hints may sound Victorian and impossibly idealistic, but if we cannot still be idealistic about young people we have sunk deep indeed into the morass of cynicism.

Reading can train straight and nourish the twig and the acorn, if only the planters and gardeners give a thought and have a care.

COMIC BOOKS: CULTURAL THREAT?

In a rather pathetically titled article in *Life*, author John Hersey asked the question, "Why Can't My Child Read?" Perhaps Mr. Hersey asked a little too much. Perhaps his child can read, if not his father's quite excellent novels and reportage (*A Bell for Adano, The Wall, Hiroshima*), at least most of the things one would expect a child to read. But if young master Hersey is indeed somewhat backward in reading, there is at least the possibility that one reason for it is that he "reads," most likely all unbeknownst to father, too many of a certain type of comic book.

This, at any rate, is the suggestion that probably would be made to Mr. Hersey by Fredric Wertham, M.D., psychiatrist, director of children's clinics, author, and most outspoken foe of the crime-and-horror type of comic book, who has published the most exhaustive and devastating study of this kind of comic book that has appeared to date. It is a 397-page volume called *Seduction of the Innocent*, which most definitely should be called to the attention of all parents. If even one third of what Dr. Wertham says is true, then crime-and-horror comic books are a cultural and moral menace to our youth and to the country, and means must be discovered and used which will cauterize the evil. At the very least, every responsible parent ought to be alerted.

It is the purpose of this and a following article to summarize Dr. Wertham's findings, to reinforce them from other sources, and to examine his conclusions about possible methods of control. The present article will deal with the comic books as a cultural threat; next week I shall emphasize the moral danger.

But first, some distinctions and some facts and figures as background. Dr. Wertham is concerned only with comic books, not with comic strips appearing in newspapers. The distinction is vital, because "newspaper comic strips function under a severe censorship exercised by some fifteen hundred newspaper editors in the country, who sometimes reject details or even whole sequences. . . . For comic books there exists no such censorship by an outside agency which has the authority to reject."

Again, it is evident, as Dr. Wertham admits, that there are some good comic books. He does not specifically mention many of them, but he would no doubt include among the good books such comics as the Walt Disney series and some of the "classic" comics, though he has reservations even about some of them. He is concerned, as must be repeated again and again against those who pooh-pooh all his charges, only with the crime-and-horror type of comic book.

These books constitute, at a modest estimate, one fourth (Dr. Wertham says one third) of the 80,000,000 comic books published monthly. These are the figures given by the Senate Judiciary Sub-committee on Juvenile Delinquency during its investigation in New York of the comic-book industry. (I shall refer to the work of this committee later.) It is estimated that the comic-book industry grosses annually $120,000,000.

On a pro rata basis, it appears that crime-and-horror comics gross some $30,000,000 a year. It is truly big business, which appeals to the acquisitive instincts of, among others, various papermaking concerns which supply the pulp. Dr. Wertham wryly remarks that the charge that he is a Don Quixote has some truth in it, except that he is "not tilting against windmills, but against paper mills."

How many children read these 20,000,000 crime-and-horror comic books? Nobody knows. There are some 34,000,000 young people in the United States between the ages of five and nineteen. Suppose just one third of them read such comics and suppose these 11,000,-000 youngsters read them, as Dr. Wertham states regular readers of comic books do, on an average of from two to three hours a day. Does the problem begin to loom up in something like its real proportions?

But is it a problem? That is precisely the question. All these facts and figures have been merely by way of prelude to the real issue. Defenders of the comic books, of all comic books, and those who think that only a tiny fraction of the books are harmful, say that the problem either does not exist or that it has been vastly exaggerated by people of the Wertham school. As far as the cultural effects of the comic books go, they argue, on the positive side, that comic books lead children on to the reading of real books, and, on the negative side, that today's comic books are no worse than the penny dreadfuls and even the classic nursery tales of the past.

What is Dr. Wertham's reply to the first of these claims? Protracted reading of the comic books interferes, he claims, with the purely mechanical matter of the

. . . acquisition of left-to-right eye movements, which is so in-
dispensable for good reading. The eyes have to form the habit
of going from left to right on the printed line. Reversal tendencies and confusions are common among children at the age of
six. . . . The comic-book reader . . . acquires the habit of reading irregular bits of printing here and there in "balloons" instead
of complete lines from left to right. . . . Reading difficulties
among children have increased and are continuing to increase
with the rise of the comic book.

Against this, we have the word of Josette Frank in *Your Children's Reading Today:* "The comics do engender a familiarity with
the written word." More about Miss Frank later.

On the cultural level, says Dr. Wertham,

the responsibility of comic books for reading disorders is mani-
fold. They have prevented and are preventing early detection of
reading difficulties, by masking the disorder and giving parents
the impression that the child can read. . . . They cause disorders by luring children with the primary appeal of pictures as
against early training to real reading; they attract the child just
at the age of six or seven, when basic reading skills ought to be
developed, and again at pre-adolescence, when, on a higher level,
good reading habits should be fostered.

But supposing the comic books do introduce children to reading,
in the purely mechanical sense, would they also be an introduction
to real books, to literature? This has been claimed and still is, especially for the "classic" comics. But Dr. Wertham states:

I have yet to see a child who was influenced to read "classics"
or "famous authors" in the original by reading them in comic-
book versions. What happens instead is that the comic-book
version cuts the children off from this source of pleasure, entertainment, and education. Macbeth [for example] is offered to
your child "streamlined for action." It is a "dark tragedy of
jealousy, intrigue, and violence adapted for easy and enjoyable
reading. . . . Packed with action from start to finish." Shakespeare and the child are corrupted at the same time.

But are not the comic books the children's "folklore" of today?
If folklore is defined as "the oral poetic creations of broad masses

of people," then the comic books, says Dr. Wertham, are "just the opposite":

> They are not poetic, not literary, have no relationship to any art. . . . They are not authentic creations of the people, but are planned and concocted. . . . Can you imagine a future great writer looking for a figure like Prometheus . . . or Dr. Faustus among the stock comic-book figures like Superman, Wonder Woman . . . or Congo Jim?

All in all, Dr. Wertham makes out a most convincing case that the comic books are, as one publisher rather boasts, "retooling for illiteracy." At the least, they do not prove to be a "bridge to books," as is claimed by Josette Frank and many others who have not dealt so extensively with delinquent and backward children as has Dr. Wertham. Moreover, they actually prevent the development of purely mechanical reading habits. "A very large proportion of children who cannot read well habitually read comic books," that is, "they gaze mostly at the pictures, picking up a word here and there. . . . They are bookworms without books. . . . Low-grade literacy is the result."

I do not and could not underwrite all Dr. Wertham's charges. But at least I have never seen a more completely documented indictment. Many disagree with his strictures, but no one, to my knowledge, has adduced an array of actual cases against him equal to his. If those cases convince a reader that comic books—the crime-and-horror comic books, be it remembered—are a definite menace to the proper cultural development of our children, they prove much more convincingly that such books are also a moral menace. This I will treat next week.

Meanwhile, Mr. Hersey, you and others who wonder why your sons cannot read might do much worse than give some consideration to *The Seduction of the Innocent*.   (June 19, 1954)

COMIC BOOKS: MORAL THREAT?

Dr. Fredric Wertham's charges that the crime-and-horror type of comic book is a serious threat to the cultural well-being of the nation were grave enough, I thought, to cause responsible parents to give more attention to what their children are "reading." His further and much more alarming indictment that such books constitute a moral threat surely ought to be a summons to some action that will minimize the danger. That indictment has actually been such a summons, as we shall see, but just what action parents and others can take is still doubtful.

By far the greater portion of Dr. Wertham's book is devoted to this moral threat. It will not be possible here, however, to do more than present in capsule form what he considers the "correlation" between juvenile delinquency and the reading of the crime-and-horror comic books. He has no doubt that there is such a relationship. Children who read such comic books are impelled toward delinquency, and those who are delinquent gravitate to such reading.

Dr. Wertham works up to such a conclusion by easy stages, so to speak. He begins, not by charging that a youngster who reads such comic books immediately rushes out to commit some heinous crime, but by stating that

> . . . the most subtle and pervading effect of crime comics on children can be summarized in a single phrase: moral disarmament . . . [which] consists chiefly in a blunting of the finer feelings of conscience, of mercy, of sympathy for other people's suffering. . . . Readers [of such comics] do not learn about any normal aspects of sex, love, or life.

Once this blunting process has operated for a time (and remember that the average comic-book reader pores over such books for two or three hours a day), the child is conditioned to drink in the "lessons" that crime does not pay and is for that reason alone wrong, that the villains in the story are invariably dark-skinned and therefore some races are superior to others, that women are either gangsters' molls or superwomen who scorn men and therefore there is an ineradicable and sadistic cleavage between the sexes.

On this point of the approach to sex in the comic books, Dr. Wertham is particularly outspoken and particularly convincing. Claiming that "in no other literature for children has the image of womanhood been so degraded," he details (with a section of graphic illustrations) how lurid language, suggestive costuming, sadistic and masochistic overtones appeal to the vivid imaginations of the youngsters. Some of these comic books go so far as to feature apparently innocuous illustrations, which, when partly covered, leave revealed most suggestive nudity. Parents may not know this, but let them not assume that their children haven't heard of the technique.

Catholic parents should not complacently assume that their children do not read these books. Dr. Wertham mentions one parochial school (not further identified) in which a study of 355 boys and girls from better-than-average homes revealed that the school authorities, who assumed that the children did not read the "bad" comic books, were shocked to realize that "under their very eyes many of the children were being seduced by the industry."

Lest it be thought that Dr. Wertham is playing with loaded dice, I have before me an unpublished thesis written (in 1948) by a nun who studied the comic-book reading habits of fourth-, fifth-, and sixth-grade parochial-school children. She obtained an eighty-five-per-cent return on 20,000 questionnaires. It turns out that seventy-five per cent of the boys (and almost as many girls) like comic books for the following reasons: excitement, facts, crime, war, fighting, killing, airplanes, Westerns.

The types of comic analyzed in this study are a cause for concern. They were found to be generally materialistic and godless; they glorified brute force, encouraged un-Christian attitudes, and offended against decency of speech and dress.

The author found that "only five per cent [of the 17,016 parochial-school children surveyed] did not read comics."

A similar survey made by *The Queen's Work* about the same time revealed that

. . . though very few children read no comics at all [the average for all is four a week], most youngsters believe that crime comics teach how to use weapons and commit crimes . . . questionnaires from big cities showed strong preference for crime comics.

This, be it remarked again, is among parochial-school children.

Finally, Dr. Wertham's indictment that crime-and-horror comics are a definite incitement to juvenile delinquency is bolstered by his roster of the various ads in such comics which push the sale of switch knives and judo lessons (so that youngsters can learn to protect themselves, while, of course, also learning how to maim an opponent). Another type of ad plays on adolescent fears and inferiority complexes ("Are you skinny, flat-chested, pimply? Write to us and you will soon be able to beat any boy in the block or outglamour any girl"). This, of course, is old stuff. I can remember when I sent off for "literature" on muscle building, but this generation, says Dr. Wertham, is the first that has had such appeals to juvenile vanity and hopes definitely tied to "reading" that glorifies crime, debases sex, and, at the same time, reaches millions of young readers.

Is there any wonder, he asks, that since 1947, when the crime-and-horror comic book began to be big business, juvenile delinquency has increased twenty per cent? And the chilling thought is not merely that delinquency has grown numerically; it has become graver in kind:

> . . . younger and younger children commit more and more serious and violent acts. . . . Up to the beginning of the comic-book era there were hardly any serious crimes such as murder by children under twelve. Yet there was a war and a long depression. . . . Children [he quotes a judge as saying] still in knee pants, who would have come in contact with the law in former years for swiping apples or upsetting pushcarts . . . are now defendants in crimes of violence.

Much more could be reported from Dr. Wertham's casebook, especially from the hundreds of instances in which he avers that he has traced a direct connection between the comic books and actual juvenile crime. But perhaps what I have cited is enough to lead us into the most interesting and puzzling question: why has so little heed been paid to his startling—if angry—crusade since it began in 1947?

One answer is the fact that the crime-and-horror comic-book industry has organized its defenses well. For every expert like Dr. Wertham inveighing against the cultural and moral threat, the industry could line up two "experts" ready to testify that such books were only today's "folklore," or contemporary Nick Carters. So, for example, Josette Frank, claiming that comic books are "a bridge to books," is revealed as being a consultant of the National Comics Publications—at a salary. Four other similar experts are listed on page 223 of *Seduction of the Innocent.* As late as June 1954, the Child Study Association of America, of which Miss Frank is a part-time staff member, was still trying to justify its connection with the comic-book industry by claiming that it has resulted in the improvement of the comics. To this Dr. Wertham simply asks: "What improvement?"

Another reason for the tardy reaction to the doctor's hair-raising charges has been the reluctance of state legislatures to tackle the problem. There are few such bodies in the country, to my knowledge, which have gone into the problem as thoroughly as has the New York State Joint Legislative Committee to Study the Publication of Comics. That committee was set up in 1949. In 1951 its report stated that

> . . . crime comics . . . published by a small, stubborn, willful, irresponsible minority of publishers . . . are a contributing factor leading to juvenile delinquency . . . instead of reforming their bad practices, the publishers of [such comics] have banded together, employed resourceful legal and public-relations counsel, so-called "educators," and experts in a deliberate effort . . . to fight any and every effort to arrest or control such practices.

In its 1954 report, the same committee stated that "the situation with respect to the publication and sale of objectionable comics within this state remains substantially unchanged since the date of this committee's last report." Well may Dr. Wertham repeat his question: "What improvement?"

The New York committee recommends legislative action, at least to the extent of prohibiting "tie-in" sales, a process by which distributors of comic books force retailers to take a certain proportion of crime-and-horror books in order to get good comic books. Such tie-ins are already banned in New Jersey and Idaho, but many localities are loathe to adopt such measures. A 1948 report on the comic-book situation in New Orleans, for instance, while admitting that one third of the comic books are bad, merely concludes that "co-operation" between parents, the police, and the industry will solve the problem, especially if the publishers will stick to the voluntary code they adopted in July 1948.

To this Dr. Wertham replies that the code is simply a dead letter, since the crime-and-horror publishers will not abide by it. Dr. Wertham is therefore in favor of federal and state control, pointing out that the United States is almost the only civilized country in the world that allows unrestricted sale of comic books. Other countries—England, France, Canada, Sweden, Holland, Italy, Belgium, West Germany—presumably as devoted to democracy and freedom of speech as we are, regulate what is so damningly referred to as the "American-style" comic book.

Needless to say, Dr. Wertham's ideas on control are violently opposed by such organizations as the American Civil Liberties Union, which blenches at the very mention of the word censorship.

Into this dusty and noisy arena stepped the United States Senate's Subcommittee to Investigate Juvenile Delinquency, which was under the chairmanship of Senator Robert C. Hendrickson. After two sessions in Washington, the subcommittee moved to New York, determined, despite pressures from "vested interests," stated Senator Hendrickson, to find out if there is a connection between crime-and-horror comic books and juvenile crime. The findings have not yet been published, but the news reports give some leads.

The subcommittee's work has aroused great interest, much fear, and has already borne good results. The interest is among parents, who, says Senator Hendrickson, show by their letters that there is "quite a boycott of the comics under way at the parent level." Fear has been manifested by some comic-book publishers, who have gone so far as to defend their wares before the subcommittee as being even "in good taste." Finally, when the subcommittee resumed public hearings in New York, a representative of the Newsdealers Association of Greater New York, a group newly formed to combat the bad comics, announced that his association would refuse to handle "lewd, horror, or indecent magazines that may fall into the hands of juveniles."

In these various ways the tide seems to be moving against the crime-and-horror comics. The idea of local legislation—at least to the extent of banning tie-in sales—seems to be gaining in favor. Parents are being alerted. The irresponsible publishers are definitely on the defensive. It is to be hoped that the published hearings of the Senate subcommittee will go far toward dealing the death blow to the crime-and-horror comics. If they do, Dr. Wertham's angry, not well-organized but sincere and truly patriotic *Seduction of the Innocent* will deserve no small share of the credit. May I repeat that it is a book that every Catholic parent ought to ponder.

(June 26, 1954)

HOW TO READ THE FAMILY TOGETHER

If we are correct in our recollection, it was *McCall's* that coined the word "togetherness." The word may sound as awkward and nerve grating as the phrase "like a cigarette should," but the concept—sentimental overtones apart—is sound enough. It denotes the desirability of a certain community of interest, a certain bond of union, especially in families. On the religious level, Father Patrick Peyton has long been plugging the concept of togetherness by his slogan, "The family that prays together stays together." On a less rarefied plateau, we can endorse "togetherness" by observing that a family that reads together is knit together, too.

But togetherness in the summer? This is the one period in the year when individuals in many families are riding off in all directions at once. Perhaps for two or three weeks the family is together away from home, off on a vacation trip. But for the rest of the long summer days, the young people are probably in the house less than during the school year. How can there possibly be any family reading together, when the youngsters show up at home only to gobble a meal and then, sunburnt and exhausted, tumble into bed?

Well, there is a togetherness that does not depend on physical propinquity; it depends rather on a meshing of our interests. A novel and suggestive development of such interest in the matter of reading recently came to our attention in the spring issue of the National Book Committee's quarterly. In the section devoted to "The Development of Lifelong Reading Habits," Richard J. Stonesifer, assistant to the dean at Franklin and Marshall College, Lancaster, Pennsylvania, tells about the college's "book-a-semester" plan:

> The idea in essence is this: each semester the entire faculty and student body are encouraged to read at least one book in common. . . . The intent of the basic idea is also simple: to provide at least one area for common discussion on a campus all too often fragmentized by specialization in a score of different disciplines.

The results were amazing. Over four hundred fifty students bought the paperback edition of D. W. Brogan's *The American*

Character; the next month about seven hundred purchased William H. Whyte's *The Organization Man.*

Can this scheme be applied to the home, with its different age levels? In a modified way, yes. Suppose, for example, parents were to read some one book that John and Mary had read as part of their college work. The book might be Dawson's *Religion and Culture* or Maritain's *Art and Scholasticism* or Father Walter Ong's *Frontiers in American Catholicism* or Ricciotti's *Life of Christ* or Bloy's *The Woman Who Was Poor*—and so on. It really doesn't matter what the book is, so long as it's one that was an element in the young people's training, one that caught their interest and thus offers parents the chance to share that interest.

It may sound infantile, but the sharing of interest can work even on more elementary levels. Many a parent would be amazed and delighted to find that a *Winnie-the-Pooh* or a *Treasure Island,* if read with the desire to find out why the children liked it, will prove fascinating for its own sake as well.

When you get back from the vacation on wheels and the long summer evenings stretch out ahead, sneak into the children's rooms sometime and browse through their books. They will be astonished to discover that you are as learned and informed as they are; more, you will have established a community of interest that will draw your family closer together, and even closer to God. (June 28, 1958)

JUVENILES' ANNIVERSARY

Tales adapted to the child's capacity must go back to Cain and Abel upon Eve's knee, but the first record we have of English juvenile literature, published specifically for the young folk's exclusive reading, is no earlier than 1744. In that year, John Newbery, bookseller, established himself in St. Paul's Churchyard, London, and published the *Little Pretty Pocket Book,* a collection of ABCs, Rules of Deportment, Rhymes and Proverbs, and a series of Letters from Jack the Giant Killer.

Of course, there had been books for children before this. Saint Peter Canisius, to take but one example, had revised his famous cathechism, first written in 1555 for advanced students, into an edition *ad captum rudiorum accommodata* (for school children) in

1556. But Newbery's book is the first in English, at any rate, of what we may call literary books for children.

Since that day, juvenile literature has passed through many vagaries. It has been cautionary, goody-goody; it has drawn from the wealth of folklore; it has reflected the oh-so-scientific horror of modern psychiatrists over the dangers of Mother Goose and fairies; it has stepped from the covers of books into animation on the screen.

But it is safe to say, I think, that all children's literature, until fairly recent times, has always been cut from the same cloth. Stevenson and Kenneth Grahame, the Brothers Grimm and A. A. Milne were all lineal descendants of Saint Peter Canisius and earlier Christian educators and indeed of the First Educator Who wrote no children's books, it is true, but Who must have been a wonderful storyteller for the little ones, of whose like is the Kingdom of Heaven, when they gathered around Him.

For all those who write for children with a love of children have always been interested in values. They have always taken for granted, as part of the heritage of the race, the existence of another world, the importance of being good, the necessity and sanity and glory of the little word "ought." If you would see more at length how this spirit has leavened the whole of children's literature, take down once again Chesterton's *The Ethics of Elfland.*

But a sad and dour modernism has begun, these latter years, to invade this clear-eyed and eager-for-ideals age. No less a person than the brilliant English author, C. S. Lewis, who is by no means interested primarily in juvenile literature, has noticed the trend in his Memorial lectures, given at the University of Durham and recently published under the title *The Abolition of Man.* The whole point of departure for his really profound argument takes its rise from a phrase he found in an elementary textbook intended for "the boys and girls in the upper forms of school."

This phrase or sentence runs as follows: "This confusion [of applying the adjective 'sublime' to a waterfall] is continually present in language as we use it. We appear to be saying something very important about something; and actually we are only saying something about our own feelings." After some pertinent further remarks, Mr. Lewis goes on to say: "The schoolboy who reads this passage will believe two propositions: firstly, that all sentences containing a predicate of value are statements about the emotional state of the speaker, and secondly, that all such statements are un-important."

From this, Mr. Lewis goes on to prove very cogently that much modern education, by making the whole question of values a matter of subjectivism, inevitably sabotages the moral law and debauches the whole of life and action to the level of "what I like."

The argument, of course, arrives at a dismal finality which the ordinary common sense of the majority of people would reject. But the horribleness of the business is that young people everywhere are actually absorbing such principles from which we may not just go on blindly hoping that their inarticulate and unconscious Christian capital may continue to save them. If they once begin to act out the consequences of such principles, then we will have embarked on an era that will truly be the abolition of man.

Children's reading, then, is a vitally important thing. Your children's school reading, thank God, will be protected against such dangers; at least it will if a Catholic school supervises it. But the home reading is another thing, and there parents cannot be too vigilant. And even more important than a censorship of the books that come into the home is the censorship that motherly and fatherly love and the instinct for the faith will supply to the reading and explanation.

Mr. Newbery may not have thought about it at all, but children's books do reflect the age.   (November 11, 1944)

READING AROUND THE HEARTH

Am I wrong, or is it true that lullabies are passé? Do young mothers still sing to their children, or have they learned from the latest book on child care that singing baby to sleep is sure to give him a mother fixation or a repressed desire to grow up to be a crooner? I am not too sure about this—whether mothers still vocalize for their offspring—for I have of late years not witnessed the off-to-bed time of too many babies. But of something else that is akin I am sure: the art and custom of family reading has yielded largely to the radio bedtime story, and children and parents are missing one of life's greatest joys and privileges.

In these days, when we hear so much about all the forces that are tending to break the unity of the home, here is one hearth-centering attraction that ought not be unconsidered. Family prayer is one supreme means right at hand to make the house a home; family recreation and play draw the circle more intimately and lovingly together; and family culture, too, in the form of reading, has its part to play in making parents and children, not in the palsy-walsy, condescending modern way, but in the truly Christian way, friends.

The first and most obvious means of practicing family reading is still in use, praise be. Mothers do still read Mother Goose to the very young ones; perhaps, more rarely, father will have a try at it, and he would more often if he only knew how those hours would be a mutual treasure in future years. But when the child goes off to school and masters the strange art of seeing a whole new world in some funny little black marks on paper, then the family reading days fast dwindle.

This is a shame and a distinct loss. There is no lovelier picture, it strikes me—save a whole family at the Communion rail side by side—than a family in the living room together, mother, father, and the children, from the young teenagers down to the four- and five-year oldsters, listening to and sharing as part of their family life a page or two, or a chapter, of some well-beloved book. We may smile at the daily communal Bible reading in Victorian families, but quite apart from the puritanical spirit that may have motivated much of it, it was sound family psychology and gave a core of interest, a unity of family activity, that our modern "each one do what he pleases" attitude can never obtain.

Beyond the passing pleasure of the hour itself, when mother and father will have the happiness of watching the youngsters' souls mirrored plain and entrancingly on their faces, this reading to children is the surest way to make their own reading fruitful and a joy. It is when children see the pleasure that the parents take in books that they will begin to love to read. Children do not, as Mrs. Annis Duff writes in her fine *Bequest of Wings: a Family's Pleasures with Books*, "just happen" onto a love for reading, because

reading for young children is rarely a pleasure in isolation, but comes through shared pleasure and constant, discerning exposure to books, so that they fall naturally into the category of pleasant necessities, along with food, sleep, music, and all outdoors.

And with the children's gains, the parents who read to them gain, too, for in the fresh response of the young minds, they will see, all over again, the wonder and adventure that lie in the world's great books. Perhaps, in reading to their children, they may become more childlike themselves, and in so becoming, will slough off all the adult prejudices and antagonisms and racial tensions that alarm all thinking men today. For, in that reading, they, too, will enter the "World Republic of Childhood," about which M. Paul Hazard writes in his *Books, Children and Men:*

> Children's books keep alive a sense of nationality; but they also keep alive a sense of humanity. They describe their native land lovingly, but they also describe far-away lands where unknown brothers live. They understand the essential qualities of their own race; but each of them is a messenger that goes beyond mountains and rivers, beyond the seas to the very ends of the world in search of new friendships. Every country gives and every country receives—innumerable are the exchanges—and so it comes about that in our first impressionable years the universal republic is born.

Certainly, even the most rabid Irish nationalist could not read the *Winnie-the-Pooh* books aloud to his entranced little brood without experiencing himself some little feeling of admiration for some aspects of England. Certainly, even the most ardent booster of Jim-Crowism could never read Don Lang's splendid juvenile, *On the Dark of the Moon,* and see his youngsters take the little Negro hero to their hearts, without feeling himself that the color line is an adult distortion, not an instinctive, rooted-in-nature reaction.

Yes, reading to the family, communal reading in the family circle, even when the children verge on young adolescence, is a marvelous means of having the children grow properly older and the parents properly younger, until they meet in that ageless place where family prayer and family fun and family culture all join together to shape and deepen and sanctify family love.

Even when the children are grown and gone and starting their own families to read to, family reading can still play a part for husband and wife. What a pall of silence often settles over those evenings—husband and wife buried in their own reading, or he huddled behind his newspaper and answering in grunts the conversation of his knitting or sewing wife. One couple I have heard of have broken through this wall of family isolationism by getting a book on the Mass, which they read aloud for a half hour or so, and there they have a ground of common interest, there they have a topic of conversation; she may not be too interested in details of his office or in the strategy in the Pacific, which he follows with the keen interest of a Monday-morning quarterback; he may be bored with the doings of the neighbors; but in common reading on a mutual interest there grows a respect for and interest in each other which continually waters the deep roots of love that are, of course, there already.

Beyond this aspect of reading aloud in the family, there is another that is of even more importance. It is supervision of the books that come into the home—for all the ages gathered under the roof. Recently, near the editorial offices where weekly travail brings forth these pages for your delectation, the present writer heard a youngster of fourteen or so, whose countenance gave quite unmistakable signs of his Irish ancestry, shouting to his friend: "Hey! Have you got my book? Have you got *My Days of Anger?*" This happens to be one of Mr. Farrell's least "realistic" effusions, but it is certainly no fare for adolescents. What was the home like, we wonder, into which such a book could be taken?

I can remember the first time, at the age of fourteen or so, I ran across Gray's *Elegy*. It was the most marvelous thing I had ever read; the language kept running through my head for weeks; I clipped it out of the magazine and promptly started a scrapbook of poetry. I added about a dozen others, I suppose, before some other fad engulfed me. Certainly I did not catch all the philosophical overtones of the poem; I missed a great deal of its meaning, but that experience was a real widening of spiritual frontiers. What poem, what book, thrilled you as a youngster? Take it up some day and read it to the family. See if, in recapturing the fine frenzy for yourself, you do not kindle a spark in them.

Many a child at school just does not understand and appreciate the poem, the essay he must read as his assignment. It becomes a mere task he must struggle through. What added life and interest the homework would take on if a chapter, say, of Stevenson's *Travels with a Donkey*, or a section of the *Idylls of the King*, were read aloud, if father were to put down his sports page or the business report he has brought home and say: "All right, son; let's read it together and see what we can make of it."

Idealistic? Well, perhaps so. But, after all, the home is rather an ideal place, if homemakers will keep working to make it so. And it is not really work, for here, too, Saint Augustine was right: *Ubi amatur, non laboratur,* "where love is, is no toil."

Sharing and guidance, then, are two means we have at hand to make family reading, among other things, an antidote to "home is where you hang your hat," that restless, rootless philosophy that governs many a youngster's life, and which many a parent bewilderedly and helplessly fosters by not knowing one of the many ways of making home a source of unfailing interest. Children do not love their home simply because they happen to have been born into it. The making of a home, the fostering of the home spirit is an art; it needs practice and stratagems; mother and father must plan it so; part of the plan should include some communal activity in the world of books. For the family *will* read—why should it not read *as* a family?   (May 6, 1944)

BOOKS THAT FORM THE YOUTHFUL MIND

Hungary and Poland and the recent apocalypse in those countries of the human spirit's unquenchable thirst for freedom may seem a good country mile away from these thoughts on reading for the young. But perhaps a little thought will serve to show that the gap is not so great after all. There is no way of telling what the young Hungarians and Poles who led the revolts had read in their younger years, but I would hazard the guess that they had not read, as their exclusive intellectual diet, the state-controlled publications of the Red regimes.

The fact that some ten years of attempted indoctrination so evidently failed to root out from the minds of the young Polish and Hungarian freedom fighters their love of country and hatred for despotism has been pointed out by commentators as one of the most remarkable phenomena of the current upsurge against Communist domination.

Perhaps the explanation is that even ten years of a controlled press, of slanted book publication, was not long enough. Perhaps it was that the religious and cultural traditions of Poles and Hungarians were still too deeply rooted for even a decade of thought control completely to wipe out. One can wonder now what chances there are for similar revolts within Russia itself, and one feels a sinking sensation with the realization that the Russian youth have been reading, for much longer than ten years, just and only what the Kremlin has wanted them to read. In that long and dread period of intellectual starvation, have all remembrances of freedom and liberty, as literature enshrines and hands them on, faded out among the younger generations of Russians?

This much is sure. Russia is one of the leading publishing countries in the world. We pride ourselves on our literacy, and with reason, but for the 12,000 new book titles a year that we can boast of, Russia can point to some 43,000 titles. Every one of these, of course, comes from a state-controlled press. There are no independent publishing houses in Russia, and if an edition of 50,000—or 500,000—copies of one title seems a good thing for the indoctrination of the people, those editions roll off the presses and are on sale at small cost in all the government stores.

But how do books for youth fit into this picture? This way. One fourth of all books published within the Soviet Union are juvenile books. And every one of the juvenile titles is devoted to the task of warping the young mind into the mold of Communist mentality.

This is why books for the young today are of an importance undreamed of generations ago. There is a fight for the human mind going on, and in this war there are no noncombatants; the very youngest within the orbit of communism's untrammeled influence are being shaped and molded.

American children, too, are having their minds formed. There is not yet—and we hope there may never be—a planned indoctrination that is state-controlled. But in the values we think of as typically and healthily American, children are having their minds set to a way of thinking, and their hearts formed to a way of acting, that will, we hope, fortify them against any future blandishment that may turn them to the Red utopia.

Most children's books are doing that job of helping form the young mind to a healthy patriotism, a sane internationalism, to an awareness of social problems such as racial tensions, minority-group sufferings, poverty, and subpar housing. It may sound pretentious to refer to "books for kids" in these rotund terms, but those are the topics that the better children's books actually deal with. The sweet little stories we may remember from our youth—*Black Beauty* and the like—do still appear, but the vast bulk of current juvenile literature is really serious-minded stuff.

By this it is not meant that the authors of these books are mounting their respective soapboxes and blaring forth their shibboleths in such wise as to frighten away the youngsters who are looking for entertaining, adventure-filled, engrossing reading. The stories, just as stories, are as good as ever, but there is a sense of social responsibility pervading them that was unknown years ago.

Needless to say, this is precisely where the challenge lies for the writer who would produce good books that appeal particularly to the Catholic child. There are a goodly number of such books this season, perhaps more than in the years immediately preceding. But there is still a lack of planned (not by the state, but by Catholic publishers) series of books which will take the youngest reader and carry him along in gradated stages till he is ready to embark on the great profit and pleasure of adult reading. (November 17, 1956)

Chapter Two

WOMEN, ADS, SEX, AND CRIME

What an horrendous collocation of subjects! But if the culture to which our young people are subjected—or which they enjoy—is a matter of concern to the surveyor of the scene, the role of women calls no less imperatively for some consideration. And, unfortunately, in our "sensate" American civilization the media that influence so many of our attitudes equate women with nothing more than sex and call this distortion blatantly to our attention through advertising. And the crime to which I refer is the type of crime that is intimately connected with that emphasis on the triple distortion of women, ads, and sex. Two reflections on the idea and the ideal of authority and respect for law round out these comments which, I fear, will seem unduly acidulous to many.

All I can do to allay a judgment that I am a crusty misogynist, an advocate of the abolition of advertising, a puritanical crusader for the suppression of sex is to aver with hand on honest heart that I do not "underestimate the power" of the first, am as attracted by truly clever and persuasive examples of the second as any other gullible person, and have upheld the God-given sublimity of the third in many of the preceding selections.

But I do firmly believe that if American women universally properly estimated themselves—that is, as God intends them to—there would be less cause to worry about the ads, the sex, and the crime.

So—into this hazardous breach. . . .

MODERN WOMAN—IF SICK, HOW CURED?

Authors have been brooding considerably of late over the state and plight of modern woman. It is becoming increasingly the accepted (by men, anyway) impression that most, if not all, of the ills that afflict modern society can be traced, more or less directly, not to the men, who have made a fairly well-known mess of running the world, but to their mothers. Such authors as adolescently omniscient Philip Wylie lash out savagely at the failure of modern womanhood, notably in his A Generation of Vipers and in magazine articles. A more sober and eminently fairer scholar, Dr. Edward A. Strecker, basing his conclusions on the thousands of young Americans rejected by Selective Service as emotionally unfit, indicts equal thousands of American mothers as suffering from "momism," a disease whose name is self-explanatory.

But by far the biggest, most thunderous gun to be discharged against modern woman is the book, Modern Woman: the Lost Sex, by Ferdinand Lundberg and Dr. Marynia F. Farnham, M.D. It is a large and handsome volume, published by Harper, of 377 pages, plus ten appendices. It has attracted a great deal of attention, with feature reviews in many large papers and one appearance, to my knowledge, on a radio panel discussion. It is an important book, a challenging one, but it is wrongheaded, illogical, and dangerous.

The general thesis of the book is this: there is today in the world a veritable tidal wave of unhappiness, shown by such developments as rising alcoholism, divorce, birth control, rapidly falling birth rate, greatly increased crime rates, and a dozen other manifestations. These all spring from psychological disorders, emotional strains—in a word, neuroses. Modern psychology proves, we are told, that the vast majority of these neuroses develop in the childhood home; the mother is the main influence in this home; therefore, the neuroses and their swelling outward manifestation are directly and mainly attributable to women. Further, instead of recognizing her responsibility and correcting her attitudes, modern woman, through the feminist movement, has vastly aggravated the evil.

To establish this thesis the authors have amassed a staggering

amount of historical background, have assessed the findings of all
shades and stripes of modern psychologists and psychiatrists, have
tried to demonstrate the influence of almost every field of human
knowledge on this problem of modern woman—with the glaring
exception of one field of knowledge on whose omission I shall
comment later.

Now, with many of the conclusions the authors reach there can
be no cavil; in fact, for many of their statements there can be nothing but sincere applause. Perhaps I should be far more accurate if
I said that for many of their premises this is the reaction, for that
is where almost the entire value of the book lies—namely, in diag-
nosing the malady, in pointing out what has to be cured. The
invalidating weakness of the book lies precisely in the conclusions
reached, which are often in total and radical contradiction to the
effect presumably desired.

As a sample of the admirable statements which dot the rather
journalistic pages (the product of Mr. Lundberg's pen, no doubt,
for he is not the psychiatrist of the twain), let me quote:

Despite the supreme importance placed today upon motherhood,
in theory, it is readily apparent to the most casual observer that
the role now carries with it for women few concrete benefits. It
carries with it, for one thing, no prestige whatever, and it has
long been the prevailing mood of the intelligentsia, which establishes patterns of thinking, to look upon it with scorn. The
woman generally conceded to have value in society today, and
accorded the concrete recognitions of value, is much more apt to
be the childless legislator, editor, writer, actress, professional
worker, business executive, and educator than the lowly mother
and Hausfrau (p. 124).

And, carrying on the same thought in more startling style:

Public opinion is uncertain about the value of a woman who has:
1) selected a physically and mentally healthy male to whom she
has wished to remain married and who has wished to remain
married to her; 2) who has successfully reared, for instance, four
physically and mentally healthy children who have found themselves, upon attaining maturity, able to function with satisfaction
to themselves and others, being neither particularly distinguished
nor extinguished; and 3) who in the process has obtained a deep

sense of enjoyment and self-fulfillment. The same public opinion has no doubt whatever about the value of a woman who has, let us say, acquired two college degrees (magna cum laude), written five novels (all good), emerged from three marriages as from train wrecks, given birth to no children (or to two, both obvious misfits and even costly public problems), been elected to the United States Senate and is prominent (noisy, at least) at national and international conclaves (pp. 202–3).

You will note, no doubt, that even in the admirableness of these statements, which are certainly on the side of the angels, there lurks none the less a strain of exaggeration and pontificating—after all, public opinion, if not the vociferous element of it, is somewhat formed by 25,000,000 Catholics and other sincere Christians and Jews who may not be of the "intelligentsia."

Again, there is a lot of good sense in the authors' strictures on the earlier and sillier stages of the feminist movement (which are not even yet fully outgrown). They comment shrewdly on the "deep suicidal destructiveness" of the movement in its drive to "liberate women from the 'slavery' of childbearing," a "slavery," they comment, which women generally have never rebelled against, "for the good and sufficient reason that in bearing children lay almost their whole inner feeling of personal well-being and their vast social prestige" (p. 122).

Further, their remarks on the fact that, as procreation is ruled out of the marital relationship, the very pleasure that nature intends sags or even becomes displeasure is but another way of saying what moralists have been saying in more general terms for ages—that it is intrinsically wrong to distort natural functions, a wrong which frequently reaps its sad fruits even on the physical plane. Lastly, in a quite sensitive summary (p. 317) of the qualities that make for a good mother, we can but applaud the warmth and humaneness with which they pay tribute to the ideals of motherhood.

But, all this having been said for the sake of fairness, the book still remains what I have said of it above.

First, it is filled with historical backgrounds that are either simply not true or distorted in their interpretation. A few samples of untruth:

All the early Christian leaders expressed themselves repeatedly as opposed to sexual relations in and out of marriage and regarded sexual relations as an unqualified evil (p. 68).

Again:

> Originally polytheistic, the Hebrews became monotheistic under the leadership of Moses. . . . An ultra-ascetic cult among the late Hebrews was the Essenes, from which Christianity was directly derived. Jesus was an Essene, although himself not militantly ascetic. . . . Asceticism . . . rests ultimately on nothing more than the desire to appear different, and therefore "holier," nearer to the "true" God, who is true because he is one's own. Asceticism has no more inherent value than priapism, which it really is in inverted form (p. 252).

Examples of distorted misinterpretation abound. For instance, speaking of the revolution in thought that the Copernican theory of the heliocentric universe brought about, the authors conclude:

> If Copernicus was right, then the Church's teachings about the central place of the world in the universe and in the esteem of God were untrue. . . . It was now evident that man's place of abode in the universe was quite incidental to the universal scheme, raising the dark question of whether man, too, might be incidental.

This is an important point in the development of the authors' argument for, according to them, it was the Copernican findings, together with Freud's making even man's "self-opinion" of free will untenable (another untruth), which deprived man of all props of inner self-esteem and drove him ineluctably into the worship of external "progress"; this, in turn, went far in undermining the home and setting up those tensions from which today's neuroses rise.

Now this is a reading of history which is beset with the capital sin of historical interpretation—namely, reading today's way of thinking into the thoughts and minds of prior ages. In all the medieval writing with which I am familiar, there never rises the conclusion the authors draw from Copernicus's discovery. It is true that the physical world was seen more and more to be but a speck in the universe (even that fact had been known to Ptolemy, however), but man and his place under God's providence were never felt to be shadowed by the "dark question" of not mattering in God's

eyes. It was for a later, materialistic generation to draw that untenable conclusion from the physical facts. The authors are saying
that, because they feel that way now, people of the Middle Ages
and the Renaissance must have felt so, too. True history is not
written in this cart-before-the-horse fashion.

But enough of these more or less incidental defects. They are
serious enough and filled with danger for the unsuspecting reader,
but they are not precisely what most vitiates this book. The utterly
incomprehensible thing about the book is its non sequiturs, its
appalling lack of logic. This point is eminently worth dwelling on,
because it is one of the weakest chinks in the armor of the birth
controllers, the planned parenthooders. Arguments from morality
carry no weight with them, but perhaps if other batteries are massed
against them, they may be brought to see the inconsistencies of
their ways. It can be shown, I believe, that ordinary good citizenship cannot be reconciled with the materialistic philosophy that
underlies planned parenthood just as surely as it underlies communism. Let us see if our present authors' fundamental illogicality
does not show that they are certainly not the people to be trusted
with the fate of our future generations.

It is interesting and quite relevant to note, by the way, the simi-
larity between the original Soviet sex program, outlined on page
217 of this book, and many of the planks in the platform of today's
planned parenthooders. The Communists twenty-five years ago
tried what American birth controllers are now experimenting with;
they woke to the practical unwisdom of their ways; our PPs have
not wakened yet. We can imagine with what sardonic humor our
national suicide is being regarded from the Red watchtowers.

The authors are believers in planned parenthood—I hope it is
not invidious to say that Mr. Lundberg is reported on the book
jacket to have one child; Dr. Farnham has two; both authors are
in their forties. This is, in part, what they have to say of the results
of planned parenthood:

> "Natural" sterility apart, the decline in the birth rate [through
> the nineteenth century] stemmed primarily from contraceptives
> and, what is of central importance, from the disposition to make
> liberal use of them (p. 123).

They further admit that

. . . if one of the largest church organizations did not flatly inter-
dict contraceptive appliances, the American birth rate would be
very much lower than it is (p. 291).

Again, they state:

The widespread use of contraceptive measures to limit offspring
—significantly paralleled by sharp rises in infanticide, abortion,
and outright child abandonment—is rationalized in various ways.
[The chief rationalization is economic ability to provide better
care.] Yet so many parents who are economically well off have
only one or two children that the argument falls to the ground.
And in cases of millions of men and women, limitation of
children turns out to mean refusal to have even a single child
(p. 298).

Yet in the face of these admissions, which certainly shriek for
only one solution—the abolishing of dissemination of contraceptive
information—the authors unbelievably state: "We would go a great
deal further than the contraceptionists in advocating the establishment of public birth-control clinics—but for different reasons." For
what different reasons? Why, we would control them for the production of perhaps less children, but certainly of less neurotic children. But the very thing that the authors have established is that
birth-control information cannot be controlled. Whatever the
pseudoidealistic purposes of the clinics may be, people have used
and will continue to use the immoral information for purely selfish
and nationally fatal ends.

What an age of warped thinking is this! Divorce is spreading and
it must be checked. Granted; and how will we check it? Why, by
making it easier to get a divorce. Birth control, from the mouths
of the planned parenthooders themselves, is decimating America
and the whole Western world. And how will we bolster up the
sagging birth rate, or at least hold our own? Why, establish still
more centers from which the paralyzing information can be got as
easily as you call Information on the phone . . . the vagaries of the
human mind are indeed a spectacle for the angels, but then, of
course, there are no angels!

No, the use of contraceptives can be controlled on no basis this
book indicates, and the book itself shows why. "What is of central
importance," the authors have been quoted as saying in the matter

of contraceptives, "is *the disposition to make liberal use of them.*"
(Italics are mine.) They are right, but what they fail to acknowledge is that that disposition is a matter of the will, and when we
have said that (and *pace* Lundberg-Farnham, the human will is
still free), we have said what is absolutely fundamental to the whole
question, not only of birth control but of modern woman and her
place and successful, happy functioning in the contemporary world
—we have said that only religious motives, sanctions, helps, and
fruits will give woman the fundamental guidance she needs.

We have nothing against the positive aspects of psychiatry or
any other science which can clear away the surface rubble of twisted
aims, misjudged impulses, and nervous tensions, but deep beneath
all these must lie, as long as humans are human, the sense of duty—
why, the very thing that will send a woman (or a man) to consult
a psychiatrist in the first place is the feeling that she *ought* to be
a better wife, a better mother.

And yet, supreme illogicality of all, the authors lay down as their
platform at the beginning of the book the demonstrably false statement that

. . . virtually all questions raised about women are deeply practical ones, having little relation to reactionary or progressive attitudes and *even less to do with morals per se* (p. 7, my italics).

But on pages 3 and 4, the questions listed as samples of what
women must determine about themselves and their functions are
at least eighty per cent moral questions:

Should they go in for a career or concentrate on homemaking?
If they marry, should they have children? If they have children,
how many should there be? . . . While unmarried, should they
recognize the authority of their fathers? Unmarried, should they
be freely permitted sexual relations with men? . . .

And so on. If the authors were only on the merest speaking terms
with Catholic moral theology, they would know that precise and
unequivocal directions for these and many another problem that
vexes "modern" woman have been at the disposal of bishops, teachers, parish priests for many a year.

However, and this is the final illogicality of the book, the authors
really attribute no inherent dignity to women—nor to mankind in
general. According to them, that dignity derives "from the tragedy

of man's having attained to acute self-consciousness." This is a purely materialistic and evolutionary concept, and as the authors have logically been wary of accepting the idea of "progress," so they ought to pursue the logic here: if man has attained his dignity through mere evolutionary development, there is no assurance that he will continue to evolve; a devolutionary process may set in at any time, and we may wonder if today's mass torture, concentration camps, secret police, drives for euthanasia, and so on are not indications that the disintegrating slump has already set in. If such devolution is possible—and it is, on the authors' assumptions—then why bother about bettering woman's lot? Within a generation or a century she may be right back where she was, as the evolutionists view her; her function of wife and mother will have reverted to mere animal mating and whelping—and she will no longer be a problem.

There is no alternative. Either womanhood, with its responsibilities and its glories of partnership and motherhood, is maintained on the level that God intends, or it slithers into the gutter, no doubt for the time being; but gutters are made to take care of filth, and tomorrow or the next day the scientifically planned gutters of a materialistic philosophy of women and marriage will overflow with the sad and nauseous wrecks of marriage which such books as *Modern Woman: the Lost Sex* will have multiplied, because, recognizing the evil, they have prescribed a cure infinitely worse than the disease.   (March 8, 1947)

WHEN THEY'RE BAD THEY'RE HORRID

"Not very long ago it would have been regarded as shocking to find girls in their teens reading the kind of books they are now writing." This was the conclusion Robert Clurman reached in his "In and Out of Books" column in the New York *Times Book Review* for August 19, 1956. Mr. Clurman had been discussing Françoise Sagan (*Bonjour Tristesse, A Certain Smile*) and alerting his readers to the proximate emergence of an "American Sagan." The winner of this dubious distinction, says Mr. Clurman, will be eighteen-year-old Pamela Moore, whose novel, *Chocolates for Breakfast*, "contains sections that make Mlle. Sagan look a trifle prudish."

But Miss Moore is not the only contender in what *Time* calls the "Sagan sweepstakes." Messner has published *Peyton Place*, a novel which, according to the blurb, "lifts the lid off a small New England town" and "brings Tobacco Road up north and gives it a Yankee accent." For once blurbs are guilty of understatement; what they should have said is that the lifted lid lets loose a stench that becomes unbearable and that the Yankee accent is couched in some of the foulest language yet to be printed in our uninhibited age.

The suspicion can't be avoided that publishers of such muck have only one reason for spewing it on the public—to make a fast buck. Can it be possible that *Peyton Place* is published in the sincere, if misguided, conviction that it adds a jot or tittle to the world of literature or to a better understanding of life? Between the grossly described scenes of sexual passion, stock characters fill the scene—the atheist doctor with the heart of gold, the young boy warped by a too-possessive mother, the girl from the wrong side of the tracks who spunkily rises to social acceptance—but the scene remains throughout a fetid moral jungle.

Such a book is, of course, not typical of the literary output of American women authors—we still have, thank God, books like *The Nun's Story* which follow the high road of idealism so unswervingly blazed by a Willa Cather. But if *Peyton Place* is not typical, it is sadly symptomatic of one socially dangerous aspect of the exaggerated "feminism" that proclaims that "women are equal to men." Not a few women authors are flaunting an equality in their literary lasciviousness.

The case might well be made that, in proportion to their numbers, American women authors rate higher in pornography than men. No purpose would be served by listing titles here, but to recall such monstrosities as *Forever Amber, The Manatee, Duchess Hotspur* may help to bring home the point that Jane Jones yields nothing to her male counterpart in her ability to shame and shock us from here to eternity.

The expression that "a drunken woman is much more disgusting than a drunken man" is an unfortunately valid commonplace in modern society. It is also true—and becoming more of a commonplace—that when a woman sits down to write salaciously, she bolsters the old adage about the female of the species. And even more indicative of a moral breakdown in society is the eagerness of some publishers to market such work and the general lack of outspoken moral indignation by critics and reviewers.

Those who believe and hold as an ideal that little girls can be very, very good have the duty to protest when they're horrid.

(September 22, 1956)

CLEAN UP THE ADS

To Eric Johnston, president of the Motion Picture Association of America, Inc., we recommend a campaign. Let neither Mr. Johnston nor the industry suspect that we are trying to lay an unwarranted burden on them, for the need for the campaign we want was suggested by Mr. Johnston's own words in his first annual report. While reaffirming the industry's pledge "to maintain its high moral standards in films," he declared that the voluntarily adopted codes governing film content, titles, and advertising were "an enlightened policy of self-discipline based on the solid foundation of respect for common principles of morality and decency."

Now, those are fine phrases and worthy of applause but, as a sorry matter of fact, whatever be the self-discipline of the industry in the matter of film content, the advertisements that spread their allure over the pages of our newspapers and on the billboards leave much to be desired. Open your paper to the movie page this night or any night in the week. You will find without fail that what you have is a spread of not-too-subtle sexiness. Even films that are themselves relatively free of that taint will be advertised with the most suggestive pictures.

It may be asking too much to inquire why all movie ads cannot be as simple and in as good taste as those which announce the attractions at New York's Radio City Music Hall, but it is not asking too much to expect the industry to set about a cleanup of this aspect of the business.

Hollywood owes this duty to the people of America. It owes the duty first of all to those who go to the films and owes it to those who may never set eyes on a screen, but who are still assailed with lurid and suggestive scenes whenever they pick up their newspaper. There has to be some protection from this sort of thing, for the sake of family life. You may keep the children from attending movies you suspect, but it is rather an impossibility to keep them from the daily papers.

The Legion of Decency and other review agencies exercise no influence in the matter of controlling the ads. This is the industry's sole responsibility, though, of course, the newspapers could show a greater measure of restraint in the ad copy they accept. But Mr. Johnston has issued his assurance that moral controls will be continued. We wait with fingers crossed to see whether that will apply to the ads as well. It ought to. We suggest that Mr. Johnston take a look at the movie page of his favorite paper and see what he honestly thinks.   (April 6, 1946)

ADMEN URGE CLEANUP

You may have noticed that *America's* columns have over the past months been waging a running battle against suggestive ads, especially of motion pictures. We have been particularly concerned that so distinguished a paper as the New York *Times* would countenance such ads. Apparently we are not the only ones to feel this way.

Variety, the weekly show-business magazine, reports that Vincent Redding, manager of the *Times'* advertising acceptability section, feels that "some of the ads . . . have exceeded the boundaries of good taste." The *Times* has accordingly "invited a small group of persons associated with the industry to gather with us at an informal meeting and discuss the matter," with a view to "readying a cleanup job."

That's good news—and there is more. Two trade magazines, *Printers' Ink* and *Advertising Agency*, have come out with blasts against sexy ads. Writing in AA, George Moses said that the ads for Bestform products have passed the limit of good taste; Hal Stebbins stated in PI that the Sarong ad campaign has been "offensive," as "bold and brazen as you can make it," violating "all the laws of taste and sensitivity."

The British reading public got a glimpse of the worst kind of American advertising in an illustration in an issue of the London *Bookseller*. It portrayed Jayne Mansfield, ensconced in her bath, reading a copy of *Peyton Place*, noxious best seller.

This, says the *Bookseller*, is one of several occasions in the film *Will Success Spoil Rock Hunter?* (Twentieth Century-Fox production), in which a copy of the book is plainly visible. "No prizes are offered," the journal concludes, "for correctly guessing which film company has bought the rights to *Peyton Place*."

This sort of tie-in between a current film, a "star" famous for more (or less) than acting ability, and a book almost universally singled out as one of the smelliest of our times is in exceedingly bad taste.

A domestic cleanup of ads is highly desirable. Let's also clean up those we export. The impact of our films abroad would be much more in keeping with the aims of our foreign policy if admen gave some thought to the harm they are doing in foreign parts.

(August 31, 1957)

MOVIE ADS AND DECENCY

Two ripples do not make a tidal wave, but when the calm surface of the advertising industry is roiled by two tremors in the same week, we suspect that there must be some greater turmoil beneath the surface.

Advertising Age, "The National Newspaper of Marketing," has delivered a stunning one-two punch against suggestive and misleading movie ads. The first was by advertising consultant James D. Woolf. He quoted at length and approvingly from a monthly advertising newsletter, "Baker's Dozen," published by Lynn Baker, Inc. The newsletter blast was called "A Disgrace to Advertising" and said, in part:

If the advertiser of a manufactured product should grossly misrepresent his wares—and if, furthermore, he should fill his ads with smirking hints of salacious satisfactions in his products— he would speedily be disciplined. . . . Yet such practices are openly tolerated . . . in certain printed advertisements for motion pictures. . . . No mature reader will take such ads seriously, but they are taken seriously by the impressionable young. . . . Misrepresentation is added to unhealthy titillation.

The charge continues: "It is thus far a reproach to the advertising

fraternity that the voices which are making the most energetic protest are from outside our own business." Bosley Crowther's New
York *Times* column, excoriating the ads for the films *Lust for Life*
and *The Bad Seed*, is instanced as one of the outside protests. Moreover, "the examples cited by Mr. Crowther are not isolated. You
can find comparable examples on almost any newspaper page carrying movie advertising."

In calling for self-control by the advertising fraternity, the account concludes:

> It is strange that highly respectable newspapers, which would
> question a single dubious word in a 14-word classified ad, will
> print some of the stuff submitted to them by motion-picture
> advertisers.

In the same issue, *Advertising Age* carries a humorous account
by Clyde Bedell of how the ad for *The King and I* was concocted
so as to hint at suggestive situations that never appeared in the film.
Movie ads, says Mr. Bedell, are "the slippery eel and the corner-
cutter of top rank in advertising."

Three of these four professionals may never have heard of the
Legion of Decency or of the National Office for Decent Literature
(NODL). Mr. Crowther has and suspects both of being un-
American. But would not all four, by their own standards, be im-
pelled to agree with a recent statement of Bishop William A. Scully,
chairman of the Bishops' Committee on Motion Pictures?

The bishop stated that while the number of pictures rated *B*
(objectionable in part) or *C* (condemned) by the Legion has de-
clined, the intensity of objectionableness has deepened. This was
particularly evident in the advertising of many films. These "lurid
and sensational details" and the "obvious dishonesty through misrepresentation," Bishop Scully proclaimed, call for "immediate
remedy by the motion-picture industry, lest our films here and
abroad be characterized as a complete glamorization and deification
of the flesh."

The purposes of the Legion and the NODL are as American as
decency and honesty ought to be. It would be good to hear those
who mistrust the organizations say just once, and for all the world
to hear, that they agree at least on those goals. (December 8, 1956)

BARDOT AND THE ADMEN

Which paper do you read? It doesn't matter much. The more sensational United States press, the in-betweens, and the dignified journals have all been for some time regaling their readers with titillating bits about one actress (?), Brigitte Bardot. This is not by any means the first time that a so-called French bombshell has deafened our eardrums, but we doubt that ever in the history of movie advertising has a second-rate actress, who has nothing to offer save a certain disproportion in anatomical make-up, been given such a build-up—something she needs least.

Ever since *And God Created Woman* (the coy asides on this title insist that the devil created Brigitte Bardot) began to gross all-time highs at some "art" theatres, the press seems to have abandoned all restraint. The problem now becomes more acute since the rights to the Bardot pictures have been taken over by a major United States distributing agency. What was a minor pestilence now threatens to become a major scourge. Your neighborhood theatre will soon be plastered with posters enticing you and your children to come and see the lady who "breathes sex in a bikini."

The astonishing thing is how the more responsible press in the United States has succumbed to this offense to good taste. We might perhaps expect *Confidential* or daily counterparts of that delver into sewers to run suggestive text and pictures. But what is our verdict when such a paper as the New York *Times* violates its own standards? We have admired that paper for years for the reticence with which it treats sex crimes in its news columns. Names of attack victims are never given; in the Lana Turner case, the lurid love letters were admirably played down in the *Times* news columns. But in its movie-ad columns, the *Times* frequently runs text and pictures it would ban from its news columns. Why the double standard?

The *Times* is on the record as having "advertising acceptability standards." They are contained in a little brochure at hand as this is being written. "The chief purpose of the *Times*' advertising policy," we read, "is to protect the reader." Under this general rubric, we find category number six: "Advertisements that are indecent, vulgar, suggestive, repulsive, or offensive." Whatever the Bardot ads are, they are without doubt vulgar. Does the *Times* have no responsibility to "protect the reader" from vulgarity?

If this indictment seems to come down particularly hard against the *Times*, it is because we expect more from a newspaper that publishes "all the news that's fit to print." Cynics have twisted that noble slogan to read "all the news that's print to fit." We don't believe that the *Times* tailors its news columns just to fit, whatever the objective truth of the matter. We are coming to feel, however, that the *Times'* movie-ad columns are getting to be such as to give us fits. The same can be said for the displays that debauch the similar columns in the New York *Herald Tribune*. Is this the first wave in the movie industry's campaign to recoup its waning business? Is it no holds barred from now on in?

We don't believe we are asking too much. If there is any journalism in this country that is bound to set standards, it is the type of journalism represented by the New York *Times*. Why can't we go to the movie-ad columns in that journal with the same confidence we feel in reading its news coverage?

"Bardolatry" is scarcely a healthy cultural influence. The press that panders to it is denying its claim to be a good influence on United States taste and public morality.   (May 10, 1958)

PANDERING TO PRURIENCE

Sexual Behavior in the Human Male was the first in a series of books based on an extensive study of the sex habits of Americans. The study was conducted by Dr. Alfred C. Kinsey and a staff of assistants at the University of Indiana; they have had the sponsorship of the National Research Council and financial support of the Rockefeller Foundation's Medical Science Division. It has been claimed that the book is strictly scientific and that its findings and the ultimate conclusions of the entire series will be an invaluable addition to our knowledge of the actual status of sex, as against generally accepted suspicions, hopes, impressions, and superstitions.

The sound conclusions of genuine science are part of God's truth and as such are never to be disowned, flinched from, hushed up. But there is a vast difference between the recognition and use of scientific truth by those who have a legitimate interest in it and its helter-skelter popularization among those who have no ground for interest save curiosity. As well might one popularize for the masses a strictly scientific treatise on the compounding of poisons. It is not that sex is a poison—it is one of God's most noble creations, but the aberrations of sex can be poison; and certainly what this age needs is less emphasis on sex, not more.

These observations are forced on us by the fact that Dr. Kinsey's scientific work was plugged for best sellerdom just as though it were any ordinary book designed for general reading. A stream-lined article on it appeared in *Harper's* magazine, an issue of '47 carried another potboiler, which adds the refinement of quoting various state statutes of "crimes against public morals," some of which, even under their legal terms, are detailed enough to suggest experimentation to the prurient. Other magazines which brought the book to wide public attention were *Science Illustrated, Readers' Scope, Look,* and *Newsweek.*

We say nothing here on the value and integrity of the book itself. It may well be a monumental, pioneering, epoch-making work, as is claimed. What we do question is the ethical justification of such advertising in national magazines which reach the home, fall into the hands of adolescents, of the mentally immature, on whom the book itself will have one of these two results: either the study will be so scientific, with charts, graphs, technical language, as to be unintelligible—and hence the merely curious reader will have been duped into buying it; or it will be intelligible and, by the very nature of the subject it treats, suggestive—and hence the curious reader will be stimulated into a course of thought and action against which he, above all, needs to be steeled.

It is too late to annul the irresponsible ads; there should be none in the future.   (January 3, 1948)

MAKING THE COUNTRY KINSEY-CONSCIOUS

Three facts cast around Dr. Alfred C. Kinsey's long-promised *Sexual Behavior in the Human Female* an unpleasant miasma of sensationalism, whatever may be the intrinsic scientific value of the book. It is standard practice among publishing houses to request that their books not be reviewed until after publication date. However, a select group of reporters and commentators were allowed to see advance sheets and write reviews of no more than 5,000 words as early as one month before the publication date—provided their copy was cleared with Dr. Kinsey and his staff. The publishers and Dr. Kinsey, it seems, were not willing to let the book stand or fall on its own merits, but were angling for the hurried, uncritical, and often sensational support they must have foreseen, particularly in the daily press. It was a rare paper that had the courage not to run a preview—a paper like the San Francisco *News*, which declared: "It is impossible to publish this material for those seriously concerned with the social sciences without pandering to the taste of a great many others whose interest is mainly pornographic." The second fact is that Dr. Kinsey, a scientist, was by this bold promotion method most unscientifically giving a vast public his conclusions first and not even offering the grounds on which he based them till a month later. Finally, as the previews indicated (and Dr. Kinsey's earlier book, *Sexual Behavior in the Human Male*, betrayed), scientific objectivity goes out of the window with the constant insinuation that moral standards are purely relative, that anything becomes "right" if enough people do it. We have no doubt that the book has some scientific value; we deplore the hucksters' approach in its promotion.   (September 5, 1953)

NORMAL ISN'T AS NORMAL DOES

One of the most controversial figures of our age recently went through the normal process of dying. Dr. Alfred C. Kinsey, author of *Sexual Behavior in the Human Male* (1948) and *Sexual Behavior in the Human Female* (1953), had been damned by many, lauded by perhaps an equal number, and objectively and fairly assessed by some few before he succumbed to a heart ailment at the age of sixty-two. It was regrettable, when his books were stirring up a furor, that some of those condemning him were simply obscurantists, who believed scientific research had no business prying into a private matter like sex habits. Truly scientific work in this delicate field does have a legitimate place and can prove an

invaluable help to clergymen, social workers, law-enforcement officers, and the like.

On the other hand, much of the praise that was lavished on Dr.
Kinsey seems to have been ill-founded. It is still doubtful, to say
the least, that his method of research was scientifically trustworthy.
As Charles Wilber, himself a biologist, remarked in *America* for
October 3, 1953, when commenting on Dr. Kinsey's second book:

> Dr. Kinsey and associates make use of the method of the public-
> opinion polls. The work is garnished with impressive statistical
> treatment of the results, but all the statistics in the world cannot
> make scientific an essentially uncontrollable interview method of
> gathering information.

This fundamental and devastating criticism has often been
repeated, as in *Kinsey's Myth of Female Sexuality*, by Edmund
Bergler and William S. Kroger.

Granted the validity of research into sex habits and granted that
even a basically unscientific method may have chanced on some
useful suggestions for future investigation, the question still remains
whether Dr. Kinsey's work tore down more than it built up.

In one most important aspect the whole bent of Dr. Kinsey's
work did incalculable harm by giving countenance and even "scientific" respectability to an utter misuse of the word "normal."
Statistical norms are a valid tool in scientific research, but they
cannot be employed as an arbiter of morality. In Eskimo culture,
for example, female infanticide by exposure may have been statis-
tically "normal"—that is, since so many infants had been so exposed
in the past, such and such a number of exposures might be anticipated for the future. But the practice was never morally "normal"—
in accordance with objective standards or norms of right and wrong.

Such confusion in the use of the word "normal" takes on a particular virulence in these times when the word "democracy" is also
used with considerable looseness. If democracy rests on no more
solid basis than a flimsy philosophy of the "common man," then
any mode of action that is uncommon will be suspected of being
undemocratic. Transfer this woolly thinking to the field of morals,
and whatever is commonly—"normally"—done will little by little
become the morally acceptable thing. Right and wrong will become
a matter to be determined by a counting of noses. But not all the

noses in the world, though they were as prominent and determined as Cyrano's, can determine the norm of morality.

(September 8, 1956)

SENSATE SOCIETY AND CATHOLIC OPINION

Veteran Harvard sociologist Pitirim A. Sorokin has long been an outspoken critic of what he has called our "sensate" civilization. He has insisted in his earlier works (Social and Cultural Dynamics, The Crisis of Our Age, Reconstruction of Humanity) that in such a civilization

> . . . the force of many religious, moral, esthetic, and social values that taboo all premarital and extramarital sex relations has been progressively weakened . . . and many of these inhibitive values have been replaced by values that commend and recommend a freer satisfaction of sex passion.

A "vast body of evidence" is at hand, claims Mr. Sorokin, to prove conclusively the replacement of "the dominant medieval (religious) values by the sensate (secular) values during the past five centuries."

Mr. Sorokin's latest work is an explosive little volume, The American Sex Revolution. In it he weighs what is happening to Western, and particularly American, society as a result of the long dominance of these "sensate" values. He begins with an examination of the extent to which we are deluged with sex. Literature, the arts, radio and TV, advertising, social, and political customs are all passed in review. The reader who begins in a skeptical mood will more than likely find himself persuaded that obsession with sex colors all American cultural life to a much greater degree than he had realized.

At the door of this unbalanced and unhealthy obsession Mr. Sorokin lays a great part of the responsibility for broken homes and marriages, irresponsible and delinquent children, the general breakdown in public morality. The indictment is so sweeping and uncompromising that some may charge the prosecution with gross exaggeration. To this Mr. Sorokin would respond that the very fact that we are unconscious of the sex saturation to which we are subjected proves the insidiousness and mortal peril of the "sexualizing" process. "Most peoples and leaders of decaying societies," says Mr. Sorokin mordantly, "were unaware of their cancerous sickness."

Even if Mr. Sorokin's observations are only half right, his studies throw much light on how a "climate of opinion" is formed and how that climate inevitably affects our day-to-day action and general mores.

It is at this point that Mr. Sorokin's latest work takes on particular interest for the Catholic. If we believe that Christian ideals of private and public morality can and must act as a leaven in the world, then we must face the fact that they will be operative only when held and professed corporately—by all of us as a body. Here precisely is the deeper purpose of such agencies as the Legion of Decency and the National Office for Decent Literature. The moral rating given to an individual book or picture is indeed important for the guidance of action, but far more important is the work of forming the corporate right thinking that will stand as an unbreached bulwark against the forces of "sexualization" and "sensatism."

Mr. Sorokin quotes (p. 130) a striking phrase from Gandhi: "The future is for the nations that are chaste." Under this test, he harbors grave doubts about the future of America. But if Catholics were united as a body to resist progressive "sexualization"—even where sin is not involved—how much the Church in this country could do to assure America's future!   (February 9, 1957)

A QUESTION OF AUTHORITY

The Truman-MacArthur controversy, though terminated in official hearings, still bubbles and seethes in the emotions of many a partisan. The torrent of charge and countercharge, recrimination and diatribe it released have, it is true, subsided. But the very fact that they were released ought to impel any serious-minded citizen to withdraw a little into the depths of his own conscience and take some thought on the restraints which Christian morals place on criticism of public officials.

A column in *America* drew attention to the easy and dangerous practice of imputing motives to the statements and actions of public figures. "Political criticism," it was remarked, "ought to be restricted to observable conduct, without questioning anything as unobservable as personal motives. . . . Those who engage in such tactics give ground for questioning their own motives."

It is true, of course, that when a man takes public office his actions become, as it were, more "observable." A wider sphere of his actions is opened to public scrutiny; he forfeits some of his privacy. But his intentions and motives, unless they are clearly discernible in the actions, are his own responsibility, for which he will have to answer to his own conscience and to God. To trespass on that privacy of a soul is a violation of justice and charity.

The fundamental reason for our present-day reckless imputation of motives is rooted deeper, it would seem, than in a failure in justice and charity. These fail because another foundation has not been laid or is being undermined. That foundation is proper respect for authority. I believe that charity and justice with regard to public officials fail because there is a growing disregard for authority and a forgetfulness of the source from which authority springs. I believe further that Catholics, who ought to have the deepest realization of what authority is and the keenest reverence for its source, are too often changed by some strange and debilitating alchemy into the most blatant, if perhaps unwitting, flouters of civil authority.

How many times, for instance, have you listened to discussions in family gatherings, in locker-room sessions, in business meetings, that centered around "that man in the White House?" When F.D.R. was "that man," the remarks, I need hardly recall to you, often waxed positively vitriolic. He was a hypocrite, a fraud, a Groton-Harvard-educated Benedict Arnold. The unfortunate marital adventures of some of his children were openly adduced in such discussions—as they are still openly bandied about in the splenetic columns of Westbrook Pegler—as proofs of a personal moral flabbiness that unfitted him for the duties of the presidency. Even the physical handicap of polio was stated in knowing whispers to have been a manifestation of an afflicted brain.

Now that "that man in the White House" is H.S.T., admittedly a less colorful figure than his predecessor, one might have expected the invective to be more moderate. Perhaps it is in some circles, but the chorus is still raucous and alarming. H.S.T. was labeled a pip-squeak, a nonentity. The fact, to be sniggered over, that he had the bad fortune to fail as a haberdasher is sufficient proof that he is a disgraceful President. Because he has a pleasant-looking daughter who apparently makes a nice impression in her travels abroad, H.S.T. is a shameless exploiter of his own flesh and blood for the build-up of his puny ego. And the fact that he wrote a letter to a music critic (foolishly and impulsively, to be sure, but certainly not un-understandably to any man who has a daughter of whom he is proud) is enough to prove that the Marshall Plan, the Atlantic Pact, and all the other monumental achievements of the administration must be silly, sinister, and un-American if "that man" had anything to do with them.

Divergent political philosophies notwithstanding, the fact remains that the President of the United States has his authority vested in him by God, following the free determination of the people. As President he has the right to the respect of every citizen; every citizen has the duty to respect him.

Let's look back at some fundamental truths we once heard in the catechism and have heard again and again if our ears have been open to papal pronouncements on the question of civil authority. Civil authority is a moral power, that is, the power to impose obligations on citizens with respect to the proper goals of civil society —the temporal welfare of the citizens. Toward those who are vested with this authority we have the duty, says the catechism, "to show respect, fidelity and conscientious obedience; to pay taxes imposed by them; to assist them in their dangers and necessities." We sin against them by "hatred and contempt; by reviling and blaspheming them; by refusing to pay the taxes due to them; by resistance and rebellion; by any sort of treason, violence or conspiracy against our Government and country."

These duties arise, papal pronouncements say incessantly, because civil authority has its source in God. Examples could be multiplied almost endlessly, but perhaps the words of Pope Leo XIII in the great encyclical *Immortale Dei* will suffice: "Hallowed in the minds of Christians is the very idea of public authority, in which they recognize some likeness and symbol, as it were, of the Divine Majesty."

The purpose of this authority is the common good, namely, to order the activities of the many groups that exist under the common authority. The purpose of authority is not its own aggrandizement, but the good of the subjects. For that reason, subjects, in respecting and obeying authority, are actually serving their own good, for they are the beneficiaries of its proper functioning.

But is this a "hallowed" concept in the American Catholic mind? Are the official pronouncements of the President—and of other officials, too, in their degree—accepted with spontaneous respect? Or are they hooted at, sneered at, belittled, and smeared, and for no other reason than that they come from "that man?"

Perhaps the most disturbing thing about all this whittling away at respect for authority is that it is poison for the young. It's a poison that's not hard to detect at work in all too many Catholic homes. Here is a young boy, let us say, who, during the New Deal years, listened to his impassioned (and thoughtless) father throwing the book at F.D.R. His father, thinks the boy, is a smart man; he knows what he is talking about. After years of such biased indoctrination, what are the chances that the boy will not have the attitude that all authority is just a "racket?" Presidents, senators, representatives, Supreme Court judges—they're all alike, just a bunch of phonies, in it for their own laurels or their own pockets. Anybody who is crazy enough to get into politics is openly confessing that he loves to wallow in dirty waters.

Perhaps the eloquent father always kept in mind the essential distinction between the man and the office, though he never expressed it. He was not—oh, by no means—criticizing the President as such; he was criticizing the man. It's a valid distinction, to be sure, and one Catholics ought to keep clear, for we have had to use it once in a while in answering charges that there have been bad Popes and unworthy priests. But what chance is there that the impressionable boy will make that distinction?

And why should the youngster confine his contempt for authority to the top levels his father has been debunking over the years? Why won't the boy reduce it to action in more immediate spheres? Why not show his contempt for the policeman on the beat? Any time he can get away with something under the nose of the cop, is he not putting into practice what has been pumped into his subconscious mind for years?

And finally, consider the dangerous boomerang the father has been fashioning. For he, too, professes to have authority. But why should his authority be respected, if none is respectable?

Public officials, of course, are not immune from criticism. The proper bounds of just criticism are difficult to define. How far can legitimate and necessary faultfinding go before it verges on contempt for authority?

Here are three considerations that may help set the boundaries and keep us from the slippery path that ends in contempt for the civil authority that, under God, is established through our own consent to provide an orderly government.

First, criticism of policies ought never to be based merely on dislike of personalities. Policies are adopted to meet human needs. Fair criticism must be based on an objective estimate of the needs and an informed evaluation of alternative solutions. Again, it is extremely unlikely that either policies or administration are ever wholly vicious or, for that matter, wholly flawless. The critic ought to try honestly to see what is good and what is bad in each, remembering that, until clear evidence is found to the contrary, the presumption is in favor of policies adopted through the exercise of legitimate authority.

Second, it should be remembered that the people have a right to elect a senator, for example, who will disagree with the policies decided upon by the legislature and find fault with their administration. He ought to accept the decision of the majority. At the same time, wherever decisions are reversible, he is within his rights in working for their reversal. Unless a critic makes a career of carping, his animadversions should not be dismissed on the assumption that a program we favor is ideal in every respect.

Third, criticism should always be made with the clear realization that the critical object of your wisdom and eloquence is an official who has his authority ultimately from God.

Have no fears that a thoughtful observance of these cautions will result in an obsequious kowtowing to all and any authority. The result will rather be a sturdy—if watchfully critical—loyalty to the legitimate authority we ourselves have chosen.

The same natural-law principles which give just governments the authority they need to govern also gives citizens the right to protect themselves against unjust policies and tyrannical governments.

Most of us would like to feel this refreshing breeze of temperance fanning out first of all from the halls of Congress and the political rostrums. One begins to wonder how any American will ever learn to respect authority when he witnesses many in authority acting and speaking as they do. But that is precisely the test of the grasp we have on the principle of authority. When we can see its splendor

and its source through the abuses that at times soil it, then we are
the loyal and faithful citizens that our catechism, the papal pronouncements, our American tradition, and informed common sense
tell us we ought to be.   (September 22, 1951)

Chapter Three

CENSORSHIP, MOVIES, TV

Ban a book (especially in Boston, it used to be said) and its popular success is assured. Hint that a certain motion picture is naughty and human nature responds, "I wonder." There is a certain resentment that naturally arises when we are told "don't," though the naturalness of the resentment is no guarantee that it is rational.

"Censorship" is the awful word we have been hinting at. There is no word in the English language at present—at least in the United States—that will more readily rouse the hackles of defenders of the "democratic way of life." There is, to be sure, censorship and censorship, but frequently the unreasoning detestation of all and any censorship rises from an inadequate grasp of what law is, and especially of the coercive aspects of any and all true law.

The first portion of what follows were essays toward a rather complete treatment of censorship on the American scene, which I ventured in Catholic Viewpoint on Censorship *(Hanover House, 1958). I must refer the reader to that book for a fuller development of the subject than he will find in the following samples.*

There follow a few observations on the motion pictures and TV. I would like to observe here that the movies, despite their rather recent decline in mass popularity, still front us with vast moral and cultural problems which are merely touched on here. As regards TV, my original tremors that we would rapidly become a nation all eyes have subsided a bit. The one-eyed monster in the living room has not yet killed reading, not even among the young. The quality of what we get on TV is another thing. For a penetrating discussion of this aspect of this particular cultural medium, I commend to my readers a provocative book, The Image Industries, *by William Lynch, S.J. (Sheed and Ward, 1959). I wish I had thought to say —or thought to think—many of the incisive and profound things on American culture to which Father Lynch will treat you.*

IS ALL CENSORSHIP INTOLERABLE?

Censorship is a hard word, and who can bear it? Nobody, said the American Library Association, gathered in convention at Atlantic City, June 14–16. At least this was the mind of the ALA as reported on consecutive days in the New York *Times* by Benjamin Fine, and finally summarized in the Sunday, June 20, issue. Mr. Fine claims that at the library convention "censorship of any kind, whether by church, government officials, or private individuals, was denounced vigorously." Judging from the earlier reports of the convention by Mr. Fine, this conclusion seems much broader than the premises, since in all the actual statements by librarians and guest speakers that Mr. Fine recorded there was no condemnation in such absolute terms. The statements of all speakers referred constantly to "improper," "undue" censorship.

However, though Mr. Fine may have exaggerated the consternation of the librarians, there was consternation. The American Library Association members roused themselves to a proper frenzy during the convention and departed for their homes determined that they were going to do something to stop the trend toward censorship which they seemed to discern in the current American scene. In view of the association's large alarm and of its very slipshod and even demagogic appeal to "freedom of speech," it seems in place to spend some time reviewing what must be fundamental principles in any consideration of "censorship" and its relation to freedom of speech.

The first principle that must be kept in mind is that freedom of speech is not an absolute freedom. That is to say, it is not a freedom which can ever be totally divorced from or uninfluenced by other factors. In a legal sense, "freedom of thought" is much wider and much more absolute. Though I am not morally justified in thinking whatsoever I please, under American law I can think whatever I wish. I may think that the thing this country needs most is an immediate armed revolution, but at the very moment I try to say this I find myself in conflict with a circumstance that curtails my freedom of speech, namely, the law of the land. Freedom of speech, therefore, in so far as it is a legal right, finds itself subject to the checks and balances of legal duties and hence is not an absolute right.

The law of the land, then, is one factor that modifies absolute freedom of speech. Are there other circumstances which legitimately modify such freedom?

Yes. There are at least two. The first is what we may call our social environment. People are today much concerned with tolerance between racial groups, with anti-discrimination, with good will and good Americanship. In this situation, though there may be no laws on the statute books to that effect, a man may not, nevertheless, say exactly what he thinks without regard to the social environment. An author may be convinced in his own mind that it is a scientific fact that Negroes are an inferior, degenerate race. Quite aside from the moral evil of such a viewpoint, in some country or other he might be free to say that Negroes are inferior and degenerate. In this country, under present circumstances, he is not free to say it. Or, if we want to be pedantic, he may be free to say it, but those whom he has maligned are likewise free to take steps to correct the saying as far as they can. Since in all likelihood they cannot force the author to write a book proving the contrary thesis, the only means at hand is to do what they can to have his book denied circulation.

If such an action on the part of the defamed group is to be labeled censorship, so be it. Actually, it is not censorship at all. It is a limitation of freedom of speech imposed by social circumstances on an author who has abused that freedom. If we care to go further and hold that our hypothetical author still has a right to his freedom of speech, then we must likewise hold that the maligned racial segment has a right to defend itself against lies. In the conflict of these two presumed rights, there has to be a settlement for the common good. The peace, harmony, and well-being of the country may depend upon such a settlement.

Third, in addition to the law of the land and social environment, there is another factor which conditions freedom of speech, and that is simply the factor of truth. Here again, hewing to our line of legality, there is nothing criminal in a man's teaching in a book that two and two are five, or that George Washington was in the pay of the British king. If he does so teach, however, his freedom of speech is subject to objective criticism, and there is no question of censorship if a book which patently teaches untruth is protested against by individuals or groups who know and wish to propagate the truth. We are faced once more with the prime consideration that an individual's right to say what he thinks is always subordinate to the common good. It is much more important that the public read the truth about mathematics or George Washington than that an individual author be free to exercise some hypothetical freedom of speech in their regard.

I imagine that the majority of the librarians meeting in Atlantic City would very probably agree with these general principles. What exercised them most, it seems to me, was the problem—and it *is* a problem—of whose responsibility or right it is to try to apply the general principles above. Perhaps the following paragraphs may clear this up to some extent.

Any group or organization which, under American law, has a legitimate end is also granted by American law the right to employ any legitimate means to attain that end. If such a group or organization, then, feels that the attainment of that end has been jeopardized by a book, it has the right to take legal means to have correction made. Much as we detest communism, for example, it is the legal right of the Communist Party (in states where the party is legal) or of the *Daily Worker* to protest a book which sets out to prove, let us say, that it is part of the Communist creed that non-Communist infants should be roasted and eaten. If such a protest by the Communists succeeded in removing such an untruthful book from library shelves, it would be stupid to let our detestation of Communists stampede us into saying that they were endeavoring to saddle us with censorship.

Under the principle that a recognized body can adopt legitimate means toward achieving a legitimate end, it follows that the government, for example, may, through some proper arm, such as the FBI, protect itself against books whose clear purpose would be to indoctrinate readers concerning the desirability of armed revolt. It is within the competence of the National Association for the Advancement of Colored People to take legitimate means to have books removed from library shelves which teach objective untruth regarding Negroes or incite to passion and prejudice. It is perfectly legitimate and American for a Catholic diocese to work to the same end regarding books that infringe upon its right to achieve its legitimate ends by legitimate means.

In this connection I should like to quote the statements made in public hearing in Newark, New Jersey, at the time the banning of the *Nation* from Newark public schools was being discussed. In all the furor which was stirred up in the columns of the *Nation* at that time, the *Nation* never once showed a spirit of fair play by actually quoting the grounds on which the superintendent of schools in Newark "banned" the magazine. (As a matter of fact, the magazine was never banned—four issues of it were removed from some students' libraries; it continued to be at the disposal of teachers.) The *Nation's* account of the whole controversy presented it as a religious issue. Here is the real issue:

For the past four years the Newark school system has been devoting its best efforts to the development of a program of Good Will and Understanding in Improved Human Relations, with the unanimous sponsorship of the Board of Education. . . . The Newark schools have given leadership in this field to the State, as recognized by the State Department of Education, Rutgers University and other educational institutions. On June 27, 1947, the Board of Education adopted a resolution formally setting forth the devotion of the school system to the principles of democracy and denouncing all subversive attempts to undermine the democratic way of life.

In line with the foregoing, the following statement is presented to indicate the background for the withdrawal from the students' libraries in four high schools of [the *Nation*].

1. It is the accepted philosophy of American public school education that the teaching of all religions is prohibited by the public school; furthermore, it is a recognized principle that the discussion of the pros and cons of the religious doctrines or dogmas of any sect is taboo within the school. As a corollary, any literature which has for its objective the propagandizing of principles and arguments for or against any religious faith violates the neutral position of the school and, therefore, should not be employed by the school in the training of American youth.

The *Nation* was withdrawn primarily because, in three successive issues, it featured anti-Catholic articles by attacking the doctrines and dogmas of the religion practiced by thousands of Newark high-school students. These articles, which contained false and derisive statements, were an insult, not only to the Catholic high-school students but to their parents as well.

2. The *Nation* not only features articles by a recognized anti-Catholic writer and lecturer, but this magazine apparently intends to continue its steady attack upon the Catholic doctrine. . . . With all of these there is no quarrel. Any magazine has the full privilege and right to set its own editorial policy. However, publications that are patently anti-Catholic, anti-Protestant, anti-Semitic, anti-Negro or anti-American have no place as teaching or reference materials in a public school where adolescents of the community are being educated for social unity and the American way of life.

This, I hold, is entirely American and entirely irrefutable. The Newark superintendent of schools, I hold, was doing a service to American thought when he reminded the *Nation* that its "freedom of speech" should have been tempered by the whole American social environment of good will, understanding, and co-operation. He was reminding the *Nation* and others that freedom of speech is not an absolute right. Whether or not the Newark decision was the best possible on tactical grounds is another point.

As a matter of fact, the American Library Association convention, despite its perturbation at the specter of growing censorship, by no means even approached a solution of the problem. One section of the "bill of rights" adopted at the convention insisted upon "the responsibility of the American library to provide adequate and accurate information on all sides of current questions." Obviously, then, it is not the responsibility of the American library to provide inadequate and inaccurate information. If one specific group of American citizens can spot a book which deals inaccurately with its aims and purposes, is it not performing a service to American librarians when it endeavors to prevent such distortions from being widespread? Otherwise, how are we going to have what the Library Association itself prescribed—a truly educated American public?

These observations by no means solve the problem of censorship, of restriction of speech in books and its relation to freedom of thought. Together with the American Library Association, I deprecate a great deal of indiscriminate book banning, particularly in individual bookstores. I must admit, on moral grounds, that many a book should be withheld from indiscriminate distribution; but the raids on bookstores by vice societies and similar organizations always manage to spread the evil they would curtail. These observations will not be of much assistance to harassed librarians who find themselves assailed by individual irate parents, or groups of them. But it may be that the above observations will serve to produce some fundamental thinking on the rights and wrongs of censorship.

What the Library Association succeeded in proving was merely that librarians at times yield too quickly to protests by various groups; but we cannot, under our American way of life, deny these groups their right to make a protest. If the act of protesting is to be called censorship, it is certainly an extension of the term. Those who do the practical censoring are librarians (or libraries) who remove the books from their shelves, stampeded by the protest.

It strikes me that the Library Association, instead of considering, as it did, the drastic step of blackballing libraries which yield to censorship, would have done a much more practical and democratic thing had it set up committees in each state, whose function it would be to receive legitimate protests, adjudicate their worth in the light of some of the principles I have mentioned, and then issue a policy statement on individual cases as they arise, for the guidance of all members of the Library Association.

That, I think, would have been a much more fruitful resolution than the large, spread-eagle but meaningless statements that censorship is to be deplored. Some censorship—though I prefer some such word as selection or limitation—is implicit in our American Constitution itself. Other censorship is unavoidable due to social conditions. Still further censorship is implied in the very concept of education, for education is concerned with truth; untruth may not be presented under specious credentials. (July 3, 1943)

THE CENSORSHIP PROBLEM CRIES FOR CO-OPERATION

Readers of Harvey Breit's column, "In and Out of Books," in the New York *Times* (June 24, 1956) perused four long paragraphs devoted to praise of a very high order indeed. The subject of Mr. Breit's laudation was an article by Reverend John Courtney Murray, S.J. in the June-July issue of *Books on Trial*.

"The best statement on censorship we have read—and we are not qualifying . . . [spoken] with a courteous logic that is rare and illuminating," is how Mr. Breit characterized Father Murray's treatment of the thorny problem. "What is happiest about the article, 'Literature and Censorship,'" Mr. Breit concluded, "is that it is just the kind of thinking we need, and too frequently do not get from our philosophers and theologians, to give most of us who are thrashing about in the immediate politics a view of the problem— and a possible solution—from a timeless morality."

It is impossible to do justice here to Father Murray's careful thought, especially when he deals with the most acute aspect of the problem, the "censorship" tried or achieved by private groups as distinguished from strictly legal censorship. Mr. Breit's concluding remarks, however, suggest a rather important topic for our further reflection.

We believe that it is not the philosophers and theologians (at least the Catholic ones) who fail to come up with "a view of the problem—and a possible solution," but rather those who consistently cry havoc when the very word "censorship" is mentioned.

Father Murray sets down as a principle, for instance, that in a pluralistic society such as ours, "no minority group has a right to impose its own religious or moral views on other groups, through the use of the methods of force, coercion or violence." He then goes on to contend that, though the use of "informal coercion— economic pressures, etc.," may be "incongruous" or imprudent,

> it is not possible to prove the position, taken by some, that an action like the boycott of a moving picture is somehow "unrightful" or "unconstitutional" or "undemocratic." No one can show that such an action lies beyond the limits of a primeval American right to protest and object.

But month after month the *Censorship Bulletin* of the American Book Publishers Council lists censorship actions taken by various private groups (frequently enough Catholic). True, the *Bulletin* is careful to report that such and such a campaign was "to obtain the consent" of newsdealers not to display certain titles. But it usually gives the impression that this consent was arrived at through implied threats of economic coercion, which take on, in the *Bulletin*, the connotation of being "undemocratic" and "un-American."

Father Murray is but recalling the constant mind of the Church when he states that the justification for any social restriction lies in the preservation of a higher freedom. The Book Publishers Council and others who combat censorship incline to the view that any restriction threatens a higher feedom. Both sides agree on one thing: the necessity to protect a higher feedom. What is that higher freedom and how may it best be protected?

We suggest that the answer to that question can be approached calmly, courteously, and democratically, if only the Council and others concerned with censorship would avail themselves of the co-operation of many who, like Father Murray, are equipped to "speak from a timeless morality."   (July 7, 1956)

REVIEWERS AND CENSORS: I

It is time, I think, to put in a word for Catholic literary critics and book reviewers. Theirs is a profession that is by no means overcrowded and their efforts to evaluate the cascading volume of contemporary books, particularly fiction, from sound literary and moral principles deserve all the encouragement and constructive criticism possible. Instead, I notice in some critics of the reviewers too much of a readiness to interpret Catholic reviewers' efforts as being spineless compromises with worldliness.

This castigation of Catholic critics is occasioned, in great part, by the diversity of opinion in the Catholic press on the moral quality of many contemporary books. Novels like *So Little Time, A Tree Grows in Brooklyn,* and *Blessed Are the Meek* are condemned in some journals, ignored in others, given qualified approval in still others. I do not maintain that this confusion is a good thing in itself; I do maintain that its effects have been viewed too alarmingly. Certainly no Catholic needs to be told that fellow Catholics, and even priests, can have different opinions on the matter of the practical application of moral principles. To expect any strict and undeviating unanimity of agreement in the critical judgment of modern books would be to predicate either that Catholic critics don the robes of infallibility when they pick up their pens or that they are subject to a rigidity of intellectual regimentation that fore-stalls any honest difference of view.

Nevertheless, these diversities of opinion have had one bad effect that far outweighs, I feel, the lamentable but inevitable confusion that may result among the laity when priest-critics disagree. This bad effect is the defeatist attitude which says, in effect: "All this disagreement that crops up about the morality or immorality of modern fiction and which is aired in the discussions of the various critics is a confusing business. The one way to solve it, therefore, is to have no more discussion."

This, I think, is not an oversimplification of the case. Two articles have appeared which seem to boil down to just about that. They are important articles because their influence will be widespread; they deserve examination and comment because if their influence spreads far enough, not only book reviewing but the possibility of conducting English courses comes to an inglorious and intolerant end.

The first article, "Evaluating the Critics," appeared in the *Homiletic and Pastoral Review*. In it, the author, the Reverend Kilian J. Henrich, O.F.M. Cap., decided that all the disagreeing Catholic critics need a common norm on which to judge the moral quality of modern fiction. That norm, he feels, can be found, and found in only one place, namely, in a study of the methods of the ecclesiastical censors. Critics ought, he stated, "ask themselves when in doubt: 'would an official censor give the *nihil obstat* to the book as it is?' They should act according to the answer. . . . No critic should express his personal opinion without regard to the mind of the Church." The use of this norm is imperative, he stated, because of the "obvious and growing tendency in the appraisal of novels to make them acceptable to Catholics by all kinds of debatable reservations," such, for example, as the inclusion of qualifying phrases like "for adults, for mature, for discriminating readers, for those professionally interested." This is but shilly-shallying, he contended; the Church knows no such method of dealing with books: the Roman Congregations "approve or condemn; they know no zigzag middle way with published books."

This proposed norm I find to be not only utterly impractical but even dangerously misleading. Before discussing it, however, I should like first to register a protest at the implication that the Catholic reviewers whom the author is evaluating pay little attention to the mind of the Church in their criticism. The problem of applying moral principles to specific books is thorny enough, at times, without having the issue beclouded by calling into question the priestly zeal of the reviewers and their devotion to the Church and its ideals. It might be asked in passing whether the National Legion of Decency, sponsored and supported by the whole hierarchy, also betrays a lack of proper deference toward the mind of the Church when it makes use of such qualifying phrases as "unobjectionable for adults, objectionable in part" in the rating of motion pictures?

However, the real difficulty with the so-called norm is that it is no norm for the evaluation of the ordinary contemporary novel. This is so because the average novel of today simply does not fall within the scope which the Church has set for itself in the condemnation of books. If and when the Congregation of the Index determines that the danger to souls is so general and pressing that any and every book that deals with sex, for example, must be forbidden, then Catholic critics will faithfully agree. But until such an eventuality, it must be remembered that the Church, in the categories of prohibited books, condemns outright only those (note that I am discussing only the matter of immorality in fiction) that are *ex professo* obscene.

This does not mean, of course, that one may read any and every book that does not happen to be obscene from studied aim and intent. Many books may still be too lurid and vivid, even in passages that are totally incidental to the general theme, to be read by most people without immediate temptation. But the fact that the legislation on prohibited books restricts its explicit condemnation to such *ex professo* obscene books does certainly mean that in judging books of lesser potential danger there is a certain leeway, a certain twilight zone, so to say, wherein critics, all equally zealous, all equally devoted to the spirit of the Church, may differ.

Father Kilian's practical norm, then, seems to me to leave the problem just exactly where it was before. This is inherent in the nature of the Church legislation on forbidden books, for that legislation is aimed at establishing general norms, whereas the problem that faces the reviewer is the specific problem of *this* particular book. To ask oneself whether the book, as it stands, would be granted the *nihil obstat* is by no means to appeal to a workable rule, for the answer will be dictated by the reviewer's own particular bent, taste, and judgment, the very tools that he uses today and which give rise to the contemporary disagreement.

The proposed norm, then, is impractical; it must be, for it is based on a wrong assumption that the Church does not make use of distinctions in its prohibitions of books. It does distinguish; by the very fact that it does not formally and explicitly consider a whole vast class of books (those not professedly obscene), it leaves the judgment on these books free to be determined by circumstances of person, place, environment—all the elements that go into a moral evaluation.

Further, this attitude in criticizing literature I feel to be dangerously misleading. It is so because it is too utterly simple; it reduces this moral problem (and I am, please God, not minimizing it; I know the dangers that lurk in it) to the too easily contrasted black and white. In practice it works out so blandly and insidiously that its proponents come to feel that if you read A *Tree Grows in Brooklyn* you are a bad Catholic; if you don't read it, you are a good one. This is not an exaggeration; witness the too open implication in the article under discussion that the Catholic critics being evaluated are actually falling but little short of compromising with immorality. This is another facet of that false perfectionism that can take easy root among Catholics—to praise with reservation a book that contains one minor moral blemish is to encourage pornography; and an analogous attitude can be discovered in political and social spheres, as well as in the cultural one.

I remarked earlier that such an approach not only stifles any literary discussion of current books but it also would effectively put a stop to most of our English courses. If my primary and indeed almost exclusive criterion of a book is that it is either good or bad, with nothing in-between, and that its goodness or badness depends mainly on whether there is illicit love in it, then Virgil is bad, and Shakespeare is bad, and even the sacred Scriptures themselves are bad.

And of what use is it to ask: "Would the ecclesiastical censors give the *nihil obstat* to *Othello* or to the *Canticle of Canticles* as they stand?" If it is true, as the author remarks in the second of these articles—which I shall take up for discussion later—that there "is nothing intermediate" between what is good and bad in books, and if it is true that whatever is bad in a book vitiates the whole book, then I find it difficult to recall a single book in the whole field of English literature that can safely be used in our courses. Not all the classics treat of sex, of course, but there are other badnesses than that which would also exclude them from the curriculum.

I am fully aware of the pastoral difficulty that Father Kilian is trying to solve—the problem of books unsuitable for adolescents finding their way into their hands; but it is no solution to the problem to keep the books from the youngsters by putting an unfair burden on the adults. And it is simply not true that because an adolescent cannot read a certain book, *ipso facto* and unequivocally all adults fall under the same ban.

Actually, there is further Church legislation in the matter of dangerous books that goes beyond the general categories established in connection with the Index. I shall discuss that more detailed legislation in a following article, as it is the basis of Father Kilian's second article. The discussion thus far has aimed only to show that if we go to the source of all the regulations of Canon Law limiting and restricting the reading of books, we shall not find there the practical norm that Father Kilian desiderates for the evaluation of the greater part of the so-called spotted books. It is not there, because the Church—as far as our discussion has taken us at this point—simply did not care to include that type of book under the general rules.

Apparently the Church believes that Catholic critics can be trusted to think together with Her while using their own best judgment.   (December 9, 1944)

REVIEWERS AND CENSORS: II

Having laid down as a norm for Catholic book reviewers the mind of the Church as shown in her legislation on prohibited books, Father Kilian J. Henrich, O.F.M. Cap., has discussed in the *Homiletic and Pastoral Review* a specific Roman document which, he has asserted, puts a definite end, once and for all, to the matter of "compromising" with spotted books. Let me first, however, before going on to examine that document and its bearing on the question, restate the conclusions of the first of these two responses to Father Kilian's stand. The conclusion was that the Index legislation, by the very fact that it centers its attention on books that are *ex professo* obscene, actually does, therefore, leave room for discussion, for qualification, about books that do not clearly fall in that condemned class. The mind of the Church, accordingly, as shown in the restrictive legislation, can be and must be a general norm that Catholic book reviewers regard always; of its very nature it is not a specific blueprint of the judgment on this or that particular book, and that, of course, is what Father Kilian desiderates.

Leaving that wider field, then, Father Kilian has come more to grips with the problem (and be it remarked again that I hope that I am not underestimating that problem) in his second article. Here he has a document which seems to offer him the *ad hoc* set of rules he desires all reviewers to follow, so that there will no longer prevail a diversity of judgment among Catholic reviewers about the same book, much, he feels, to the confusion of souls. The document, which may be found as one of the introductions to the later editions of the *Index Librorum Prohibitorum*, in the original Latin, or in English in Father T. Lincoln Bouscaren's translation (*Canon Law Digest*, 1917–33, pp. 687–91) is an "Instruction on Sensual and Sensual-Mystic Literature." The Instruction is aimed at "that type of literature which exploits sensuality and lust, or even a certain lascivious mysticism." Such literature is the product of writers who

> depict immodesties in flaming imagery, relate the most obscene details, sometimes guardedly, sometimes openly and shamelessly, without the least regard for the requirements of modesty; they describe even the worst carnal vices with subtle analysis, and adorn them with all the brilliancy and allurements of style, to such a degree that nothing in the field of morals is inviolate.

Even worse than this, the Instruction continues, is the type of literature in which the authors do "not hesitate to give to their sensuality the appearance of rectitude by blending it with sacred things. Into their stories of impure love they weave a sort of piety toward God and a very false religious mysticism." The official document then goes on to say that no excuses will justify this type of literature, not the excuse of elegant style, nor of psychological insight, nor even the excuse that vices are depicted only to be reprobated. No such intention on the part of the author "can prevent the readers who, owing to the corruption of nature, are usually very weak . . . from being gradually enmeshed in the allurements of those unclean pages."

This is, of course, an official guide and as such is binding on Catholic reviewers. It is an important document, and in this discussion the farthest thing from my intention is to minimize its importance. But it is one thing to recognize the importance and weight of the law and quite another to apply that weight indiscriminately and lightly to cases where its application is, to say the least, doubtful. This remark is not a matter of my own private interpretation; the spirit and the letter of Canon Law itself is that restrictive legislation is to be interpreted at its minimum, not at its maximum.

Now, from this document, Father Kilian derives some conclusions that seem rather wide. "From this," he states, "it appears that a classification of objectionable books as spotted, for adults and for the educated, cannot be maintained, because these discriminations are based on excuses which are invalid." Further, "the Holy Office clearly disapproves of all excuses and subterfuges sometimes found in Catholic publications or issued in pamphlet form palliating and compromising with evil in books."

The Instruction clearly does no such thing. What it is clearly talking about, to use its own words, is literature which "exploits sensuality and lust," which "depicts immodesties in flaming imagery," which "relates the most obscene details." It is a literature whose "unclean pages deprave heart and mind"; it is "a deadly literature, a filthy literature."

Now if Father Kilian fears with any justification that Catholic reviewers and Catholic publications fail to recognize that type of literature for what it is, then the Catholic press and the Catholic conscience in this country are indeed in a parlous state. What grounds he may have for thinking that Catholic reviewers are thus blind to their duty, I do not know, but it is a charge to be most cautiously made.

I am most willing to agree with Father Kilian that the far greater proportion of present-day best sellers are books of no particular worth, but the fact that so many of them are not immortal nor even a manifestation of good craftsmanship, the fact that many are a supreme waste of time, is no reason for giving the impression that the same amount of them are "filthy, degrading, deadly." Such indiscriminate fulminations, leveled at "modern literature" in general, only serve the purpose of bringing the very law that is invoked into disrepute. If every traffic violation had to be tried before the United States Supreme Court, the importance and weight of that tribunal's decisions would soon be dissipated; there are some (minor) violations in modern books that have to stand before the judgment of the individual reviewer, because they simply do not fall within the scope of this more solemn law.

So much for the general interpretation. When Father Kilian essays to use the Instruction as a rule of thumb for this or that particular book, he leaves the problem advanced not one whit. The beginning of his second article remarks: "What is good or bad in books (there is no intermediate degree) seems to be in Catholic periodicals more or less a matter of private interpretation, although actually such is not the case." And it is no longer a matter of private interpretation, he concludes, because of this Instruction. But is it not clear as sunlight that however plain the Instruction be, however uncompromising, however strong and severe, the particular and troublesome question at issue is always whether this book that I am reviewing actually does fall under its castigations? That application must always remain a matter for the private interpretation of the individual reviewer, unless, of course, the authority of the Church, whether diocesan or universal, steps in and removes the particular book from the field of discussion. But until that time comes—and it is doubtful that it ever will with sufficient immediacy and comprehensiveness to cover the current output of books—the reviewer cannot humanly do more than trust his own judgment, informed and guided, it is true, by what he fervently hopes is his most inmost devotion to the mind of the Church, but his own individual judgment still.

Several incidental remarks in the article under discussion also call for some comments. Father Kilian states that "books which are even partly objectionable (often referred to as 'spotted') may not be used for any legitimate purpose, because these ends can be reached by good books." The generalization here made, as this whole discussion may have shown, just cannot be that flatly stated, but apart from that, the reason adduced is not universally true. There are many ends that can be reached by partly objectionable books which are not, as a matter of fact, reached by "good books." *Othello*, for example, is partly objectionable, for the simple and unvarnished reason that its imagery, as scholars have pointed out, is predominantly concerned with sexual intercourse, but the end, the impression, the artistic and spiritual catharsis of the play, is *Othello's* own unique possession.

Finally, Father Kilian's one open contradiction puzzles me. After having stated that "there is no intermediate degree" between what is good and bad in books, he later admits that "naturally, there is a degree in the bad parts found in a book." If there is such a degree in the bad parts, then does it not seem rather logical that there can be a degree in the condemnation passed? And if there is a degree in the condemnation, are we not right back to the use of those "compromising" discriminations—"for adults," etc., which it has been Father Kilian's intention to eliminate?

No, as one moral theologian remarked in an issue of *Theological Studies*, in discussing this whole question of morality in modern literature, the answer is not quite so simple. "Father Kilian," he says:

> . . . found a great deal more in this Instruction than I can find in it. His interpretation of it, and of the problem itself, seems over-simplified to me. His object is to put an end to compromise and settle the whole problem with one sweeping generalization. I wish that the solution to moral problems were as obnoxious to complete simplification as he appears to consider this one.

So much for the disagreement between Father Kilian and some other Catholic book reviewers. I think I can assure Father Kilian that the fact that we do disagree will not shock Catholics and perplex souls. After all, most Catholics have got, at times, opposite advice in Confession, diverging practical applications to a perplexing problem, and have not felt that either priest was denying principles or compromising with them. As long as moral guidance, yes, and even the sacraments, are given and administered by human, fallible instruments, there will always exist this perfectly understandable possibility of conflicting views on questions that are, as this present discussion shows, debatable.

It is not by extending ruthlessly the Church's wise regulations on immoral reading to cases which fall beyond its explicit provisions that the problem will be solved. How will it be solved? Perhaps in two directions: by the Catholic reader being so spiritually poised and grounded that he will not be shaken off base by an incidental vulgarity or too realistic frankness in an otherwise sound book; by the Catholic reviewer deepening, as Father Kilian and I both wish, his simple and loving devotion to the mind of the Church and by keeping foremost in his own mind not only his office as literary critic but his thousand times more glorious and important office as a guide for souls.   (December 30, 1944)

MALAISE OF THE MOVIES

The movie industry that existed in 1946 "is gone forever." Such was the chill conclusion of a year's survey completed for the Hollywood Federation of Labor Film Council by Dr. Irving Bernstein.

Here are some of the reasons for the statement. Combined net earnings of the Hollywood film industry dropped from $121,000,000 in 1946 to $32,000,000 in 1956. Average weekly attendance was 90,000,000 in 1946; ten years later it had shrunk to 46,530,000 (34,830,000 at drive-ins, only 11,700,000 at "conventional" theatres). Since 1949 there has been a steady growth in United States films made abroad, resulting in a drop of films made in Hollywood from 356 in 1949 to 272 in 1956.

So mounts the roster of Hollywood woes. "The huge theatre audience is lost. . . . There can never again be as many conventional theatres, as many films . . . produced in Hollywood, as lush corporate profits, as many people employed."

The survey singles out ground for modest optimism, however, in the "great teen-age boom" that will come in the 1960s and '70s. There were 35,000,000 young people between the ages of ten and twenty-four in 1955; there will be about 60,800,000 in 1975. Hollywood must set its sights now to win the young people of the next twenty years.

If these teen-age statistics sound cheerful to Hollywood, they ring ominously in the ears of others, for it is exactly in a drive to capture the teenagers that Hollywood will be tempted to use any device that promises to make the cash register ring. The industry's decline is no signal for those concerned with movie morals to let down their guard.   (April 19, 1958)

WILL HOLLYWOOD NEVER LEARN?

Public indignation was deeply stirred in the early 1930s when Hollywood began a trend of glamorizing gangsters and criminals. It was this degeneracy that led most directly to the formation of the National Legion of Decency; all the documents which projected the formation of the Legion in 1934 echo this charge.

Today, a short two decades after Hollywood got its knuckles cracked, we are being submitted to another wave of films in which a criminal is the hero up to the last few feet of film. Then the moral, "crime does not pay," is cynically dubbed into the show.

An independent producer, American-International, released *Baby Face Nelson*. Although it got the seal of approval of the Production Code, the Legion of Decency promptly slapped a B rating on it—morally objectionable in part for all. The Code has already approved *Machinegun Kelly*, released by the same producers. Films have also been made of *The Bonnie Parker Story* and *The Al Capone Story*.

There is little wonder that J. Edgar Hoover, director of the FBI, has written to Eric Johnston, president of the Motion Picture Association of America, to express his "deep concern" over movies that go beyond "the bounds of common decency and result in the glorification of the gangster and his elevation as a false idol for American youth."

Hollywood has embarked on an enterprise that furnishes a course of visual instruction for the potential leaders of our juvenile gangs and for the full-fledged criminals of tomorrow. It deserves the reproaches of Mr. Hoover—and of the public at large.

(April 12, 1958)

THE EYES HAVE IT

One hundred and fifty-two years from now, the human countenance, I predict, is going to look vastly different. I say this on the assumption of the evolutionists, who hold that practice makes perfect, and vice versa, and that, consequently, the organs that we use most develop most and become predominant; those we don't use shrink and become vestigial. Well, if that be true, here is what Homo Sapiens will look like ere long: the top of his head, above the ears, will have disappeared; the nose will be much smaller, the mouth about the same size as now; but these losses will have been compensated for by much, much larger ears and eyes that will be enormous and considerably protruding.

A Martian creature such as is foiled by intrepid Buck Rogers? Not at all. That's what we shall look like, take my word for it. Because, of all our faculties, the ones we use most are those of hearing and seeing, especially of seeing. So the brain will shrivel up like a dried pea, and we shall become all eyes.

This melancholy clairvoyance descended on me very simply. Over in a corner of the office where I write is a pile of boxes containing jigsaw puzzles. Some anonymous benefactor dropped them at the door a few days ago and scuttled off, as though they were a foundling; he/she probably thought the editors needed some simple, gay laughter to keep them from gibbering idiocy. Anyway, as I took a glance at them, I found that they were not the simple jigsaw puzzles I used to know. They have gone high-hat; they are now "picture puzzles." That, in turn, reminded me of an article in *Harper's* on the picture magazines.

It really does seem that the signs on the highroad of our culture read more and more unmistakably: "Stop, Look—and Stop Thinking." Let's just look (there I go—see?) at the picture magazines a bit. According to the *Harper's* article, in 1942 more than 275,000,000 copies of picture magazines were sold in the United States. At a modest estimate of five readers to each copy, there were 1,375,000,000 readings.

Add to this a movie or so a week, and you see what a boon this phase of American life is to the opticians and oculists.

But does the American eye just glide over the photos or does the brain, too, get in a few licks? Speaking of the most successful of the picture magazines, the article remarks:

It is true that much of *Life* requires no mental activity at all; you can take it as a pure pastime in the literal sense of the word . . . but if you want to use your head you usually have a chance to do so. And the success of *Life* is a good sign that millions of Americans prefer a magazine that gives them such a chance.

We are not convinced—may not the millions prefer it (and much more *Life's* myriad imitators) for the "much" that requires no mental activity at all? Or, perhaps, for one aspect that "might almost be classed as constituting a principle in its own right"—namely, the slyly cautious, always sociologically captioned purveying of nudity? Just watch the next person you see with a picture magazine—see the pages flip by.

Well, and why not look at pictures; can't we learn from them? Nobody yet has invented a substitute for language as the medium of conveying ideas, truth. The whole of pictorial journalism labors from the inherent defect that pictures, and particularly a series of them, arranged to slant a story, consistently present a subtle distortion of reality. If we could only look without thinking, it would be just fun; but try as we may, the brain will start to work, and on the wrong premises. The approach to a picture magazine, I suggest, ought to be not "What fine photos!" but rather "What's wrong with this picture?"

You may have suspected all along what this fulmination has been working up to. If Catholic readers, too, must glance at not a few of these picture magazines betimes, they really, though misguidedly, do not have time and energy left to read a Catholic magazine we might mention.   (July 24, 1943)

TV AND AN AGE OF PICTURES

Anyone who saw the production by NBC-TV of *The Caine Mutiny Court-Martial* must have realized how one "picture" can be worth a thousand or more words. Programs of this type are posing, for educators and for all concerned with the cultural life of our country, a problem new in its dimensions and challenging in its consequences.

Meeting at Princeton University, some two hundred fifty alumni of the Graduate College pondered "The Communication of Ideas." It was agreed by the conferees that "people are turning more and more from printed information to pictures." Perhaps, as Francis

H. Taylor, director of the Worcester (Mass.) Museum of Art, expressed it, this is simply because "the sheer bulk of printed materials is so great" and is steadily becoming greater. The conference itself provided a dramatic illustration of the relationship between words and pictures. After seeing a fifteen-minute color film called "A Communications Primer," the assembled scholars spent seven and a half hours discussing the problems involved.

Mr. Taylor was forthright in urging his confrères to drop their intellectual "snobbery" about television. It has defects, he said, but these are more easily overcome than is the attitude of many educators who do nothing "but sit back and deplore the vulgarization of knowledge."

There is little doubt that the age of the picture is with us. But let it not therefore be thought that the age of the word is gone forever. The year 1955 was one of the most prosperous in history for United States publishers. Sales in bookstores have been from eight to thirteen per cent above the preceding year.

Indications mount that the age of the picture is even adding strength to the world of the book. Sales of books like *The Caine Mutiny, Peter Pan, Heidi*, and *No Time for Sergeants* have boomed following TV shows based on them. The picture, however, still remains way out in front of the word in the number of people it can reach. The production of *The Sleeping Beauty* by the Sadler's Wells Ballet was seen by an audience estimated at 30,000,000.

There is, of course, the constant danger that culture will indeed be "vulgarized" by the steady encroachment of the picture technique. But that danger can be met if those guiding the destinies of TV and other visual media realize their full responsibilities. Mr. Taylor, in his remarks at the Princeton meeting, told how classical music was somewhat "vulgarized" when Caruso's voice was introduced to millions through the imperfect recording methods of the day. But perhaps, he went on to remark, it was the very distortions in the records that gave hearers an appetite for the higher fidelity they could find by attending concerts.

The relationship of picture and word is a problem that will exercise educators above all others. How the use of the visual arts in many fields, including religion, can be made to assist, not destroy, the irreplaceable role of the written word is the crux of the question. But parents ought also to be alert to the question. Their judicious suggestions that a TV program can lead to a book, or a book be used to enrich a program, may take some time and thought. But if these suggestions are made, children will grow up with some realization that words and pictures are natural associates, that they can, indeed must, go together.   (January 14, 1956)

PART THREE

Miscellany

Chapter One

A CRITIC WHEN NOT AT HIS LAST

Motes, beams, and eyes must constantly haunt the dreams of one who sets out to be a critic, though I must confess that my slumbers are little disturbed save by the attempts at cultural expression I can hear from my Manhattan windows, especially in the summer evenings—and long into the nights—when the budding Carusos and the plodding Paderewskis have a fling at their art. But we hear it whispered about that every critic is a frustrated creative artist, and so, every critic is, for all I know, tempted once in a month of Mondays to try his pen at something freed from the critical fetters that may have constricted him.

Here are a few pieces that may be called essays at something like more constructive writing than pure criticism allows. They are, as one will readily discover, modest in scope, if not in ambition. They are some reflections suggested by the liturgical seasons of Christmastide and Lent, supplemented by some briefer pieces on aspects of Christian life such as suffering and prayer. They will, it is hoped, provide a more cheerful ending to the book than if I had concluded by protesting that there is still much to be criticized in our American culture.

If I may steal a lovely title from my colleague, the Reverend John LaFarge, S.J.—though I cannot pretend to the mellowness of the years and wisdom that blesses him, this brief chapter is something like my "American Amen." I mean that in the sense that I, like Father LaFarge, am optimistic about our American culture and especially about the American Catholic contribution to it. However dimly the beauty of the Catholic faith may be caught in these few pieces, the beauty is gloriously indwelling in that faith and the more it shines forth in the lives of American Catholics—be they readers, writers, or mere critics—the more robustly will we be able to say "Amen" to all that is good, vital, and hopeful in the culture this book has praised or chastised.

SANITY AT BEDLAM

Things are prone to be upside down at Christmas time. All is gloriously turned around and mixed up. How different and strange the clean midnight air smelt in our young noses as we turned the day around and went, trudging so tinglingly wide awake between mother and father, to Mass at night. And in the bright, like-no-other morning of the Day, when we all lined up in the upper hall to march downstairs and see what Santa had brought, the youngest of all led the family procession—not mother or father, but the toddler headed the family trek downstairs to the tree.

And all through the day, things are quite literally upside down, as mothers can wryly attest. Can anyone recall ever having been spanked on Christmas Day? No rules, no discipline that day—and that was an upside-down state of affairs in itself. Of course, the whole mixing up had begun way back with talk of Santa Claus. You did not realize, of course, that that jolly, munificent gentleman was no one else but father. Father felt, though, that there was a most lamentable mix-up, (a confusion worse confounded) for Santa was sure to satisfy your every extravagant desire, and father —well, not that he was unwilling, but how to stretch his few dollars to the magic measure of Santa's generosity?

Yes, Christmas is gloriously upside down. Even the very word that names Christ's birthplace, that lovely word Bethlehem, got into the mix-up. Our English ancestors, in their love for shortening names (that queer process that gives us "Maudlen" for Magdalene), used to call it "Bedlam." So an old carol tells us, in delicious disregard for chronology, that Saint Stephen, the first martyr,

. . . a clerk
In Kyng Herowdes halle,
saw a sterr was fayr and bryght
over Bedlem stonde.

which announced the fact that

> ther is a chylde in Bedlem born
> is better than we alle.

Then in the course of time, there was a priory established in London, which gradually became a hospital devoted to caring for the insane. It was called St. Mary's of Bethlehem, and as Bethlehem had been commonly called Bedlam, so was the asylum for the insane, and so gradually were all such places, so that now our word "bedlam" means confusion and disorder and says nothing to us of the little Judean town which saw the birth of the Christ Child centuries ago.

So, the quality of upside-downness has long been connected with Christmas. But it is too bad, is it not, that we have gone so far? How sad that we can so take the fine sheen off holy things, like gold coins that have been rubbed smooth through overmuch passing across the counters of the world. How lamentable that the musical and sacred word Bethlehem can be debased so, step by step, until it comes in changeling form, to be Bedlam, a madhouse, a place of confusion.

For Bethlehem was no Bedlam, we protest. There was no trace of Babylon there, no confusion. Rather, there was peace, order in tranquillity, when "all things were in quiet silence, and the night was in the midst of her course" and God's "almighty Word leapt down from His royal throne." Midnight, the shepherd-watched fields, sheep, whose gentle bleating but deepened the hush that brooded under the silent Palestinian stars, the quiet ox and ass; not a word to suggest turmoil, disorder. How sad, then, ever to have called this peaceful little town Bedlam!

So we think. The upside-downness of Christmas is as delicious as ginger cakes to a young Christmas appetite, but it should only be on the surface of the day; it should not touch the real meaning of Christmas, for that is too sacred; that was too ordered and peaceful.

Sacred? Yes, deeper than the deepest fathoming of fact or fancy. And peaceful beyond the reach of yearning. But ordered? There was an orderliness there on that stilly night, as there is always an order in God's doings, but it was a Divine order. And to our poor, dim, half-opened minds, the order of God's plans is often a topsy-turvydom. Where is the order that our prudence would recognize in the first being last, in losing your soul to save it, in the humble exalted and the exalted humbled?

So perhaps our old English carolers and preachers were right after all in calling Bethlehem Bedlam, with all that word has come to mean, for there, as in all God's great strategies, there was a Divine topsy-turvydom; there were things standing on their heads; God an infant, Joseph and Mary, royal travelers, finding hospice in a poor stable-cave, shepherds conversing with angels, beasts (according to legends that are not too incredible) kneeling in worship, wise men wooing wisdom from a village trinity, a proud king troubled over a just-born Baby.

Yes, there was confusion there, too—confusion not in the events themselves, for

He came alle so still
To His mother's bower,
As dew in Aprille
That falleth on the flower

and the stars (save one that went errant with joy) kept their courses, and the earth sang not in its quiet spinning—but confusion, confounding for the world's arrogance, its fullness of itself then and forever put to shame by God's outpouring of Himself.

It is due to this Divine upside-downness, to this sweet confusion of the first Noël, that fairy tales have in them a profound and keen truth. One Divine story, that would have been but a lovely unrealizable dream had it not been Divine, came true in Bethlehem; things were there, in the quiet of that long gone midnight, not what they seemed, and other things may not be either. Now it is not too impossible that the fairy queen may lurk in the rags of the scullery maid, since then the Eternal Word hid in the tatters of human flesh.

That great childlike man, Chesterton, who never strayed beyond the lovely light that pulses from Bethlehem's cave, once wrote of the Ethics of Elfland. He saw in all the world's fairy tales glimpses ever recurring to the world's eye of a lost Eden and happiness once had and waiting to be regained—a constant preoccupation with the fall of man. But may we not go further and see in fantasy and make-believe man's dim remembrance of Bethlehem? Only a Christian, I hold, can really appreciate Mickey Mouse or the talking animals of our fables, for in these topsy-turvydoms where things become something else, he is reminded time and again that human nature became something other once and for all time—when God consecrated it by taking it to Himself through her of whom it is sung:

Mother and maiden
Was never none but she;
Well may such a lady
God's mother be.

Should we not, then, speak rather of the Theology, than of the Ethics of Elfland?

For since Bethlehem, make-believe has become a Divine art. There was, to be sure, no make-believe, no masking there. The Infant, His eyes still closed, His first uncertain wail still echoing in the stable before pouring out to flood the world with the sweet, terrible cry of the Hound of Heaven on mankind's trail—that infant was God. But that reality, which seemed so utterly incredible, has, as it were, baptized and made Christian the make-believe that springs from childlikeness.

Because the Child was so utterly other than He seemed, saints have loved to seem utterly other than they were. Because he knew the Child and His heart so well as to give us the Crib, the Poor Man of Assisi loved to play the fool, and he was no fool, save a Bedlamite fool. Our Lady, too, was above all others a Bedlamite, filled to the brim and overflowing with that Divine and happy folly of the Crib, which stood the world's values on their head and made valid with eternal verity our trite phrase that "things are often not what they seem."

Thank God for Bedlam, then, for the Divine topsy-turvydom that there consecrated our fantasies and our fairy dreams. To accept the inversion of our human values that Bethlehem meant is a sure and mortal blow to our smugness, which makes us prate of order being Heaven's first law. It may be, but it will be God's order, not ours. If only Bethlehem can shock our self-centeredness deeply enough, perhaps we can be jarred out of our amnesia, in which we forget who we really are, back into a wakefulness that keeps vigil always at the Manger at Bethlehem, even if, as a medieval preacher said, to gaze on the "pore childe bonded in a cribbe," we have to take a very humble place indeed, even that of kneeling "betwix a nox and a nasse." Perhaps we may be shocked out of our real madness into the madness of a Bedlamite, mad with the Divine topsy-turvydom of the first Christmas night, which saw, with still-held breath and full heart, Omnipotence in bonds and man free.

(December 21, 1940)

THIS CHRISTMAS POETRY

Many lovely things bloom amid the Christmas snows over and above the rose, and not least among the lovely, to boast just a little modest bit, are the poor scriveners who thaw out their pens, perhaps stiffened by a nip of worldly frost, before the warmth of the Crib and try to snare in written words the mystery and the marvel of the incarnate Word. And among their legion is the smaller band whom we may call the elite guard of letters, for like (and how unlike!) another elite guard, they bear, at the season of His birth, an *SS*—initials of two qualities that stamp their work (if it be true work) no less than they illumine the Feast.

Christmas is, perhaps, the unique feast that joins so wonderfully and winningly the qualities of simplicity and sublimity. A baby is born: how simple, how usual! The baby is God: mysteriously sublime!

These two elements run through the whole Christmas liturgy; the simplicity of "a Child is born to us and a Son is given to us," the utterly unassuming ordinariness of "Joseph went up . . . to be enrolled with Mary, his wife, who was with child" are counter-pointed by the surging sublimity of thought and language that pulse through *Tecum principium in die virtutis tuae: in splendoribus sanctorum, ex utero ante luciferum genui te* ("with thee is the principality in the day of thy strength: in the brightness of the Saints, from the womb before the day star have I begotten thee"). The "goodness and kindness of our Saviour God" is lowly; but He is, too, the "brightness of His glory and the figure of His substance, upholding all things by the word of His power," majestically sublime.

The two elements of the Feast, then, must find their shadowing forth in all poetry that is both Christmassy and poetry. Puddings and mulled ale, trees, toys and tinsel, turkey and the blazing hearth must somehow, by the poet's imaginative alchemy, lead naturally and reverently to the Cave, which was a home, but also (perhaps, indeed, for that very reason) a place of wonder.

Nor can the poet omit the human, homely, round-the-hearth, stockings-filled-with-nuts-and-candy touch—not if he is to write a real, authentic Christmas poem. To dwell only on the splendors of the Eternal Word leaping down from Heaven while midnight held its course, and not to tell of the lamb and the donkey and hay, is to write, it may be, a majestic theological poem but not one that will tell of our Christmas which is, after His two natures, Divine and human in its joys.

Catholic poets know that; by a certain homing instinct they wing right to the heart of Christmas. They hint at, they touch upon, they stand in awe before the breath-taking truth, and their realization of the sublimity saves their thought and their verse from sentimentality; they sing of the lowly like-us-ness of the dear event, and the warmth of their humanity saves their thought and verse from overausterity. And in this, every Catholic poet who writes of His Nativity is much like to Our Lady, for she gazed, that midnight, far, far down the unending depths and up the infinite sheer heights of the simplicity and the sublimity. He was God, but He fed at Her breast.

And from the deft interweaving of these two elements, much as God interwove them in the great Fact, springs the emotion that sings and shouts in every true Christmas poem—joy. Joy that He who has become a Baby is God; joy that what He has become is a Baby; joy that simplicity is sublime and that sublimity is simple. And God will not mind too much if we rejoice a little more over the simplicity than over the sublimity; sublime things overawe us a bit; with the simple we feel, or ought to feel, more at home. If the simple, human, homely touch predominates in Catholic Christmas poetry, it is not a bad business, so long as the majesty of the great Fact tempers and leads our human joy to at least touching the hem of the Divine.

Ever since the first Christmas, there have been these Christmas poets and poems. Chesterton was perhaps the greatest of our latterday ones; so was the unknown one great who wrote the priceless Towneley *Second Shepherds' Play*, with its marvelous, natural transition from rough peasants' fun to the quaint and sweet reverence of the shepherds' visit to the Crib and of the little verses they say with their presents to Him, one of which goes:

Hail, pretty darling, Thou art God indeed.
I pray to Thee, be near when I have need.
Sweet is Thy look, although my heart does bleed
To see Thee here, and dressed in such poor weed.
Hail, Babe, on Thee I call.
I bring a tennis ball.
Take it and play withal.

Yes, Christian ages have always mingled the two in their joy at Christmas time. Fun and holiness, simple and sublime, Divine and human brought together, as He has brought them together, make Christmas poetry. The poets who can do that are makers, indeed. They are truly an elite guard, standing watch not too far from the other and winged poets who chanted the first Christmas poem, the Gloria.   (December 25, 1943)

PARATROOPER

Clearness and quiet. Those were the atmosphere of the high world he was living in. Out beyond the Plane, as far as vision's farthest reach and then beyond, were the depths of cloudless infinity fading into other depths. Blue, we call it, but he knew better; it was the limpidity of timelessness and spacelessness that has no color because it was the blend of all colors. And the clearness, the clarity, was twofold, he saw: it itself could be seen, and each stratum, layer, sphere of it was a window, too, through which other and deeper clearness could be seen beyond, and still others beyond that. Vision was satisfied with this utterly pure clarity upon which it rested, and still with yearning was drawn on to search out other clear infinities beyond.

And the quiet. It was not the mere absence of sound that is an emptiness in the ear. It was completion, as though all the loveliness of sound had been spoken at once and superbly and then faded to leave the hearing filled and satisfied, at peace with sound forever. No, more than that, there was, in the profundity of the peace, a definite sound that was not so much a sound as a pulse. Yes, he realized, that is the Engine; that is what keeps this quiet alive and tingling, and not a mere void.

Peace and quiet and clearness—out beyond the Plane as far as his vision's farthest reach. Yes, that way up and out and around—but not down. For when his vision bent down, he did not see those things. Oh, to the vision it was clear and quiet enough, but he knew the turmoil and the murk that was there. Out and around and up, Infinity where he was so much, so deeply at home; down, finiteness and the earth to which he must so soon descend.

Even as he looked down, little puffs of white dotted the field-quilted scene, as soundlessly as when a waterdrop pocks the deep dust of a country road. The sound did not reach to the high, quiet world he was in, but he knew the shock and the concussion wedded to that quietly budding smoke flower. For there was war and agony down there, incredible as it seemed in the profound peace that lapped the Plane. There were shrieks and curses, and weeping and the shrill agony of loss that cannot give voice. There were starvation and wasted bodies, even of little ones, he knew, and he loved them, for he had little ones of his own.

There was little clearness below, too. From his height every river and road, field and town was etched clear and sharp. But to the plodding fighters, to the huddled dwellers, how foggy it was, how dense the smoke and the gloom; physical darkness from the shadow of those smoke billows that swirled so lazily and quietly from where he saw them; soul darkness, too, in men killing and being killed with little clear and steadying perception of just why.

What an exchange, he realized, he was soon to make! To plummet from this lucid depth upon depth upon depth of peace and rest and clarity, from this home where truly and only he was at home, into the mean and foul and hate-corroded shambles that spread so deceptively placid beneath him—well, yes, that would be the order, would it not? He had trained for this; he was fit and ready. And the order, when it came, would not really be a command. He had volunteered for this mission; there had been no coercion, and so, when the Pilot was over the objective and he stepped to the edge and poised himself, it would not be under order so much as under a stern and proud permission. Still, the rude transition from peace to passion would be there.

And when his feet met the rising-to-meet-him earth, what would his coming mean? The tide of battle, Intelligence told him, was high and strong against his own, and would his own think that only one could not turn it? He knew it would not be so. With the lucidity that his present high, clear world made his, he knew with simple, utter comprehension that when he came down, with the exhilaration that his high world had given him, he would turn the tide of this and any battle. Oh, the war would not end when his feet touched earth, he knew, but he knew, too, that he could rally and would rally his own. He knew that this clarity and quiet could battle down any turmoil and obscurity.

Well, the time was running out, he knew. The down-below smoke puffs were more scattered now; the Plane was pulsing toward behind the lines. The place elected for his earth-plummeting was a quiet little village among the hills. There his own, a handful at first, would rendezvous with him; soon from the underground of the streets and hills and fields his till-now hidden comrades would come trickling in to join him, and the rally would be under way.

He rose and stepped to the edge of the Plane. He looked out and up once more to the dear infinity of clarity and peace that he loved. He was to leave it for a while, but he knew that he would seek it out again, so it was not good-by.

It was utterly quiet. Even the Engine now pulsed more as a feeling than as a sound. The village objective was clear and directly in range. Paratrooper tensed himself.

From out the high world of clearness and peace, rocketing down, down to the low world of murkiness and tumult—he leaped. . . .

For while all things were in quiet silence . . . Thy Almighty Word leapt down from heaven from Thy royal throne, as a fierce conqueror into the midst of the land of destruction. . . . And Mary brought forth her first-born son, and wrapped him up in swaddling clothes and laid him in a manger.

(December 23, 1944)

BIKINI-BETHLEHEM

The Technician was ready. In a few minutes now the great event, prepared for through many long months, planned with such meticulous care, buttressed by all the vast resources at His command, would burst on a world waiting more anxiously, more eagerly than it realized.

He looked about. Yes, they were all ready, too, all his assistants, those who would play their bigger and lesser roles in the great drama. Some would actually witness the shattering climax; others would later go to see and report, but they all dovetailed into His plan. He had chosen their parts for them and He knew exactly how well they would play them.

Out across the waters the target was ready, too, the place where the stupendous event would occur. It was all tranquil there now, but in a moment what awesome power would burst its bonds!

What that power was He knew. Light more brilliant than the sun (and He had measured its power too); energy to move mountains and—what was even more—to move the souls of men. He knew that when the exact second came there would be released a chain reaction that would leave the world never quite the same.

It was true, He knew, that many in the world would be indifferent to the great event. Many, despite the fact that it would be widely publicized, would think it of little consequence. A great many would never even hear about it, but not one soul in all the world would be unaffected by it. No, not one soul, for the life of every man and woman, of all the children yet to be born, would be different because of what was going to happen in a matter of seconds now.

The Technician knew something else. He knew that this tremendous power could and would be used in either of two ways. It could be used either for construction or for ruin. It could be beneficent for those who approached its mysteries with good will; it could spell destruction for those who tampered with it malevolently. It was peace or the sword, He knew.

And such world-shaking energy confined in so small a compass! A woman's arms could encircle the source of it, yet the energy it would release would penetrate the heavens. So small it was that it might easily lie unnoticed in the corner of some old, abandoned stable.

The moment was at hand. There was not a sound (a mighty roaring, as of a great wind, there would be!); around Him hardly a breath seemed to be drawn (how there would be a song of triumph!); the eternal hills far out on the horizon seemed expectant (and how they would be shaken!). There was brilliant sunlight (how it would be eclipsed!) and the waters were at peace.

The Technician stretched forth His hand. He touched the release. There was a blinding flash. . . .

Apparuit benignitas et humanitas Salvatoris nostri Dei. Her days were accomplished, that she should be delivered, and she brought forth her first-born son, and wrapped him up in swaddling clothes and laid him in a manger.   (December 25, 1948)

HIS MANGER OUR THRONE

During this Christmas time—as so often in dear Christmas times of the past—you will walk simply and humbly up the aisle of your church to pay a visit to the Crib. Perhaps you will be leading your children by the hand, leading them up, it may be, for the first time to pay their wide-eyed visit to the little King of all children and of all who become, for His sake, like unto children.

And what will you see at your Crib? How is the timeless Christmas scene depicted? If your church is like most churches, the sexton or the parish priest or perhaps the nuns will have set out the traditional figures. The sheep and the ox are there, with perhaps the donkey pushing his inquisitive head through a window. Angels hover about up near the rafters or the thatched roof. St. Joseph stands quietly somewhat in the background, as he loved to do. Our Blessed Lady kneels near the manger, protective and adoring at the same time. And the Infant on the straw—how does He look?

Your Crib will probably portray Him with His little arms outstretched, as though to welcome all the world. A smile is on His infant face, and rays of glory make a nimbus around His holy head.

The portrayal is simple, devout, traditional, and symbolical. But it is apt to cloud in our minds a great truth, perhaps the greatest truth on which our prayerful thoughts ought to be riveted at Christmastide.

Because, you see, the Christmas scene was not just like that. Oh, the sheep and the ox may keep their places without distracting us. St. Joseph and Our Lady probably took their stand as your Crib depicts them. But the Holy Infant?

The stupendous mystery and the infinitely warm attraction of the Crib lie in the fact that He did not look the way our traditional tableaux show Him. When Mary first knelt at His Crib, her eyes of faith saw the glory and the majesty of His Godhead shining through the new-born infant's limbs and countenance. She—and St. Joseph, too—knew by faith that there was an aureole of glory around His head. But they did not see it.

Our Infant Saviour, after His birth, was as helpless as any other new-born baby. His arms were not outstretched in welcome; they were making the little spasmodic and unco-ordinated movements of an infant. About His head there were no rays of glory, but only the sparse and funny little hairs of early infancy. Our Divine Lord, at His birth, was like any other infant. The glory that surrounded the manger was the glory of the marvelous Fact, not the glory of the Angels and their celestial hymns. It was to the shepherds, out in their fields, and not to Mary and Joseph at the Crib, that the heavenly host appeared in ravishing concert. From the Gospel account it would appear that Mary and Joseph did not even hear the strains of the first Gloria. They did not need to—in the reality of the little Infant form before them they saw the sweetest and most majestic symphony of all God's creation, the harmony of all the ages, the union of God and Man in the Babe of the Manger. But they saw all this with the clear-eyed vision of faith. Their eyes of flesh saw only what we would have seen (and have still to see)— an infant like any other who may perhaps have been born in some house in Bethlehem the same wintry night.

This we know, because we know with St. Paul that "He was like unto us in all things, sin alone excepted." Knowing it, we have struck to the core of the utter, infinite, and unfathomable depths of the humility of the Son, the Word of God. He entered our world as we enter our world. He appeared in the flesh as we appear in the flesh. He became, more truly than our intellects can fully grasp, one of us.

This is the strain that runs no less surely through all the Christmas liturgy than the magnificent measures that hymn the fact that it is the Very Word of God Who has come among us. We are told not only that the Supreme Word of God has leapt down from His Eternal Father's bosom but that—wonder of wonders!—he was truly nourished at the bosom of the Maid. As the hymn for Christmas Lauds touchingly puts it, "He is fed with a little milk, through whom not even the birds of the air go hungry" (*Et lacte modico pastus est, per quem nec ales esurit*).

There is always the need for us to sharpen and deepen our realization of the reality of Our Saviour's humanity. His divinity is something it never crosses our mind to doubt. That realization is rooted ineradicably in our Catholic thought and instinct. Perhaps it is so predominant that we give small consideration to the fact that the reality of His humanity is just as essential a part of Catholic teaching.

Our Saviour really was a man. He was not acting a role. He did not go through the motions of suffering on the Cross. He suffered. He did not go through the motions of being a new-born infant. He was one, with all the consequences that entails. The Second Person of the Most Blessed Trinity, the Eternal Word of the Father, He whom universe upon created universe cannot contain, Very God of Very God—that ineffable One really possessed an infant's body that developed as any other infant's body does until it grew to the full stature of splendid manhood, in which it suffered the agony of the Crucifixion as truly as—more truly than—any man would have suffered it.

And the reality of Our Saviour's humanity, which Christmas shows us in its strongest, most intimate appeal, if we but know to look, is the proof and pledge of a corresponding reality in us. It is the reality of our incorporation into His Mystical Body.

This is why God's Providence decreed that the Eternal Word should take flesh and appear in the flesh as men do—save for the sweet marvel of His virginal birth. Christmas is the visible doctrine, the incarnate doctrine that just as truly as Christ was born a real Infant, so we are by His grace born into real divinity. The reality of our partaking of the divine nature, through grace, is measured by the reality with which He takes our nature. If His sacred Humanity is a phantom, if it is just a shell He put on, a mask assumed for appearance sake, then are the words in which He promised us our divinization hollow symbols, mere metaphors, figures of speech. But if His Humanity is real, then is our sharing of God's nature just as real, no mere image, no metaphor, but the literal and astonishing truth. And to underline this truth, He underlines the reality of His humanity by taking it in its infant, weak, to the human eye, unextraordinary form.

Christmas is the visible, touchable, lovable fulfillment of the desire we express in every Mass, when we say "O God, Who hast marvelously created human nature and still more marvelously renewed it, grant that through this mingling of water and wine, we may become sharers of His divinity Who deigned to become partaker of our humanity." In the Crib we witness the Son of God filling His part of this covenant. It will be filled in us, if we will.

Christmas sets before us, on the rough straw of the poor manger, the real, the helpless, and infant physical body of God. And it sets before our eyes the Head of that Mystical Body whose mysterious and really perfect stature will be reached at the end of time, but whose growth in unity works like the Gospel leaven through all the hours of time.

Christmas is the feast of that unity. The Blessed Sacrament, which gives us again the Body of God, is its Sacrament.

As never before, the world seeks unity. The Infant from his timeless Crib looks out and sees that our efforts are feeble and stumbling. We hobble along the highway toward political unity in the United Nations. We limp toward a unity of racial, industrial, and international justice. The Christ-Child, though He sees that the attempts are stumbling, does see that they are attempts. Perhaps He but bides His own time, from Christmas to Christmas, until He sees that we have come to the end of the tether of our human attempts. Perhaps then His Infant arms will open wide and He will crown our poor efforts with a great outpouring of His grace, with an awakening all over the face of the world to the reality of His Mystical Body, of that unity of which He is the center and the soul, of that unity of which Christmas is the incarnation.

Pay your visit to the Crib, simply and humbly. But see, beneath the carved and painted images, beneath the stiff postures and the perhaps sentimental piety, the human reality of the humanity of Christ. There is the motive, the source, the soul of what the world too glibly calls the brotherhood of man and thinks too easily to attain. It can be attained fully and lastingly only when we come to realize that we men are one because Christ became one with us. That is the meaning of the Crib, the meaning of the so ordinary appearing little human body that lies in the Crib. His divine intellect did not shape His Infant lips to the uttering of a single word, but His very presence said at the first Christmas and repeats with every Christmas the sublime and wonderful words He uttered at the Last Supper:

[I pray] that they may all be one, as thou, Father, in me, and I in thee; that they also may be one in us . . . that they may be one, as we also are one . . . that they may be made perfect in one: and the world may know that thou hast sent me, and hast loved them, as thou hast also loved me . . . that the love wherewith thou hast loved me, may be in them, and I in them.

The infant humanity of the Son of God tells us that from the Crib. When will all the world hear? When it does, there will truly be one world.   (December 24, 1949)

KING-SERVANT OF THE TOILING WORLD

If it weren't for two words in St. Luke's account of the Nativity of Our Lord, the innkeeper at Bethlehem would probably be one of the most maligned men in history. We would rather believe, I think, that he was a kindly man, perhaps a family man himself, that he had no haughty disdain for the poor and that he was properly touched by Our Lady's condition. We'd like to think that he did scurry off through every nook and corner of his caravanserai (just a "tourist camp" of today) only to come back regretfully to report truly that "there was no room"—at least no room where a mother might have her child in decent seclusion.

But the two words make us take a bit of second thought. St. Luke says that "there was no room for them in the inn." "For them"; it seems as though they were singled out for exclusion for some special reason. There was room for others but not for them. And what could the reason for exclusion have been, if it were not either the lack of wealth of Mary and Joseph or Our Lady's condition, which promised inconvenience to the innkeeper?

It would be more pleasant to think that the unborn Infant's first overture of love beyond Nazareth met with human kindness in return. But it looks as though His first advance was rebuffed, that His mother and guardian were turned away from the inn precisely because they seemed poor.

And Mary and Joseph were poor. Pious exaggeration about their poverty serves no purpose save perhaps to arouse false emotions. Our Lady and St. Joseph never lived in abject poverty, nor did Our Lord later. It would be an insult to faithful Joseph, whose prototype was the Joseph who provided well for the land of Egypt, to think that he did not provide a frugal sufficiency for his family. It would be a slight on his skill as the village carpenter to think that his work was so poorly done that few customers came and that the Holy Family therefore lived in dire want.

No, they were not that poor, with the degrading poverty that stalks big-city slums. Yet they were poor, poor as the dozens in Nazareth, the thousands in Israel, the millions in the world who lived on the same social level, were and are poor.

For the thing to remember is that Mary and Joseph were actually of the working classes. Their lineage was kingly, their sanctity godly (and now to deepen unfathomably with the visible advent of God to the circle of their family life), but they were poor with the poverty of the world's toilers, because they were toilers. They were what a later age would call "of the masses."

Knowing their holiness and proud of their nobility of descent, we may fall all insensibly into the sentimental error of halfway imagining that Our Lady and St. Joseph were something like later nobles of kingly courts who would masquerade romantically in the guise of peasants. Only it was no masquerade for Christ's mother and foster father. They were not playing the part of being poor and of the poor working classes. They were not going through a pantomime for our edification; they were living the life of the poor for our sanctification.

And into that status of poverty, which is the lot of the world's millions, the Word, the Second Person of the Blessed Trinity, chose to appear and live in His humanity. He chose to be a member of a poor, working family; He chose to be Himself a worker, one of the working class, one of "the masses."

Why?

It was said to Adam, and through him to every member of the human race, "In the sweat of thy face shalt thou eat bread." Our lot is to toil, and actually the vast majority of the human race eats its bread in sweat that pours out as a result of physical, manual labor. A fraction of the human race occupy positions as industrial executives, office workers, or administrators. A fraction of the human race sit in comfortable offices behind desks. The vast and teeming masses earn their bread in the furrows, at the forge, down the mines, on the sea. The vast masses are the toiling masses, as indeed even more of us would be had not modern civilization brought the machine more and more under its sway.

But those who do not earn their bread by the actual sweat of their brows—are they exempt from the primal penalty of toil? No. Rather has their toil been commuted to another form and shape. If the sweat of physical labor does not start out on their brows, then their brains, their hearts, their energies are dampened with the sweat of anxieties, of planning, of deeper responsibilities. But the physical sweat of the laborer and the mental sweat of the executive are one and the same, because both are members of the human race.

The man who does not work with his hands, then, is in no wise a member of an elite class. Kings and presidents, senators and ambassadors, executives and even ordained priests of God, are not elevated by their office to some untouchable plane whence they may look down with fastidiousness on the sweat of human, manual toil. They may not, for the intrinsic reason that every member of the human race lies under the selfsame penalty, and for the added and most glorious reason that the Son of God did not look fastidiously on human toil, but plunged Himself wholly, really, and without make-believe into a life of it.

More than that. Those whose lives are not compassed round by physical labor, by the very fact that they are so placed in an extraordinary condition compared to the laboring millions, are faced with the responsibility of serving those millions. Though in no sense an elite of superior, more exquisite social rank by the mere fact that they do not work with their hands, they are, by the very fact of their greater influence in economic, social, and political affairs, established as leaders. But a leader, to merit the name, must in reality be the servant of those he leads.

Human thought can put these truths before us. Mere human study of sound ethics can establish the truths of the social responsibility entailed by wealth, position, influence. But Christmas suffuses these cold propositions with the warmth of love. At Christmas Our Divine Lord does what reason merely indicates ought to be done. Into the abstract truths He has infused the dynamism, the beauty, the overwhelming appeal of His personal living of those truths.

Did He have position, wealth, influence? Of course—beyond the span of thought or imagination, for He is the Second Person of the Blessed Trinity. Could He—and He alone, with justice—not have considered Himself in His humanity absolutely unique? He was the Incarnate God. Was He not exempt, by His very being, from the penalty of physical toil? Not to Him had ever been spoken, "In the sweat of thy brow. . . ."

Yet, how did He act, and what did He say of Himself and what was said of Him? "Behold, I am in the midst of you as one who serves"; "Is not this the son of the carpenter?" For thirty long years He chose the life of toil and sweat, of poverty and inattention that is the life of the billions of men from Adam down who literally have earned their bread by the sweat of their brows. Even in His public life, when He took on the office of Supreme Teacher, He but commuted one form of toil into another.

Thus some thoughts come knocking at our hearts again at Christmas time, some thoughts which, please God, may deepen into action—action that will show our realization of oneness with and love for the world's toilers and a realization of the social responsibility wealth or position may have given us. They are thoughts of how He really became one of us, one of what the human race really is—a toiling, laboring, poor human race, toiling and laboring to be less poor on earth, but above all to be rich in heaven.

I hope the innkeeper was kindly on that first Christmas night. I know that if he wasn't, if He did turn them away because they were poor, I know that Christ had chosen that, too, as His first reminder that the toilers, those who sweat to earn their bread with the literal sweat of their brows or the sweat of their responsibility, can, if they will, wear the crowns of kings, because the Infant King came to be—to *be*—one of them, and to serve them.

(December 23, 1950)

CHRISTMAS PEACE IN TIME OF STRESS

Once more returns the season of the Angels' song that rang in the Judean skies, and all our organs in church and chapel will be pulsing with it—and our hearts, too. All through the Christmas season, the Church takes up the refrain and chants it over and over again: "Glory to God in the highest and on earth peace to men of good will." The phrase is so consecrated and so dear that perhaps it has lost some of its meaning for us. Let's meditate on it a bit for Christmas time and see if it can come alive more vividly.

Perhaps the freshest restatement of the familiar sentence is that given in the translation of the New Testament by Monsignor Ronald Knox. His version runs: "Glory to God in high heaven, and peace on earth to men that are God's friends." What makes this version seem startling rises from the fact that Monsignor Knox has filled out the condensed thought that lies in the Greek word for "good will." That word, we are told by scholars, never means in the Scriptures the subjective good will of men; it means the good will that God has toward men. So the peace that is mentioned is the peace of those who are the objects of God's good pleasure—those, in a word, who are His friends.

But the phrase has another meaning, which is commonly overlooked. According to a very probable interpretation, the verb that is to be understood in the phrase is not the subjunctive *sit* in the Latin ("let there be" or "may there be") but the declarative *est* ("is" or "there is"). The Angels, in other words, were not voicing a hope that glory *would be* given to God and that peace *would come* to men who have God's friendship; they were stating a fact —that glory *was then given* to God by the visible coming of His Son in His Humanity and that peace *was the possession* of men, who were made God's friends by that very coming. The reality of the glory given to God by the Incarnate Word is absolute: the new-born Child, by the very fact of His appearance in human flesh, gives to God a glory that is infinite and immutable. The reality of the peace given to men is relative: it depends on their appropriating to themselves through their co-operation the peace that is objectively proffered to them at the Nativity. That peace they may not accept, or, having accepted, they may lose, but it is proffered by the very fact of Christ's birth.

Accordingly, those who are God's friends, those who are living a life of sanctifying grace, have the peace the Angels proclaimed as then operative in the world. They do not have to seek for the peace Christ came to give. It is already their possession, their treasure, and it can be said that the goal of Christlike living is but to deepen one's hold on that treasure and one's realization of its strength and sweetness.

For we do fail to savor the peace of Christmas all through the year. The worries and distresses of our personal lives, the inconveniences and sacrifices demanded by civic life, wars, and the threat of wars that glower over the international scene—all tend to darken the peace that does actually have its abode deep down in the depth of our souls. But all these, in God's sight, are but surface cares. Torment us as they may, they simply have not the power to shake us from the profound sense of "being at home" with God and Our Lord that is the fruit of the peace the Christ Child came to give, and has given to us.

That is not to say that Christ's peace is mere placidity, an insensitive withdrawal from the cares and struggles of the world. By the mere fact that it is Christ's peace, it is a dynamic peace, for it is the peace that is the all-pervasive atmosphere of His Mystical Body. That Body is a living and growing Body, and for us who are members of it here on earth, it is a fighting Body. Hence it is that this peace and indeed all the other means of self-sanctification that God bestows on us are never completely self-regarding—they have social ramifications; they are for the good of the Body.

The peace that is the possession of those who are God's friends, then, has nothing to do with the attitude called "angelism." This is an attitude that would have nothing to do with the world and the world's cares except on a purely supernatural basis. It is fastidious of natural means and thinks that the only purpose of the life of the Church and the life of the individual Christian in the world is the sanctification of the world. That, of course, is the main and essential purpose, but it is not the only one. The Church and the Christian have the vocation of working for the natural betterment of the world, too, for it is in the environment of the world —though not in the spirit of the world—that souls have to be saved.

Hence it is that a realization of what the peace of Christmas is and of how it is a dynamic and social-minded peace will urge Catholics to work through all legitimate means that that peace may come to be shared by others. Peace—not yet, perhaps, the peace of Christ, but the peace of good order on a purely natural plane—will be worked for in the various aspects of our national life, in industrial and racial relations, in education and politics. Peace will be worked for in international relations, even if only by the imperfect means, such as the United Nations and the Atlantic Pact, which are now at our disposal. None of these practical and painful means will be despised under the delusion that because one possesses the peace of Christ he is therefore dispensed from helping to bring about a peace that may be, indeed, less than the peace given at Christmas, but is a natural concomitant of it.

Not too many years after the Angels sang of the peace that came to us with the Christ Child, He spoke, at the end of His earthly life, of another kind of peace, which was not to be His gift to us: "I came to bring not peace, but a sword." He came to arm us against sin and injustice and cruelty and mediocrity and all the other allurements against which we have to wage war. He would not have us at peace with them. But it is because we have Christmas peace in our souls that we can so wage war against evil. Indeed, it is because we have the peace of Christmas at heart that we must strive to our degree on all the levels of our living—familial, national, international—to spread His peace to a world that hears the song of the Angels year after year and still does not know that His peace is waiting for them.

Glory was given to God at Christ's birth. Peace was given to those who have accepted it. More and more will accept it, if this Christmas finds that peace dynamic in our hearts and outgoing from them.   (December 22, 1951)

COMPANION IN LENTEN READING

Browsing recently through some excerpts from St. Thomas Aquinas (an intellectual pursuit that eludes me most of the time), I ran across several that kept echoing in my mind. The more I thought about them, the more they seemed to be applicable to a certain type of reading. The passages, by the way, were found in the admirable little book, *Philosophical Texts from St. Thomas Aquinas*, in which the Reverend Thomas Gilby, O.P., has gathered under twenty headings the key thoughts of the great Doctor. As you range through chapters that deal, for example, with "Science and Wisdom" or "Human Nature" or "Happiness" or "Community and Society," you will not be amazed at the profundity of the thought —you expect that—half so much as by the exquisite quotability of passage after passage.

It was this quality of the pellucid statements that struck me when I read the following: "Homes are not beautiful if they are empty. Things are beautiful by the indwelling of God" (*Exposition, In Psalmos*, xxv, 5). Also, "No possession is joyous without a companion" (*Commentary, I ad Corinthios*, x, lect. 5).

But what may these human and divinely friendly phrases, for all their suggestiveness, have to do with reading—and especially with reading recommended for Lent? Perhaps more than appears at first blush. Let us grasp the skein and see how far the unraveling will go.

Have you not from time to time felt that after your reading you still felt empty? What had you got from all the hours spent with eyes glued to the funny little marks on white paper? After you had put down the book or the magazine, what "take-home pay" did you have in your intellectual jeans? Could it have been that you felt empty because what you read there had itself been empty? If so, what ought to have been in the reading; what—or who—should have been in the house of books to make it beautiful?

If we set aside strictly scientific and technical books, I think that what we want in our reading is always a companion to make reading joyous. We are perhaps all unwittingly searching in the pages for the human quality that will enable the book to speak to our heart. This is why some of the best friends we have, I surmise, are—in a far deeper sense than any flesh-and-blood friend—those we first met in books we treasure. I know, to take but one instance, that I have always felt that if the "whisky-priest" of Graham Greene's *The Power and the Glory* were to walk into the room where I am now typing I would recognize him immediately, though in the book there is hardly a line of physical description of him. But I know him inside, and the book that housed him was no empty book.

It would appear that literature, though it seems several steps removed from actual life, does in fact do its share in filling up the loneliness that is at the heart of every man. It does this because we meet in its pages people who become our companions.

Well, if this seems a neat little theory woven on the looms of fancy, there is one field in which it can certainly be put to the test—and I do not anticipate that I shall be proved a false guide. It is the field of spiritual reading.

For you will infallibly find that no well-written book that deals with whatever aspect of the spiritual life is an empty book. It cannot be, for the simple reason that a Person will always be there waiting for the seriously aware reader—and that Person is Christ. If it is a life of Him, such as the superb *Jesus and His Times*, by Henri J. Daniel-Rops, obviously He is there at the center to share your interest and captivate your love. If you read the story of one of his heroic imitators, you will be but following His footsteps, in which the lover trod. If you read about the history or organization of His Church, you cannot be far from Him, because the Church is but "Christ continued."

Since we have started with some thoughts suggested by St. Thomas, perhaps we can best end with one from St. Bernard. In his beautiful homily on the Holy Name of Jesus, the fervor of his love leads him to write: *"Si scribas, non sapit mihi, nisi legero ibi Jesum; si disputes aut conferas, non sapit mihi, nisi sonuerit ibi Jesus. Jesus mel in ore, in aure melos, in corde jubilus"* (Reading pleases me not, unless I read there the name Jesus; dispute and conference please me not, unless there sound in them the name Jesus. Jesus is honey in the mouth, melody to the ear, jubilee in the heart).

If books are not empty because in them we meet a companion, spiritual books are indeed full because they are literally made beautiful by the indwelling of God—God become man, Christ our jubilee.   (March 2, 1957)

LENTEN BOOKS MAKE CITIZEN-SAINTS

I was having a mental tussle recently to get some thoughts on spiritual reading in order, when, lo and behold, what do you think happened? I am far from being a mystic, but it is quite literal to say that Saint John Chrysostom came to my aid. He did it through the pages of my breviary.

On his feast day, January 27, his office contains a passage from his own commentary on St. Matthew's Gospel. Speaking on Our Lord's words, "You are the salt of the earth," St. John brings his argument down to the following practical application:

> He who is tractable and modest, merciful and just, does not simply lock these virtues up within himself. He makes of them clear fountains that well forth for the good of others. And so, he who is pure of heart and peaceable, and who suffers persecution for the truth, none the less orders his life for the common good.

The first and paramount purpose of spiritual reading, of books

with a religious theme, is, of course, the personal spiritual development of the reader. The directly God-established means for that
spiritual development are the sacraments and prayer. These are the
ordinary channels through which His grace comes to us. They are
the wide and full-welling channels, at which all can and indeed
must drink. But there are myriad little rivulets, too, and those who
truly desire to water well the fallow fields of their souls do not
overlook them. And what are they? The sacramentals, for example,
private devotions—and spiritual reading. Those who attune their
ears to catch the delicate rippling of God's grace in the rivulets
will be all the more alert to hear the thundering floods of that
grace in the wide channels.

Spiritual reading, then, attunes the soul, sensitizes its receptivity,
makes the practice of virtue more attractive. Its first result, therefore, is growth in personal holiness.

But that is far from all. A necessary secondary effect—if indeed
it be secondary—is the gain to the community, to society. This is
true (and this is where St. John Chrysostom comes in) because
goodness is of its nature outgoing. No saint, no good person, has
ever been good for himself alone. This, in turn, is true because
of the fact (among others) that one of the marks of the Church
is holiness. The more holiness there is in the Church, therefore, the
more divinely efficient is that Church to draw all men to herself
and to Christ in her.

On a lower level there is another inevitable result. If goodness
is outgoing, if it cannot be locked up within the good man, then
the community, even in a purely civic sense, is a better community
because of the good man. The good man is then, by the very fact
of his virtue, a good citizen and, the better man he is, the better
citizen.

Spiritual reading is, accordingly, not a thing that begins and ends
merely (though that is supremely important) within the soul of
the reader. It has social consequences which today, of all times,
take on added significance.

If the world—and the United States above all—ever needed good
citizens, it does now. We are girding for a supreme effort. The need
for sacrifice faces us squarely. Thousands of families have already
made the sacrifice of husbands and sons dead in frozen Korea. The
citizenry that is needed is an informed, determined, and convinced

citizenry, but it is above all a citizenry that is virtuous. The world today especially needs men of deeply grounded civic virtue.

If all this be true, the reader who consecrates his time this Lent to spiritual and religious books need not fear that he is divorcing himself from the vital issues of our turbulent world. His reading, which deepens his spiritual life and thereby vitalizes his influence on the goodness and soundness of the nation and the world, may be—can be, in God's Providence—a contribution of incalculable worth toward peace and justice on earth.   (February 10, 1951)

THE THERAPY OF SORROW

Dr. Gregory Zilboorg, the eminent psychiatrist, commented at length in the June 7, 1958 issue of *America* on Pope Pius XII's April address to the International Congress of Applied Psychology. He remarked that "this discourse, far from putting restrictions on psychotherapy and applied psychology, delineates with greater clarity than ever before the moral sphere within which the psychiatrist must work."

The consonance between scientific advance and traditional moral principles is, of course, nothing new. The somewhat hackneyed but still valid fact that "truth cannot contradict truth" is borne home to us perhaps most obviously in the field of moral action. To take Dr. Zilboorg's point as a sample, it is remarkable that psychiatry, which a decade or so ago was assigning a very minor role indeed to religion, is now stressing more and more heavily the necessity of religious convictions for a sound and useful life.

The consonance of truth with truth is even more strikingly demonstrated when the findings of scientists corroborate principles which are not merely moral, but spiritual and ascetical. Here is a recent instance.

The use of tranquilizing drugs has become "quite a fashion," despite the fact that "there is no complete data on them yet," as Dr. Erich Lindemann of Harvard Medical School said in an interview summarized in *This Week* magazine. But, continues this authority, "Their use in grief situations makes us question the extent to which one should hide normal emotions. . . . For the bereaved individual it is very important to face up to what has happened and work it through psychologically. It is very uncomfortable . . . but it helps the person to recover and go on."

Other experts quoted in the same article stress the danger of "delayed grief reaction," which may show itself in "greater emotional suffering later on." One statement goes to the heart of the matter: "Sedatives and tranquilizers may seem like agents of mercy, but what they actually do is deprive the individual of the therapeutic experience of mourning."

One William Shakespeare was way ahead of today's psychiatrists in this matter. When Malcolm breaks the news to Macduff that his wife and children have been murdered (*Macbeth*, Act 4, Scene 3), he admonishes the stunned man: "What, man; ne'er pull your hat upon your brows; / Give sorrow words; the grief that does not speak / Whispers the o'erfraught heart, and bids it break."

But the Christian is ahead of both Shakespeare and the psychiatrists. He knows that sorrow faced up to is not only a psychological safety valve or a physical and emotional therapy. It is not only, on a spiritual level, an effect of original sin. Rather, all sorrow, whether grief for the death of loved ones or contrition for sins, is now an opportunity afforded us by the Lord Christ to unite our sorrows with His, for it is "by His stripes [that we] were healed" (*I Peter*, 2:24).

The authorities quoted above probably never thought that they were stating, in medical terms, a formula for the good sense of asceticism. But they were. Sorrow heals, if it is faced as nature intends. It heals still more sweetly and radically if accepted as the Man of Sorrows confronted His own upon the cross. Such acceptance of sorrow results in a healing that stretches out beyond one's self to co-operate with Him in binding up the wounds of the world.

(June 28, 1958)

PAIN AND THE CHRISTIAN

Pope Pius XII, in his answer to questions proposed by the Italian Society of the Science of Anesthetics, applied and confirmed the traditional teaching of Catholic moralists on the subject of pain prevention. Under the proper circumstances, which the Pope outlined, the use of anesthetics is contrary neither to the natural law nor to the "Christian's duty of renunciation and interior purification." On occasion, indeed, prudence would counsel their use. One thinks of delicate operations that require perfect relaxation and immobility on the part of the patient.

In further discussing his theme before the five hundred physicians gathered in audience at the Vatican, the Pope indicated that the endurance of suffering could at times be a strict duty: whenever, that is, one was faced with "the inescapable alternative of enduring suffering or acting contrary to a moral obligation."

The example of the martyrs comes easily to mind. But martyrdom, as the Pope reminded his hearers, is not just a matter of early Church history. In a clear reference to Communist persecution, he praised the "magnificent example of Christians who . . . endure suffering and physical violence in order to remain faithful to God and their conscience."

Short of this extreme, however, said the Pontiff, the Christian who fulfills all the duties of his state or profession, prays recollectedly, resists his evil passions, practices charity toward his neighbor—such a man "is always living beneath the sign of the cross of Christ, whether physical suffering is present or not."

With the penitential season of Lent upon us, we may profitably ponder the Pope's words. For us, suffering is not just an intolerable intruder, to be driven off at all costs. It is a means of making reparation for our sins and the sins of the world; above all, it is the truest imitation of Christ. (February 9, 1957)

NEVER MORE ERECT THAN WHEN KNEELING

Some time ago one of our popular magazines ran a poll which asked a number of people why they went to church. The replies are not at hand, but recollection is vivid that the vast majority of the answers were concerned with what ought to have been secondary reasons. Many replied that they went to church because it gave them "a sense of belonging," because the sermon gave them "intellectual stimulus," because they enjoyed the company of nice people, and so on. Probably one response in ten went to the heart of the matter and stated that one went to church primarily to worship God.

It is without doubt an obvious feature of much of our present spiritual revival, as revealed by mounting church attendance, that a utilitarian motive is behind a considerable amount of the renewed interest in religion. The temporal advantages that can be found in powers of "positive thinking," in "peace of mind" promised those who turn to some form of religious activity can be all well and good in their place. Frequently enough they are, so to speak, by-products of a religiously oriented life. But the current emphasis on them serves only too well to obscure the basic fact that man is a praying being precisely because he is a creature—and a sinful creature—of Almighty God.

This drift toward oblivion of creaturehood's first duty and basic glory, adoration, is subtly at work in the responses given by ten religious leaders (eight Protestant, one rabbi, and one Greek dissident) to a questionnaire in *McCall's*, "How to Pray . . . and What to Pray For." True, not all the clergymen were asked specifically about the nature of prayer, but it is rather symptomatic that only one answer (to the question, "Is There a Right and a Wrong Way to Pray?") explicitly stated that the primary purpose of prayer is "praise, adoration, and reverence for God."

Reinhold Niebuhr of Union Theological Seminary was the one leader who insisted that "the right prayer concentrates on the glory and majesty of God." Having made the essential point, Dr. Niebuhr then unfortunately continued with a statement that can lead only to confusion, saying: "It is selfish to pray for yourself. You are using God when you pray for your own ends." This is not true. Anything that can be legitimately desired can be legitimately petitioned from a loving Father. Only if the ends I desire are contrary to the ends God wills for me will I be striving to use God as a means.

The prayer of petition is not the highest form of prayer, but it is included in our Lord's command: "Thus shall you pray." If "hallowed be Thy Name" is His directive, so is "give us this day our daily bread."

Though it must be insisted on that the prayer of petition is perfectly valid and meritorious, it is nevertheless true that selfless prayer is more sublime. The great apostolic intentions that are recommended monthly by the Apostleship of Prayer, for example, ought to occupy an ever increasing place in our lives of prayer. Our petitions may humanly and humbly touch on our success in business, our health, our little plans and hopes, but the wider horizons of what we ask for ought to open up on the vast vistas of the intentions of the Heart of Christ.

Père Raoul Plus, S.J., reminds us in his gem of a little book, *How to Pray Well*, that man is never more kingly than when on his knees, for if "prayer is a cry of distress," it nevertheless is at the same time "a hymn of glory." (September 29, 1956)